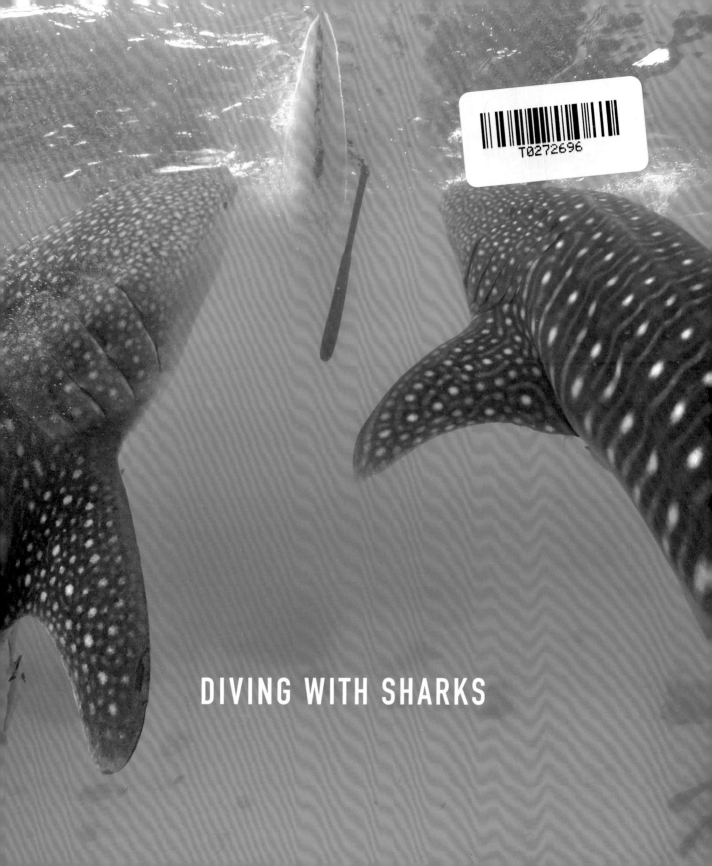

DIVING WITH SHARKS

DEDICATION
To all the wonderful people around the world fighting to save sharks.

This paperback edition published in 2022 by New Holland Publishers
First published in 2017 by New Holland Publishers
Sydney

Level 1, 178 Fox Valley Road, Wahroonga, NSW 2076, Australia

newhollandpublishers.com

A record of this book is held at the National Library of Australia.

ISBN 9781925546965

Managing Director: Fiona Schultz
Publisher and Project Editor: Simon Papps
Designer: Andrew Davies
Production Director: Arlene Gippert
Printed in China

10 9 8 7 6 5 4 3 2 1

Keep up with Reed New Holland
and New Holland Publishers

[f] ReedNewHolland
[O] @NewHollandPublishers and @ReedNewHolland

DIVING WITH SHARKS

Nigel Marsh and Andy Murch

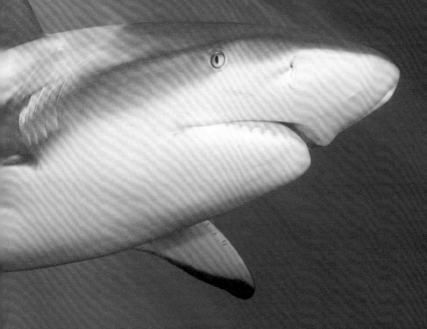

CONTENTS

INTRODUCTION

When divers first entered the seas they tried to avoid encounters with sharks, as in the 1950s most sharks were seen as man-eaters, waiting to attack anyone that entered their realm. And as most divers in those early days were spear-fishing, and often harassed by sharks, these claims appeared to be true.

However, by the 1970s many divers had swapped spears for cameras and discovered something strange and surprising – that most sharks are naturally shy and wary of divers. They soon discovered that even the so-called dangerous sharks were impossible to get close to without first placing baits in the water. Everything they had ever heard about these creatures was completely wrong, and the sharks were not interested in eating them.

Today, many divers seek out encounters with sharks, wanting to get close to them in order to observe and photograph these majestic predators of the deep. And with more than 500 species of sharks so far discovered, divers have many different underwater encounters awaiting them.

To dive with sharks it is not simply a matter of jumping into the water and the sharks are waiting. Contrary to claims in the media and perceptions of the general public, sharks are not lurking beneath the waves in teeming numbers. In reality shark numbers across the planet have plummeted during the past few decades due to unrelenting fishing pressures, while many shark species were never bountiful to start with. In order to encounter sharks, divers first have to seek them out, often paying large amounts of money to visit remote destinations where healthy shark populations still exist.

This book is a comprehensive guide for people who want to see sharks in their natural habitat, close-up and face-to-face. It details the more common shark species divers can encounter around the planet, and also includes many rare and interesting species that divers can see if they are lucky or spend time searching for them.

Within this book are also features on shark biology and behaviour, threats to sharks, shark conservation, shark research, the pros and cons of shark feeding, a listing of shark diving hot-spots, and information on how best to interact with these graceful creatures. This guide is designed to give the reader a better insight into the world of sharks, and hopefully it will inspire more divers to seek out these amazing animals.

OPPOSITE TOP – Most shark species are completely harmless, including the lovely Leopard Shark.
OPPOSITE BOTTOM – Lemon Sharks are generally wary of divers but will come close when baits are in the water.

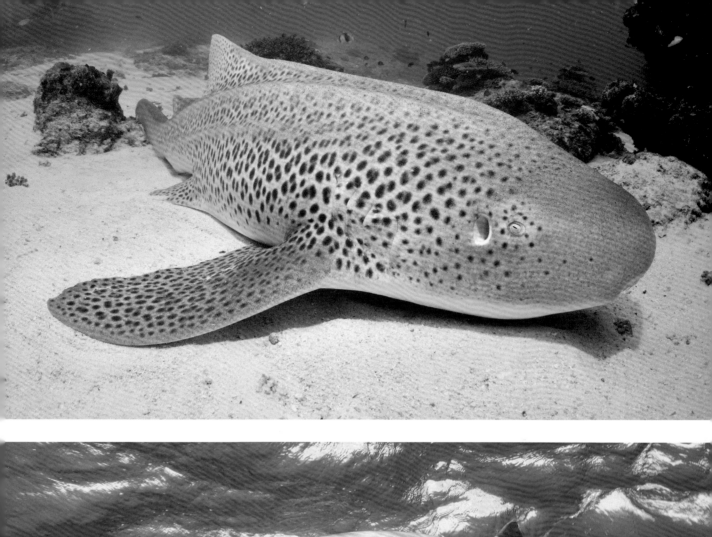
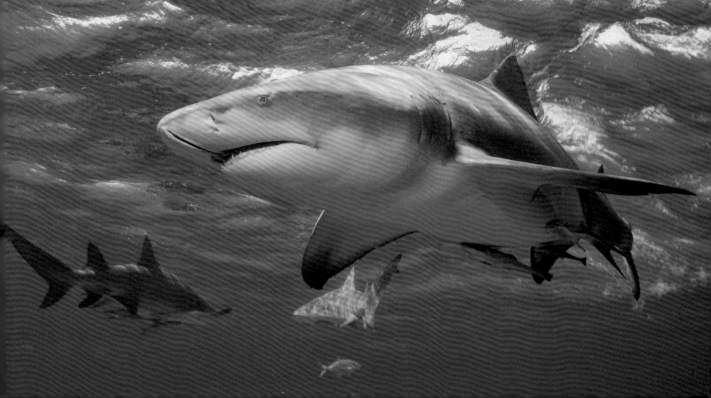

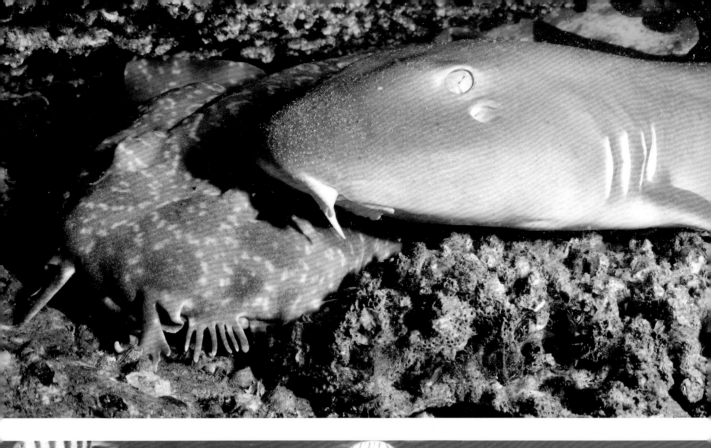
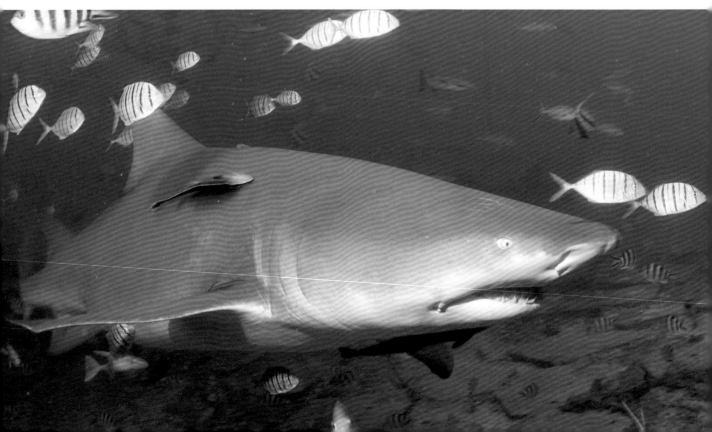

SHARK BIOLOGY AND BEHAVIOUR

Sharks and rays belong to a group of fishes known as the Chondrichthyes, or cartilaginous fishes. They differ from bony fishes, the Osteichthyes, by having a skeleton made entirely of cartilage, a rigid but soft tissue also found in the human nose. Sharks also lack a swim bladder, a device used by fish to maintain neutral buoyancy at any depth. Other differences include their skin, which is covered in dermal denticles (small teeth), while their teeth are embedded in the gums instead of being fused to the jaw. Sharks also use internal fertilisation, with the sperm delivered into the female along one of two penis-like claspers on the male. And unlike most fishes they produce only a small number of young.

CLASSIFICATION OF SHARKS

Cartilaginous fishes can be separated into two groups. The sharks and rays are known as elasmobranchs, meaning 'strap gills' as they all have between five and seven gill slits on each side of their head. The other group, not covered in this book, is the chimaeras or Holocephali, which have one gill opening on each side of the head covered by a flap.

The elasmobranchs are further broken down into two superorders based on their taxonomy: rays belong in the superorder Batoidea, which contains six suborders, while the sharks belong in the superorder Selachii, which contains eight orders. Similar family groups are determined by a number of governing factors, including fin arrangement and number, body shape, mouth position, number of gill slits and other characteristics. The following are the shark orders:

Hexanchiformes have anal fins, one dorsal fin and six or seven gill slits. Includes frilled sharks and cowsharks.

Squaliformes lack an anal fin. Includes dogfish sharks and roughsharks.

Squatiniformes lack an anal fin and have flattened bodies. Order contains only the angel sharks.

Pristiophoriformes also lack an anal fin and have an elongated snout with spines. The sawsharks are the only family in this order.

Heterodontiformes can be distinguished by their dorsal fin spines. Comprises just one family, the horn sharks.

Lamniformes have anal fins, a mouth located below and behind the eyes, and lack nictitating eyelids. Includes sandtiger sharks, goblin sharks, crocodile sharks, megamouth sharks, thresher sharks, basking sharks and mackerel sharks.

OPPOSITE TOP - Sharks come in a variety of shapes and sizes, and some are very social like this Spotted Wobbegong and Brown-banded Bamboo Shark.
OPPOSITE BOTTOM - Sharks are often accompanied by pilot fish and suckerfish, in this case a Sicklefin Lemon Shark with an entourage of juvenile Golden Trevally.

Orectolobiformes is quite a varied order. Members have anal fins and the mouth positioned in front of the eye. Contains collared carpet sharks, blind sharks, wobbegongs, bamboo/epaulette sharks, leopard sharks, nurse sharks and whale sharks.

Carcharhiniformes are very similar to the Lamniformes but have nictitating eyelids. Includes catsharks, hound sharks, whaler sharks and hammerhead sharks.

Most families of sharks contain a number of different genera, with each genera consisting of groups of closely related species. Individual species are further identified by their scientific name, based on the system of binominal nomenclature, with the first part being the generic or genus name, and the second part the individual species name that is often based on a characteristic. The classification of some sharks is still disputed among scientists, and the taxonomic situation is in a constant state of flux, with families and genera occasionally revised as new research is completed and new species are discovered.

EVOLUTION OF SHARKS

The earliest known fish-like animals were the ostracoderms. These jawless 'proto-fishes' first appeared in the fossil-record around 500 million years ago. They were eyeless, finless creatures with rod-like backbones and no jaws, instead they used suction to collect food off the seabed.

For 100 million years, proto-fishes spread throughout the world's oceans. Over time, their frontmost gill arches rotated forward to become jaws with teeth adapted from modified scales.

One group evolved into very efficient predators known as placoderms; armor-plated fishes with robust fins that provided stability, power and maneuverability.

Around 350 million years ago, the first, small proto-sharks appeared, resulting in the eventual demise of the placoderms. Feeding on their bony cousins, proto-sharks quickly proliferated. Over many millions of years, they evolved into numerous different forms. Some grew into agile predators reaching more than 2m (6.6ft) in length. The reign of proto-sharks was largely uncontested until the appearance of marine reptiles in the late Permian period. At that stage, proto-sharks not only had to compete with these fierce predators for food, but also found themselves on the menu.

One notable but short-lived family of proto-sharks was the *Cladoselache* sharks. Although primitive by comparison, these ancient predecessors of modern day sharks displayed many of the same basic traits, including sharp teeth, dorsal fins with spines, paired pectoral and pelvic fins and seven paired gill openings.

Most species of *Cladoselache* sharks died out by the end of the Palaeozoic era, some 245 million years ago, having been replaced by the hybodont sharks. These sharks had a similar shape to the sharks in the family Cladoselachidae, but more powerful jaws and teeth, and better developed fins and tails for

OPPOSITE TOP - Horn sharks, such as the Port Jackson Shark, retain a vestige from their primitive ancestors – fin spines.
OPPOSITE BOTTOM - Fossilised sharks teeth, like this Megalodon tooth, are found in abundance around the world.

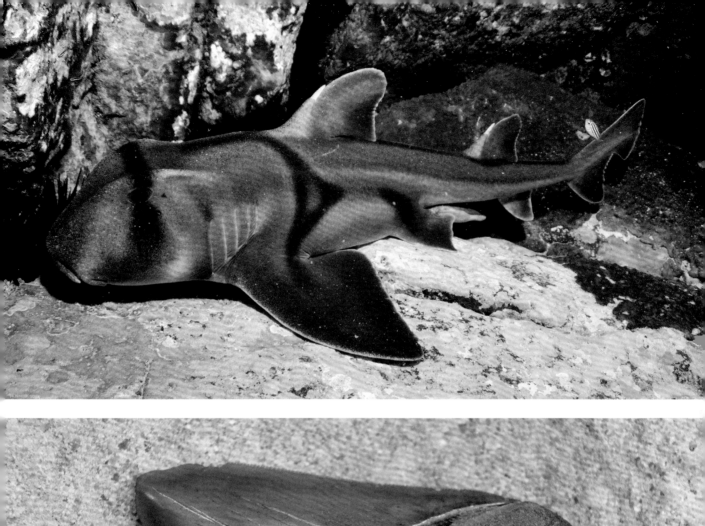

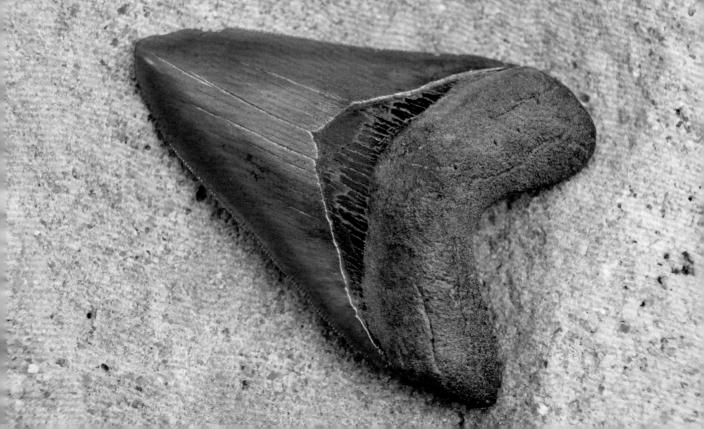

extra speed. Hybodont sharks dominated the seas for many millions of years but couldn't compete with modern sharks, and were driven to extinction in the Cretaceous era, around 65 million years ago.

Modern sharks of the orders Hexanchiformes and Heterodontiformes are thought to be the first 'neoselachians' to appear and they still retain some features of the proto-sharks. The Hexanchiformes have six or seven paired gills, while the Heterodontiformes have fin spines.

By 150 million years ago, most modern shark families had appeared, developing into the variety of species we see today. Sharks have changed little during the past 100 million years; becoming perfectly adapted to their environments they found no reason or pressure to change. However,

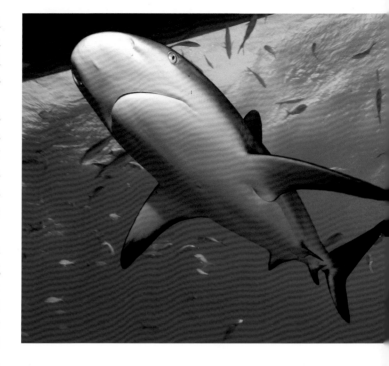

along the way, many species have become extinct, especially the mega sharks, including giant forms of makos, sandtiger sharks and the infamous Great White Shark relative, Megalodon.

Complete fossilized remains of sharks are extremely rare due to the fact that their cartilaginous skeletons dissolve more rapidly than bone. However, shark teeth are very resilient and are among the most abundant fossils found around the world. Scientists can tell a great deal from fossilized shark teeth. The family and species can be identified, the size of the animal can be calculated, and the shark's diet can be ascertained from the shape.

SHARK BODY DESIGN

During the past 350 million years sharks have evolved into a variety of shapes and sizes that have allowed them to adopt roles as the top predators of the oceans. Each part of their body has developed to take advantage of their environment – some have streamlined bodies for speed, others have become flattened to assist with camouflage and concealment, while some species have developed elongated bodies to allow them to wriggle into tight caves for food and shelter. Although shark species look quite different, they all have the same basic body structure and design.

CARTILAGE SKELETON

Sharks were once considered to be quite primitive fishes because of their cartilage skeletons. In all other vertebrates the skeleton is formed of bone, with cartilage only being used for the support of structures such as ears and noses. However, all vertebrates have a cartilage skeleton when in the embryonic stage, with the cartilage forming a foundation for the bones before gradually being replaced with calcium salts to form bone.

The distant ancestors of sharks had bony skeletons with quite heavy skulls. It is thought that sharks developed a cartilage skeleton to rid themselves of this excessive weight. Cartilage is much lighter than bone, is more flexible and possibly aids in speed, manoeuvrability and buoyancy. Sharks are not entirely without bone – as they grow and become older calcification of the cartilage usually occurs in the vertebrae, fin supports and jaw. The calcium is deposited in layers, but researchers have found that these layers are not deposited annually. It had been hoped that these calcium growth-rings could be used in order to determine the age of a shark, but it seems that more research is required.

OPPOSITE - The Caribbean Reef Shark has evolved a sleek, streamlined shape that allows it to swim fast to capture prey.
BELOW - Rows of cartilage shark jaws sold as souvenirs make a sad sight in tourist shops.

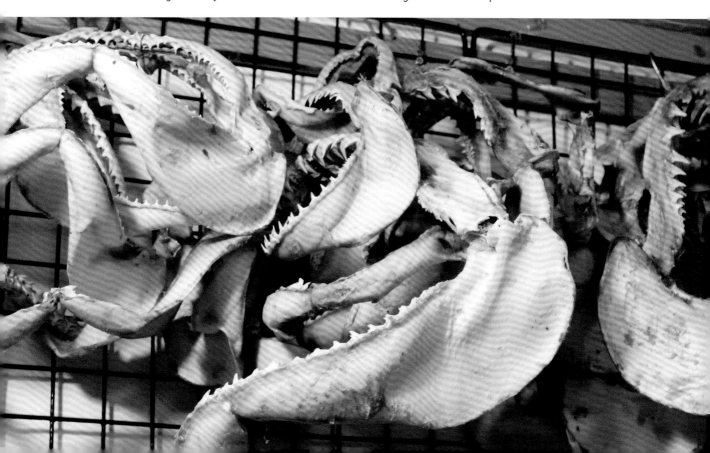

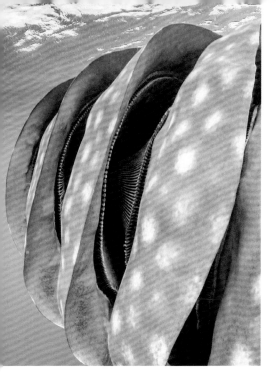
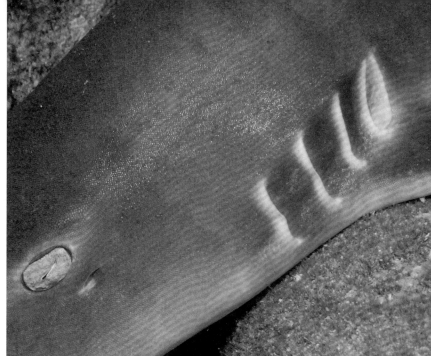

GILLS

Primitive sharks once had up to ten pairs of gill pouches located behind the skull. All modern sharks now have five pairs of gill pouches, except for sharks belonging to the order Hexanchiformes, and the sixgilled sawshark, which have six or seven pairs. It is thought that the first pair of gills in primitive sharks moved forward and modified to form the jaws we know in modern sharks. Gills are used to extract oxygen from the water, with each gill pouch arranged in a vertical arch. Water enters through the mouth or spiracle (the vestige of a gill mainly used by bottom-dwelling sharks) then passes through the gill and out the gill slits. Oxygen is collected on filaments and enters capillaries leading into the bloodstream.

Sharks lack the operculum gill cover found in bony fishes that can open and close to pump water through the gills, so they have to either suck or push water through the mouth or spiracle. For most bottom-dwelling sharks this presents no problem, but larger free-swimming sharks have to keep moving in order to push water into their mouth and out through the gills. This means that most free-swimming sharks can never stop swimming or they will drown. However, a number of free-swimming sharks have evolved to be able to suck in water as they rest on the bottom, and others have been observed resting in caves and gutters where there is a good flow of water. Gills vary in size between species but have become overdeveloped in Whale Sharks and Basking Sharks so that they also act as sieves for the collection of plankton.

ABOVE LEFT - The oversized gills of Whale Sharks are used for breathing and to capture their plankton food.
ABOVE RIGHT - Brown-banded Bamboo Sharks breath via small gill slits and a spiracle, located below the eye.

FINS

The arrangement of fins on all sharks is basically the same, but they vary considerably in size, shape and location to suit the lifestyle of the individual animal. Fins are basically used for propulsion, stability and manoeuvrability, allowing the individual to swim fast, slow, turn and stop. Shark fins are supported by an inner cartilage skeleton attached to the spinal column. The cartilage forms the base of the fin and radiating from this base are fibrous rays, known as keratotriches, which stiffen the rest of the fin. These fibrous rays are the part of the fin most prized in shark fin soup.

BELOW TOP – The free-swimming Lemon Shark has learnt how to rest on the bottom and suck water through its gills by opening and closing its mouth.
BELOW BOTTOM – The tail or caudal fin of a bottom-dwelling Brown-banded Bamboo Shark is small and undeveloped as these sharks don't do much swimming and often wedge themselves into ledges.

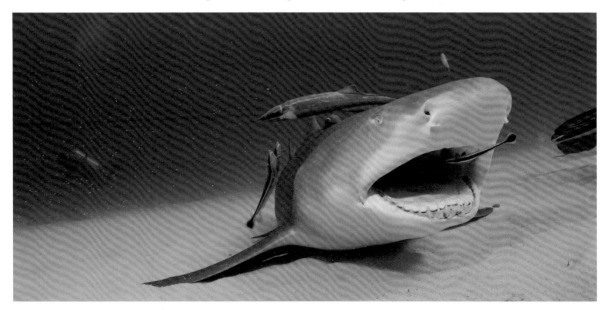

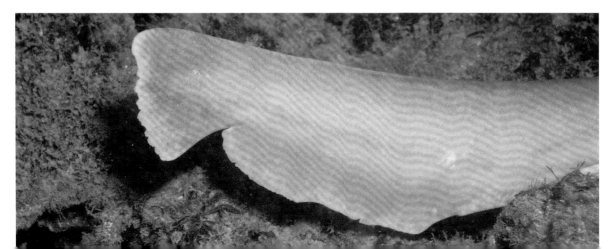

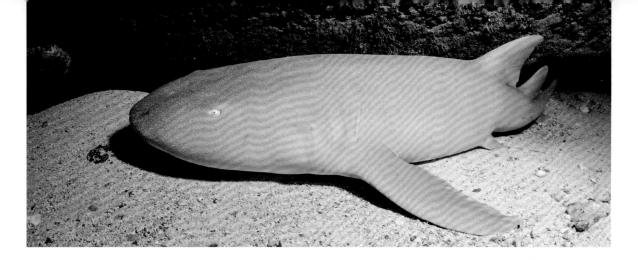

Primitive sharks, and a few modern sharks like the horn sharks and dogfish sharks, have pointed spines on the leading edge of their dorsal fins. These spines serve to support the fin structure and have limited use in defence.

Sharks generally have one or two dorsal fins which are used to provide stability, balancing the driving force of the tail as it sweeps back and forth. Sharks generate thrust in their tails by undulating their entire body, with muscles along their bodies arranged in a vertical zigzag pattern to assist these movements. Tail fins vary greatly among sharks, although the upper lobe is generally longer than the lower lobe and provides most of the kick. In the mackerel sharks both lobes are the same size, giving the tail the classic half-moon shape. Bottom-dwelling sharks like wobbegongs and Leopard Sharks generally have a longer upper tail lobe and almost no lower lobe as it is of little use when resting on the bottom. The upper tail lobe in thresher sharks is longer than the body of the shark. This greatly elongated tail is used not only for swimming, but also helps to stun prey.

The pectoral fins are located near to the centre of gravity of the shark and are joined by cartilage. These wing-like fins are primarily for steering, with sharks dipping, lifting and rotating their pectoral fins to turn in any direction. Bottom-dwelling sharks usually have small pectoral fins and some species can even walk slowly along the bottom on these fins, especially the epaulette sharks. The pectoral fins of angel sharks are quite large and project from the side of their flattened head, helping them to keep a low profile when concealed under a layer of sand. The pelvic and anal fins of sharks are paired and provide additional steerage functions.

BUOYANCY

Unlike bony fishes, sharks lack a swim bladder (an internal air sac that helps to maintain neutral buoyancy at any depth), so must constantly swim or they will sink to the bottom. A number of shark species can fill their stomachs with air, gulped at the surface, to maintain buoyancy. Other sharks, especially deep-water and pelagic species, have livers filled with light oil, called squalene, which allows them to remain neutrally buoyant.

TEETH AND SKIN

The bodies of sharks are covered in teeth-like scales known as dermal denticles. These small teeth point backwards and are very abrasive if rubbed against the grain. The skin of sharks has been used as sandpaper for thousands of years and also makes strong leather. Dermal denticles vary in shape and size, not only between species but also on individual sharks, with smaller ones on the head and fins. Most are shaped like teeth, with ridges, grooves and cusps. Denticles are constantly being replaced and an individual shark may lose 20,000 each year. Each denticle grows from a basal plate under the skin, blood pumps into the structure as it grows and the denticle has a protective coat of enamel just like a tooth.

The rough skin of sharks has evolved over the course of millions of years for a number of reasons. The dermal denticles form a very tough hide that protects the animal from cuts and scrapes when feeding and breeding. Some female sharks even have thicker skin to protect them from amorous males. It has also been found that the shape of the denticles helps to direct the flow of water to sensory organs

OPPOSITE – Lacking a swim bladder and being negatively buoyant allow Nurse Sharks to rest on the bottom.
BELOW LEFT – The dermal denticles of a Banded Wobbegong change in size and shape around the eye.
BELOW RIGHT – The jaws of a Great White Shark display a variety of different tooth shapes, with those on the top row used for sawing through flesh, and those on the bottom row used for holding the prey.

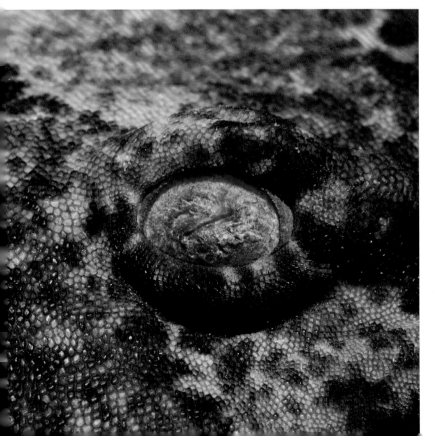

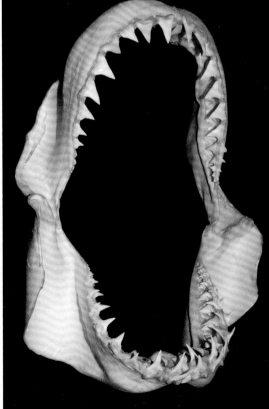

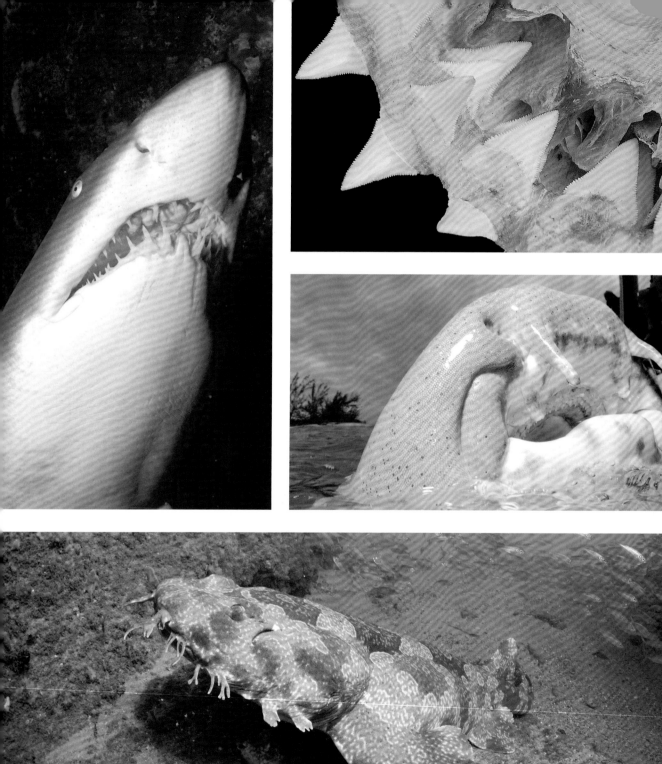

and away from the eyes. But one of the main functions of the denticles is to reduce surface resistance when swimming, allowing a smooth flow of water over the body.

All sharks are carnivores and have evolved a number of different tooth shapes to catch, bite or crush their chosen prey. Shark's teeth are quite remarkable as they are not embedded in the jaw like those of other animals, but anchored into the gums. They are also continuously replaced with new teeth every eight to fifteen days, which constantly grow and rotate forwards. At any one time it may appear that a shark has six or more sets of teeth, but only the outer teeth are functional. Teeth are lost naturally, especially when feeding.

The teeth of sharks are very strong and grow in much the same way as the skin denticles, from a basal plate under the skin. Tooth shape varies greatly, between the upper and lower jaw and between juveniles and adults of the same species. A quick look at a shark's teeth can ascertain their food and the way they capture it. Teeth with serrated edges are designed to cut flesh, allowing sharks to bite chunks out of large prey. Non-serrated teeth that are curved or dagger-shaped are designed to grip prey which will be swallowed whole. While rounded, plate like-teeth, are used to crush prey such as the shells of crustaceans, molluscs or echinoderms.

Sharks can have a combination of these teeth at one time or at different stages of their life. Young Great White Sharks have dagger-like non-serrated teeth and feed mainly on fish, while adults of the same species have large serrated teeth and take bites out of large prey. Horn sharks have small pointed teeth at the front of their jaws, which are used to grip prey, while the side and back teeth are plate-like in order to crush their prey. Even plankton-eaters such as Whale Sharks and Basking Sharks have tiny sharp teeth, but these see little use.

HUNTING STRATEGIES

Sharks use a range of hunting techniques to capture prey. Many stalk their quarry, following target species in order to pick off the young, sick, old or unaware. Plankton-feeders such as Whale Sharks and Basking Sharks also pursue prey but at a slower pace, swimming with an open mouth to gather fish eggs, krill and other small items. Many bottom-dwelling sharks are ambush predators, using camouflage or concealment to get close to their prey. A number of deep-water sharks have bioluminescent body parts that are used to attract prey. Other sharks round up schools of fish into concentrated balls, and a few species have been observed feeding co-operatively, herding schools of fish into shallow water.

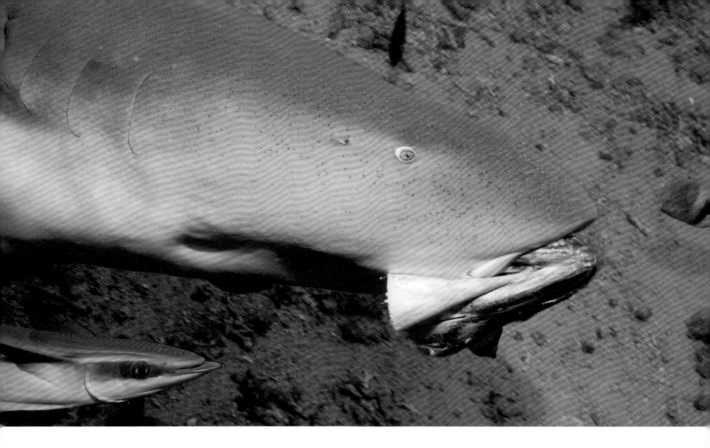

DIGESTION

No shark actually chews its food – it is either swallowed whole or in pieces, to be broken down by their digestive system. Once a piece of food is swallowed it passes directly into the stomach along a short digestive tract. Tubular glands in the stomach release hydrochloric acid and digestive enzymes to break down the food. The food then passes through the intestine which has a spiral valve to increase surface area and the intake of nutrients. Most food is broken down instantly, but larger sharks seem to be able to store undigested food in their stomachs for extended periods of up to several weeks. From the intestine the waste passes out through the rectum, while indigestible material such as bones are usually regurgitated.

Most sharks can survive on quite a small diet relative to their size, because they have a cold-blooded metabolism, with a body temperature equal to the surrounding water. The mackerel sharks are the exception, maintaining a body temperature higher than the surrounding water. This keeps their muscles warm and responsive, but they have to eat more food in order to compensate.

ABOVE - A Tawny Nurse Shark sneaks off with a fish head claimed as a prize at a shark feed in Fiji.
OPPOSITE - Shark eyes vary greatly depending on the behaviour of the animal. Coral Catsharks (BOTTOM LEFT) are nocturnal and as such have large pupils to aid vision at night, while Tasselled Wobbegongs (BOTTOM RIGHT) are ambush predators that snatch prey at any time of the day and have slit-like pupils.

SENSORY ORGANS

Over a period of millions of years of evolution, sharks have developed an array of sensory organs for the detection of prey that is superior to almost all other animals. To control this influx of information they have well-developed brains, especially in larger sharks such as the mackerel sharks, whaler sharks and hammerheads. Tests on sharks have shown that they have the ability to learn and remember. Their brain to body weight ratio is similar to that of birds and many mammals.

SIGHT

Many sharks feed at night, dawn or dusk and as such have eyes that work exceptionally well in low light conditions. The eyes are located on the side of the head to provide a large field of vision. Shark eyes work equally well by day or night. By day cones in the retina allow them to see colours and shapes, while at night rods in the retina allow them to distinguish between light and dark objects. Behind the retina they also have silvery plates known as the tapetum lucidum, which reflects very low light back into the retina for enhanced vision.

Vision is a very important sense for sharks when searching for prey. Their eyes are exceptionally good at seeing objects from a long distance, but it is thought they may not be able to focus on close objects.

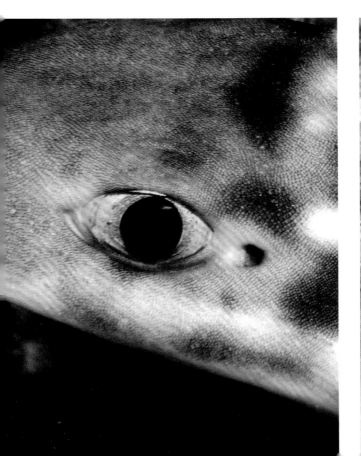
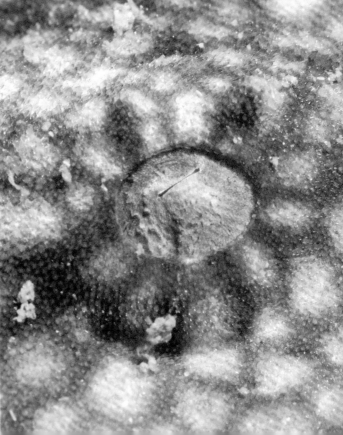

To protect the eyes many sharks have a nictitating membrane that covers the eyeball. Other species roll their eyes back to avoid damage, especially when feeding.

Unlike land predators, sharks do not possess binocular vision whereby both eyes look ahead at the same time; a trait that leads to better depth perception during the pursuit of prey. However, sharks swing their head from side to side while swimming, allowing each eye to pass through the same forward field of view; an adaptation that affords similar depth perception while also maintaining excellent peripheral vision.

SOUNDS AND VIBRATIONS

Sound travels much further and more efficiently through liquid than air and as such is an important source of sensory information for sharks. Sharks have a very basic form of hearing, lacking ear drums and other basic elements of the ear found in other animals. They instead have paired openings in the top of the head that lead to the inner ear. The inner ear, known as the macula neglecta, is linked by three canals, set in different orientation to each other. Each canal is lined with sensory hairs that detect sound, and by being set at different angles allows the direction of the sound to be ascertained. The inner ear of sharks is also used for balance, which is especially important for creatures swimming in open water with no fixed visual reference points.

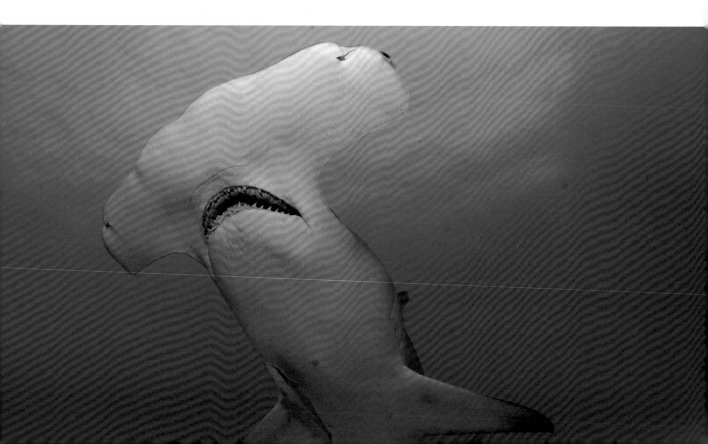

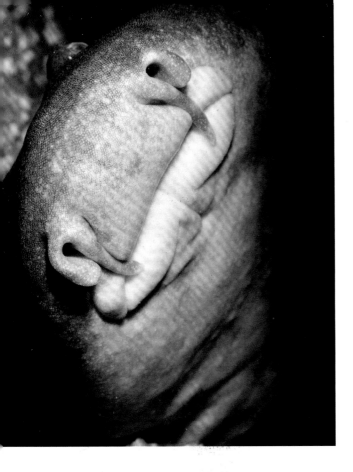

OPPOSITE - Hammerhead sharks swing their head back and forth as they swim to ensure all their sensors are put into play when searching for prey.
LEFT - The nostrils of a Blind Shark are flanked by barbels that provide additional sensory information.

In addition to their ears, sharks also have a lateral line for detecting vibrations. The lateral line extends around the head, down the body and onto the tail, and consists of tiny pores that are connected to a mucous-filled inner canal covered with sensory hairs. Pit organs are also located over the bodies of sharks in varying degrees of concentration. These organs are similar in design to the lateral line organs, but provide information to the creature about movement, position and water flow in relation to itself and its environment.

Using all this information, sharks have been shown to be very sensitive to the struggles of distressed or injured fish and can quickly locate the source, even if hidden from sight.

SMELL AND TASTE

One of the most important senses sharks use to find prey is smell. Their olfactory organs, known as nares, are found under the snout and are covered by skin flaps. Water constantly enters these organs, and molecules of blood and other proteins are detected by receptor cells. These olfactory organs are connected to the mouth in many bottom-dwelling species, allowing them to smell the surrounding water with each breath, even when stationary.

Although sharks have been shown to detect substances diluted more than 10 million times, they have to be close to a constant stream of the substance in order to follow it back to its source. Tests in the wild have shown that Great White Sharks can detect a slick of berley 8km (5 miles) from its source, but at greater distances it tends to become too dispersed for them to follow. Once an attractive scent is detected a shark will accelerate to find the source before it disappears, even closing their gills to reduce resistance.

Sharks not only use smell to find prey but also to distinguish a receptive mate in the breeding season. Males will smell the female's cloaca to determine if she is in season and ready to mate.

Sharks use their taste buds mainly to accept or reject food being eaten. Angel sharks are a prime example, as being ambush predators they ingest almost anything that swims by, then rely heavily on taste to determine if the prey is edible or not. Most sharks reject prey if it doesn't taste right.

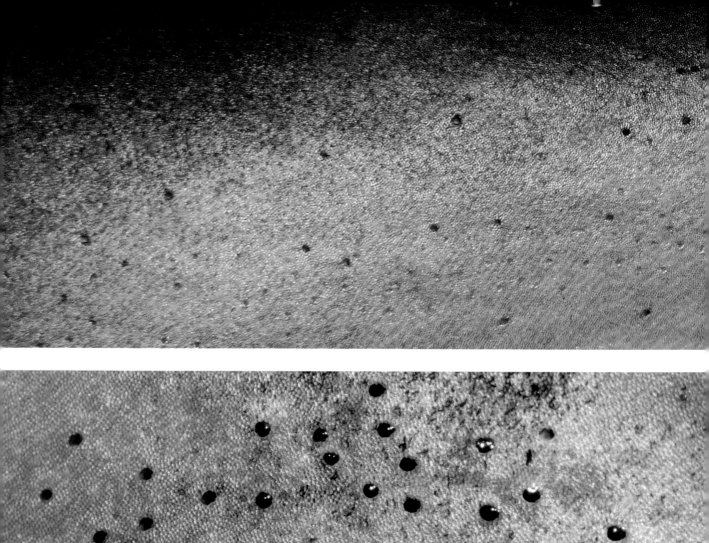
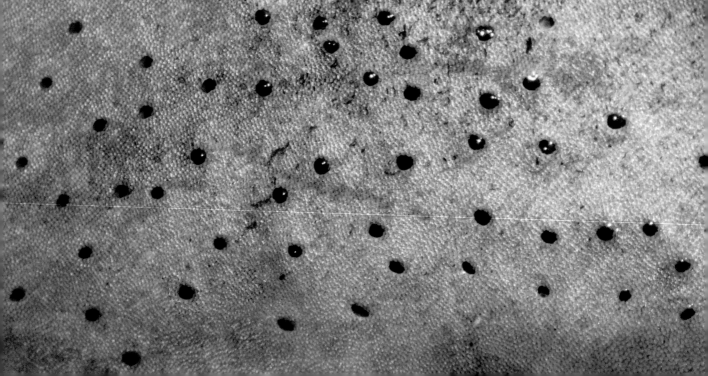

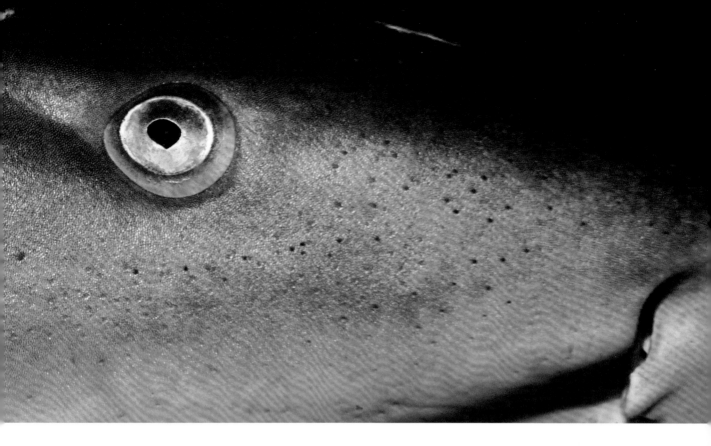

ELECTROSENSE

One special sense that sharks possess is their ability to detect the electrical fields of living animals. These electrosensory organs are located around the head and are commonly known as the ampullae of Lorenzini. They are small chambers covered with sensitive hair cells that are connected to the nervous system. These small pores are visible on the heads of most sharks and can detect even the faintest of electrical fields. The ampullae of Lorenzini are used to locate buried prey and also assist when feeding, especially if the prey is lost from sight. These electrosensory organs may also aid in navigation, allowing migratory sharks to follow the Earth's magnetic fields to return to favoured breeding and feeding grounds each year.

OPPOSITE - The ampullae of Lorenzini on a Porbeagle Shark – a member of the mackerel shark family.
ABOVE - The small black spots on this Grey Nurse Shark are the ampullae of Lorenzini and pit organs.

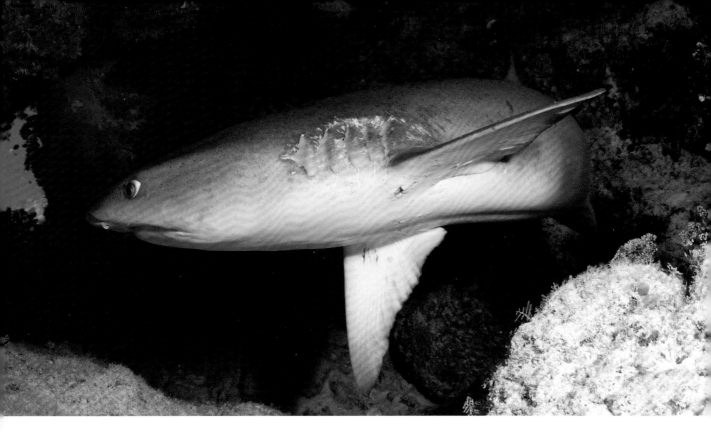

REPRODUCTION

One of the major differences between sharks and bony fishes is their reproduction strategies. Female bony fishes generally lay millions of eggs which are externally fertilised by the male. Sharks practice internal fertilisation, like mammals, and only produce a small number of young.

When in season, female sharks release eggs from the ovaries that pass into the reproductive tract. Male sharks produce sperm in the testes, which then passes along a series of ducts to be stored in sacs known as the seminal vesicles.

Mating may be the only time that male and female sharks of the same species meet. During the mating season, many sharks congregate. Courtship generally involves one or more males following a female, sniffing her cloaca to find out if she is in season. The males may bite her on the fins, tail, head and back in a rough courtship ritual. If the female is not interested or not ready to mate she may bite the males back or flee the area. If the female is receptive she will slow her swimming and allow the chosen male to get in a better position. During mating the male will bite onto the female's pectoral fin for stability and most species also brace themselves on the bottom. Mating positions vary between species; side-by-side, belly-to-belly, male on top and even snaking around one another are some of the variations.

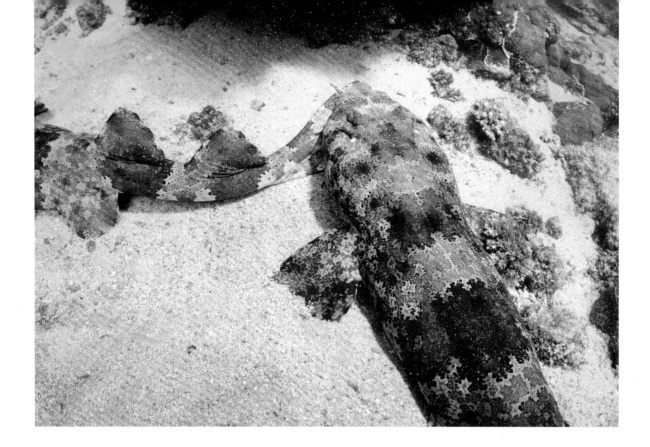

During mating the male inserts one clasper (a pair of modified fins) into the female's cloaca and sperm is forced along a groove in the clasper. Female sharks are able to store sperm for extended periods of time until environmental conditions are most favourable for their pregnancy to take place.

Eggs are fertilised in the shell gland and protected by a shell, which varies in thickness and purpose. The fertilised eggs then move into the uterus to develop in a number of different ways.

OVIPARITY

Many bottom-dwelling sharks are oviparous, laying eggs that are surrounded by a protective leathery case of keratin. The fertilised eggs are either held in the uterus until just before they are ready to hatch or laid just after mating, then left to contend with the elements and predators until they hatch. Eggs are produced in a variety of different shapes and sizes. Horn sharks lay corkscrew-shaped eggs, while most other species lay rectangular pillow-shaped eggs. Most egg cases are anchored to the bottom by tendrils and generally become covered in a growth of algae that helps to camouflage them. The developing embryo receives nourishment from the yolk and may take anywhere from two to fifteen months to hatch.

OPPOSITE - This female Whitetip Reef Shark displays fresh mating scars on her gills and pectoral fins.
ABOVE - Shark foreplay is a rough business and not always successful. This male Ornate Wobbegong was observed biting the tail of the female for over ten minutes before she finally swam away.

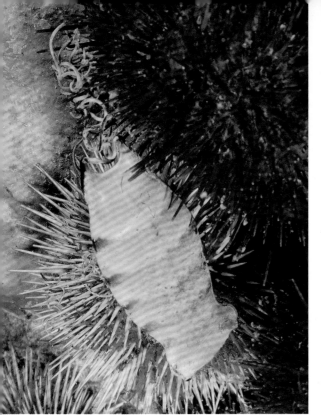
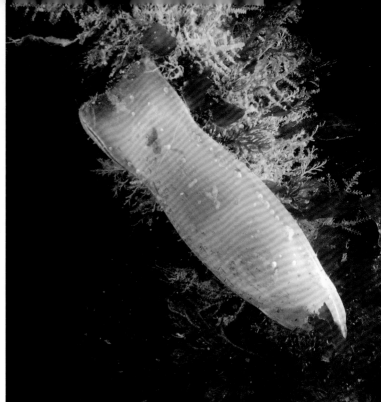

OVOVIVIPARITY

Ovoviviparous sharks also have fertilised eggs that are surrounded by an egg case, but the young emerge from the case while in the uterus before being born. Most ovoviviparous species rely solely on the yolk to nourish the embryo, but some receive additional food by eating unfertilised eggs produced by the female (known as oophagy). Sandtiger shark embryos not only eat eggs but also other developing embryos (known as embryophagy).

VIVIPARITY

A number of whaler and hammerhead sharks are viviparous, with the embryo having a placental attachment to the oviduct wall via the yolk sac. The embryo receives nourishment from the yolk sac and

ABOVE - Catshark eggs vary greatly in style, but all are anchored to the bottom with tendrils, such as this Puffadder Shyshark egg (left) and this Lesser Spotted Catshark egg (right).
OPPOSITE TOP LEFT - The Draughtboard Shark is another species of catshark and its egg cases have distinctive ridges.
OPPOSITE TOP RIGHT - An unusual cluster of bamboo shark eggs. These eggs don't have tendrils to anchor them to the bottom, and are generally wedged into the coral.
OPPOSITE BOTTOM - The corkscrew-shaped egg case of a Crested Horn Shark.

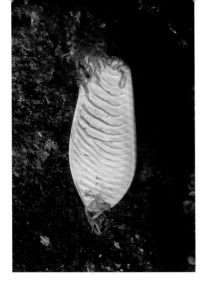
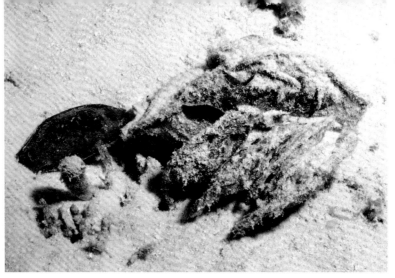

also additional uterine milk. Waste from the embryo passes back along this placenta to be disposed of by the mother.

A number of shark species have been observed giving birth and laying eggs. Some species rub their stomachs against the bottom to assist birthing, while others display agitated swimming patterns and release the young on a sharp turn.

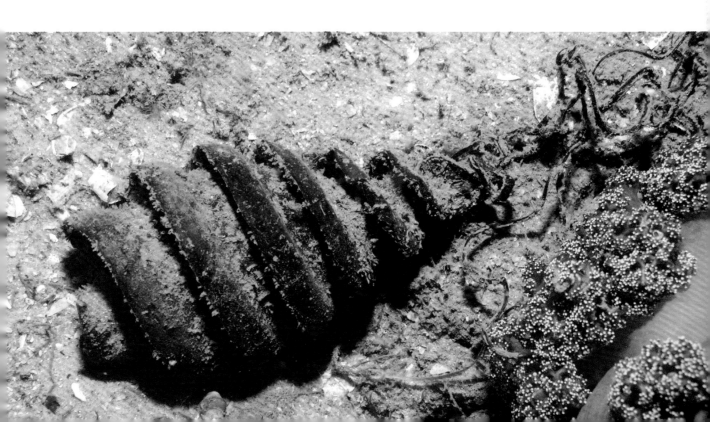

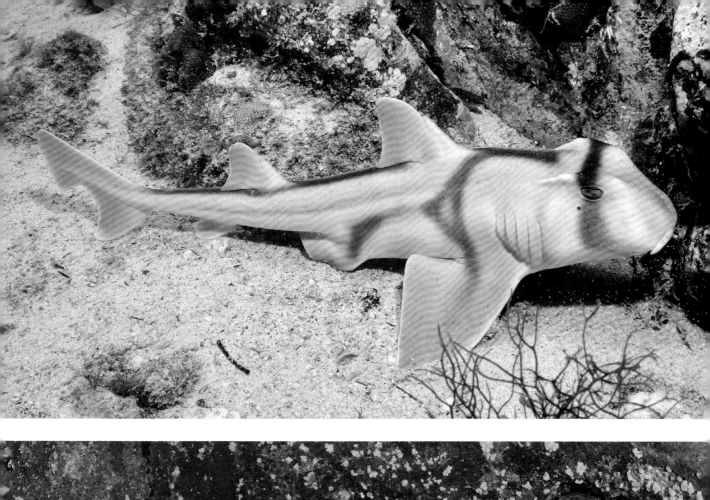

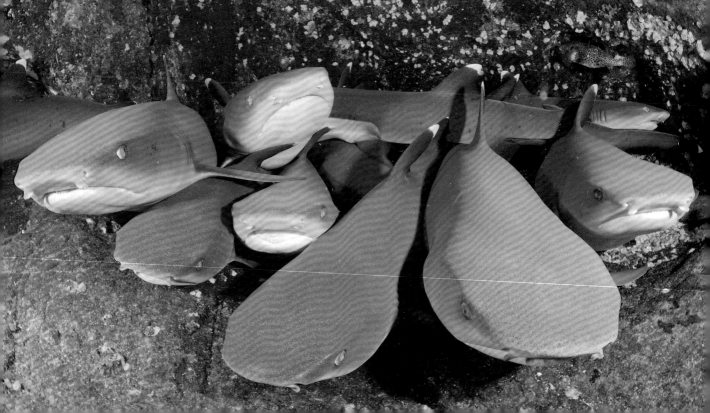

GROWTH AND AGE

On average sharks grow slower and live much longer than bony fishes. Most species live to around 20–30 years of age, but the lifespan of species varies from 10–400 years. Determining the age and growth rate of sharks has proven to be quite difficult. The growth rings of calcium on the vertebrae are being studied, but tag and release methods have provided the most reliable information to date.

Sharks reach sexual maturity at six to seven years of age in most species, but short-lived species may be sexually mature at two to three years, while long-lived species may be 20 years or older before reaching maturity. Mature animals can be identified in the wild, with the males having roughened claspers that indicates use, while females may have faint bite or scratch marks around the fins and back, indicating involvement in rough mating rituals. Size is not a good indication of maturity as sharks can vary greatly in size.

SOCIAL LIFE

Very little is still really known about the social lives of sharks. Most of what we know has come from studies of captive animals or from fleeting encounters in the wild. The most commonly observed behaviour of sharks is hunting and feeding, but reproductive behaviour and the social structure of these creatures can also been witnessed.

Many sharks are solitary creatures that are rarely seen close to another member of the same species, except when mating. There are a number of theories as to why they live solitary lives. Competition for food is one reason, as having a dispersed population allows for better use, and little overuse, of resources. Size is also a factor that separates species, as smaller sharks sometimes fall prey to larger members of the same species. But sex and sexual aggression may be the main reason, as many species have been found to be segregated by sex, either found in different depths or different temperature zones, only meeting in the breeding season. As the courtship rituals of sharks can be very rough, if this were to continue right throughout the year it would be counterproductive, as the animals would waste too much energy trying to mate with unreceptive partners.

Apart from during the breeding season, sharks do congregate on occasions if an abundance of food is available. A good example of this is Whale Shark aggregations at feeding sites such as Ningaloo Reef in Western Australia and Isla Mujeres in Mexico. Usually Whale Sharks are observed singly, but these gentle giants do sometimes gather en masse to take advantage of large quantities of food.

Many shark species also migrate, individually and en masse. These migrations are not fully understood, as they can be driven by feeding, breeding and a number of other factors. Some species, such as the Port Jackson Shark, migrate from deep to shallow water in order to breed. Others, like Grey Nurse Sharks

OPPOSITE TOP - Juvenile sharks are rarely seen, but divers often find juvenile Port Jackson Sharks in southern Australia.
OPPOSITE BOTTOM - Whitetip Reef Sharks are very social and will often rest together in a cave.

and Leopard Sharks, migrate up and down the coast driven by changes in water temperature. Some species, such as Whale Sharks and Great White Sharks, migrate long distances to favourite feeding sites, while other shark migrations appear to follow the movements of fish populations.

Schooling behaviour is known in a number of shark species. Hammerhead sharks have been observed in large polarised schools. In these schools the sharks are nearly always an equal distance apart, all heading in the same direction and turning as one giant body. Other shark species gather in less structured schools, including Grey Nurse Sharks and many whaler shark species. The advantages of schooling are obvious; their numbers can confuse predators that find it difficult to select an individual, they can also overwhelm prey, and schooling formations have been found to be hydro-dynamically efficient, so saving valuable energy. Being in a school allows for more social interaction and also saves time when searching for a mate. But the school doesn't always stay together and tracking studies of hammerhead sharks and Grey Nurse Sharks has shown that they separate and disperse at night in order to feed.

Many species of shark are observed together throughout the year, but don't form schools. Wobbegongs are commonly found resting in caves together, as are bamboo sharks, nurse sharks, Whitetip Reef Sharks and Port Jackson Sharks. They may rest together for defence, or it may just be a matter of convenience – a case of a popular resting place used by all.

Numerous species of sharks often share the same territory, patrolling and feeding in the same area without conflict. But some species appear to have a pecking order, or dominance hierarchy structure. This is most frequently observed in members of the whaler shark and mackerel shark families, especially when feeding as the largest shark will nearly always feed first. Smaller sharks are often observed changing course to avoid a larger member of their own species. This dominance hierarchy also exists between different species. At shark feeds Grey Reef Sharks and Whitetip Reef Sharks often give way to larger Silvertip Sharks, and they are all very wary if a Tiger Shark or Great Hammerhead appears.

Some shark species appear to interact without being aggressive towards each other. Spotted and Banded Wobbegongs often share caves together with Brown-banded Bamboo Sharks and Port Jackson Sharks. Considering that wobbegongs occasionally eat these smaller species, it is not clear if they are accidentally lodging together, or maybe the wobbegongs are just waiting for the right time to consume their companions.

There are many other shark behaviours that have been observed and little understood. Some shark species have been sighted following each other around head to tail. Often this is breeding behaviour, but when it involves members of the same sex this following behaviour is not understood. Sharks are also observed rubbing their side or belly on sand or rocks. This may simply be to scratch an itch or could be a display directed at another nearby shark. Many species of sharks are also known to breach, but why

OPPOSITE TOP - Spotted Wobbegongs and Brown-banded Bamboo Sharks are often found sharing a home, even though wobbegongs sometimes eat bamboo sharks.

OPPOSITE BOTTOM - Grey Nurse Sharks are very social animals, always found in aggregations that can number in the hundreds.

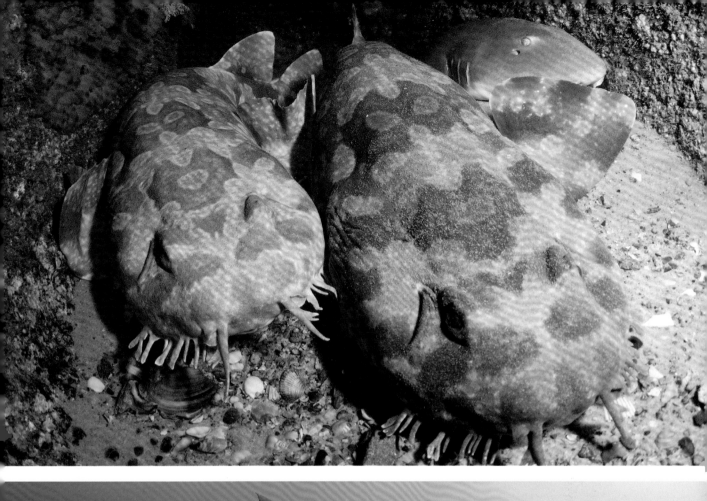
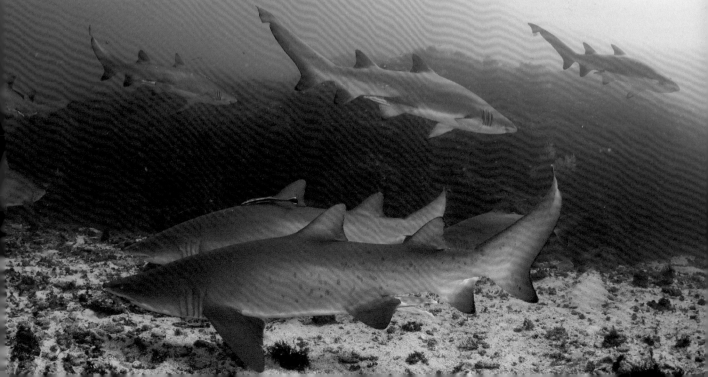

they do this is still unknown. It may be to stun prey, to get rid of unwanted parasites and freeloaders such as suckerfish, a means of communication, or a threat display to rival males, or even just for fun.

Some of the most interesting aspects of shark behaviour are how they react to and relate to humans. Most sharks are shy and avoid humans, but some are curious and will investigate a diver. Some tolerate divers closely inspecting them, but others will snap at a diver who gets too close. We actually know very little about most sharks, and diving with these creatures can help to unlock more secrets of their biology and behaviour.

SHARK RESEARCH

Considering how fascinating and feared sharks are, we still know very little about these ocean predators. Much of what we do know about them has been learned from dissecting their carcasses or from observing sharks in aquariums. Studying them in the wild is a real challenge, as most species are found in deep water, are wary of divers, and can only be observed for a limited amount of time. Plus baits are generally used to lure them close, in the process changing their natural behaviour. However, research scientists have conducted many interesting studies on sharks, which has helped to demystify these misunderstood creatures. One of the most popular ways to study sharks is by tagging them.

TAGGING

Much of what we know about shark growth rates, populations, life histories and migration patterns has come about from tagging studies. Tagging was first used to study birds in the 1890s, and was identified as a good way to study sharks in the 1940s. One of the first tagging studies was conducted in southern Australia on School Sharks in the 1940s. Using Petersen disc tags wired to the dorsal fin allowed scientists to study the growth rates and population dynamics of these sharks, which are heavily fished. They also used internal Nesbit tags, inserted into the shark's body cavity via a small incision, as the researchers found the external tags were often lost. One of these internal tags was recovered 42 years later – a record for the longest tagging period for any shark.

In the years since, many other different external tags (known as passive tags) have been used on numerous shark species. To attach most tags the shark has to be captured. This not only allows the tag to be fitted, but the shark to be measured, sexed and photographed, and for blood and tissue samples to be collected for DNA and other testing. To collect useful data from these tags the shark has to be recaptured in the future. Many years can pass before a tagged shark is recaptured, and many are never seen again.

OPPOSITE TOP – This Leopard Shark has a tag on its dorsal fin that has become fouled by algae.
OPPOSITE BOTTOM – Two types of acoustic tags used for the tracking of Great White Sharks.

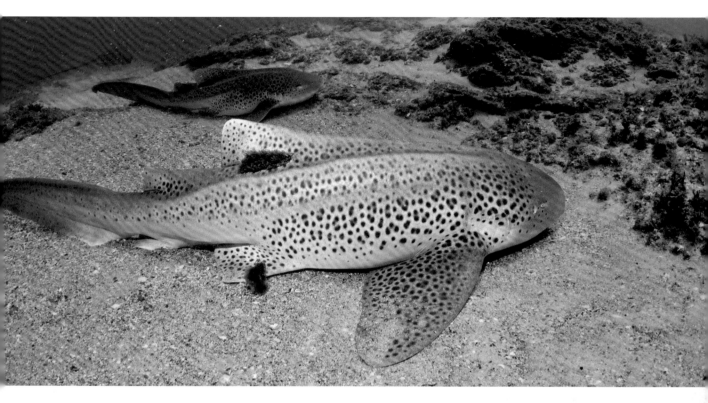

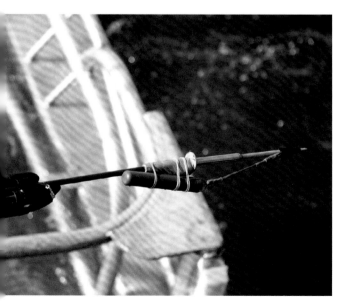

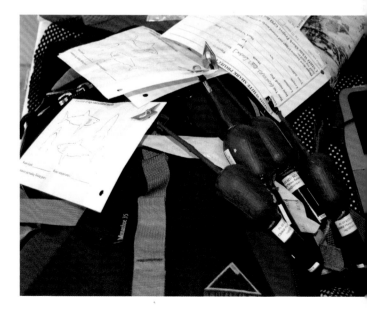

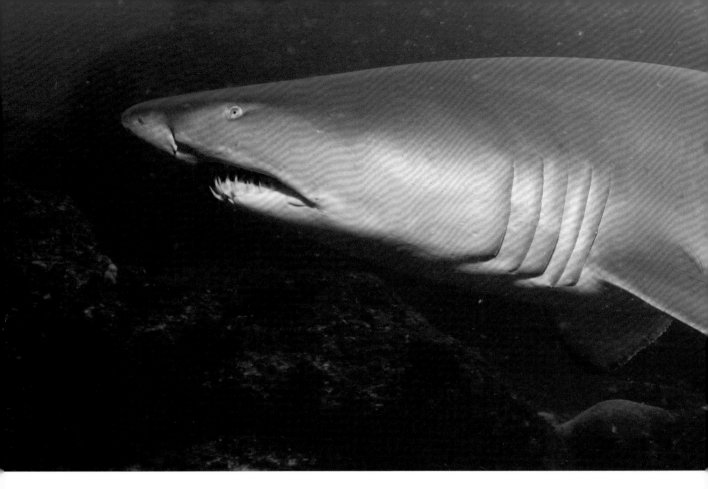

While much useful data can be gathered, these passive tags don't tell us where the shark has been and what it has been doing between captures. It is also thought that about 50 per cent of passive tags are lost before the shark is recaptured.

More recently, acoustic, archival and satellite tags (known as electronic tags) have been used to track the movements of sharks. These tags are generally externally attached to the shark. Some are simply speared into the side of the animal, while others are attached to the dorsal fin, but some are also placed internally. The simplest and cheapest are the acoustic tags, as they don't have to be recovered in order to obtain valuable data, as the key to their success are listening stations. These listening stations, dotted around the coastline, note each time the shark passes by, so can be used to track localised and more distant migrations and movements.

Satellite tags are more sophisticated, and many are used for short-term studies. As radio waves cannot transmit through water, these tags are only used on sharks that regularly come close to the surface, such as Whale Sharks and Great White Sharks. Each time the tag breaks the surface it transmits its location to a satellite, allowing scientists to study the movement of far-ranging species.

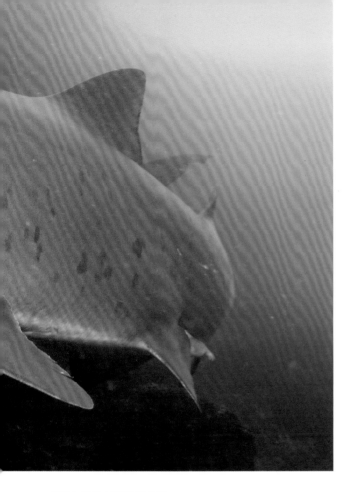

Archival tags are quite sophisticated, and can record the shark's movements, depth and water temperature. Most are externally placed and designed to release from the shark after a certain period, but others require the shark to be recaptured.

While we have learnt much from tagging, it is often an invasive study technique, requiring sharks to be captured and recaptured. Tags can also cut into the flesh of the shark, causing infections, and many tags are also lost or become fouled by algae. In recent years scientists have looked at other ways to study sharks, and have found that they can identify individual animals from their unique countershading, scars and spot patterns.

SPOT PATTERNS

Many sharks have spots and blotches on their bodies that are as individual as fingerprints in humans. One of the first shark species to be studied via its spot pattern was, and still is, the Grey Nurse Shark. Endangered on the east coast of Australia, divers have assisted researchers in studying the movements and populations of these sharks by photographing their distinctive body spot patterns. This species is also studied in a similar way in South Africa. Spot patterns have also been used to study and identify Whale Sharks and Leopard Sharks. Great White Sharks are also studied in a similar way, using photographs of their individual colour patterns and scars.

We still have a lot to learn about sharks, but what we have discovered so far reveals them to be complex creatures of the deep.

SHARKS UNDER THREAT

Sharks have traditionally been taken for food by indigenous people around the world for many thousands of years. Catches were always low until large commercial fishing operations appeared in the 20th century. However, with their slow growth rates and small reproductive capacity, sharks are easily overexploited, and today many species are now endangered because of overfishing.

TRADITIONAL FISHERIES

Many coastal people from around the world have traditionally captured sharks for food and other uses. While most landed the sharks primarily for food, they also found other uses for the skin, teeth and liver oil. The rough skin of sharks has been used as sandpaper, for sword-handle grips and also turned into leather. Shark's teeth have also been used to make weapons, jewellery and ceremonial decorations. Shark liver oil is a rich source of vitamins A and D, and was consumed, used as a lubricant, and also burned in lamps. These traditional fisheries saw little impact on shark numbers until the 20th century.

BELOW - A California Swell Shark falls victim to a gill net off Baja, Mexico.
OPPOSITE - Many sharks end up as bycatch. This School Shark was captured in a gill net intended for California Halibut off Baja, Mexico.

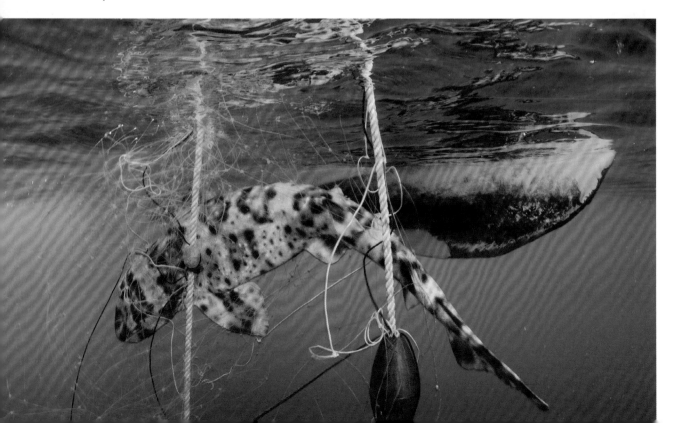

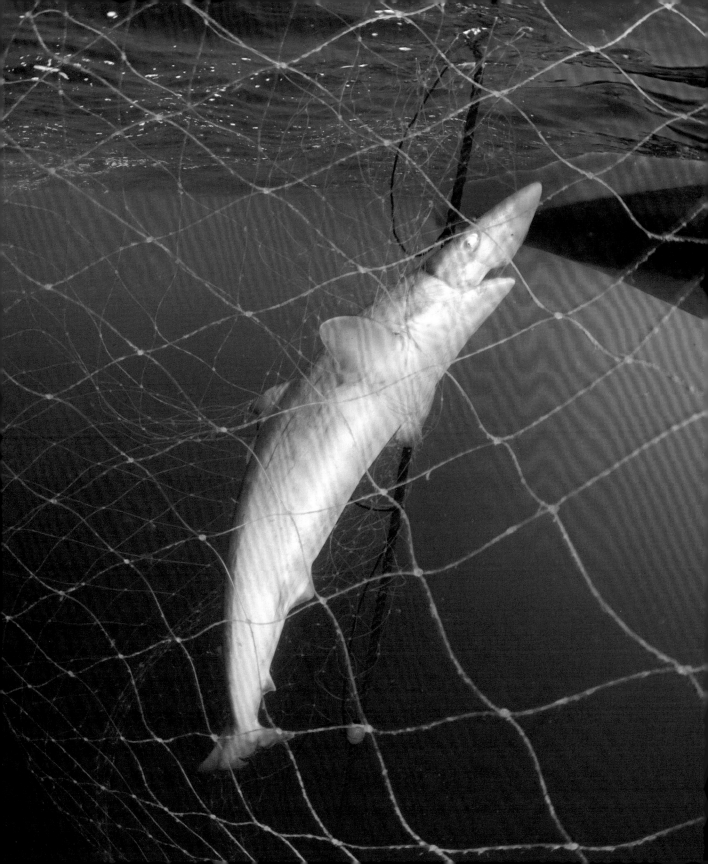

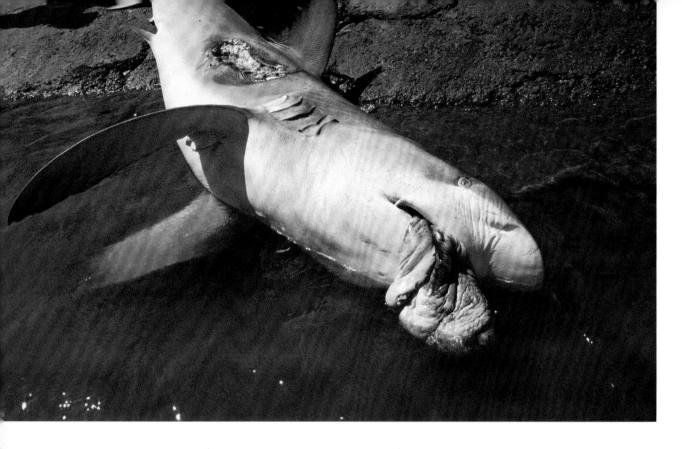
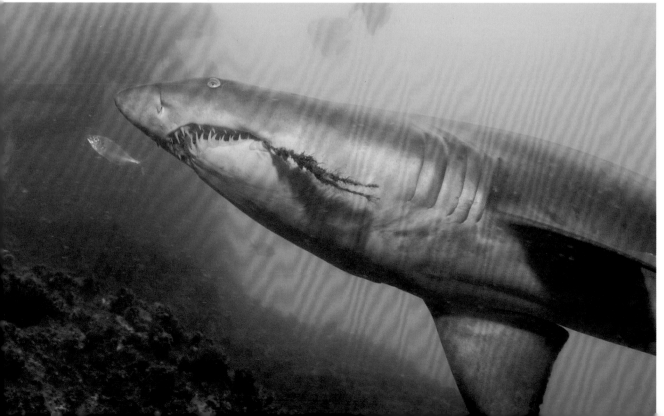

SHARK SEAFOOD INDUSTRY

After the industrial revolution, and the construction of steamships, fishing boats became more efficient and sharks could be captured in larger numbers. However, only a handful of shark species were taken commercially as a source of food, with the main target being hound sharks. These sharks have been taken in large numbers since the 1920s, and have been sold as 'flake', a popular food in the fish-and-chip trade in Australia. Many hound shark fisheries are now thought to be close to collapse, and there have been numerous calls to protect these sharks from overexploitation and extinction. A number of other sharks are also taken commercially for consumption, such as wobbegongs in Australia, Greenland Sharks in Iceland, and dogfish sharks, catsharks, Basking Sharks and even makos in other parts of Europe. However, eating shark flesh is not recommended, as being at the top of the food chain, it often contains high levels of mercury and other heavy metals.

OPPOSITE TOP - A Bronze Whaler senselessly killed for sport.
OPPOSITE BOTTOM - Endangered Grey Nurse Sharks are often hooked by fishers. The sharks can survive hooks in the mouth, but die from septicaemia if the hooks get into the stomach.
BELOW LEFT - Bags of chopped up School Shark left at a wharf in Tasmania, Australia, to be used in crayfish pots.
BELOW TOP RIGHT - Various whaler species waiting to be sold at a fish market in Dubai.
BELOW RIGHT - Pacific Sharpnose Sharks captured by longlining in the Sea of Cortez, Mexico.

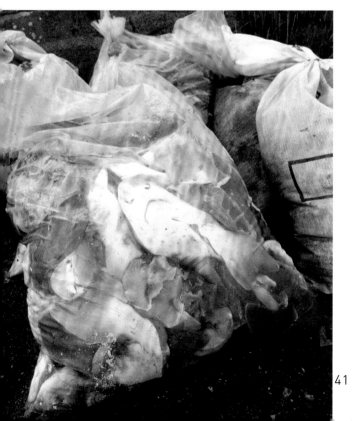

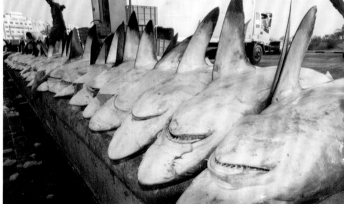

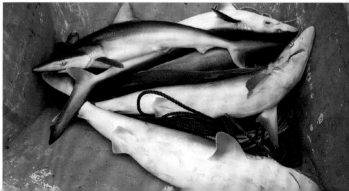

BEACH MESHING

Another threat to shark populations appeared in Australia in the 1930s. At the time Australia had seen a number of shark attacks, so the New South Wales State Government decided to put nets off the popular beaches of Sydney in 1937. Known as beach meshing, these nets are still in use today and consist of rows of nets set parallel to the beach, each one being 6m (20ft) high by 150m (500ft) long. The nets are suspended by floats and anchored to the bottom, and are designed to intercept anything that swims towards the beach. They don't actually stop sharks from reaching swimmers in shallow water, and many sharks are captured when returning to deep water. Their main purpose is to cull shark numbers, and they certainly work. Over the decades these nets have killed thousands of sharks, plus many other marine animals. A massive decline in shark numbers, and an apparent reduction in shark attacks, was seen as a great success, leading to beaches being meshed in other parts of New South Wales and also in Queensland and South Africa in the 1950s.

Statistics relating to catches have only been kept since the 1950s, with the nets off New South Wales taking almost 10,000 sharks between 1950 and 1990. Off Queensland the numbers between 1962 and 1978 are staggering, with 20,500 sharks killed. But there were also a lot of other marine animals inadvertently killed in these nets, including 40,889 rays, 2,654 turtles, 317 dolphins and 468 dugongs. In reality, most of the sharks captured, around 69 per cent, are harmless species such as wobbegongs, angel sharks, Port Jackson Sharks and small hammerhead sharks.

In Queensland some of these nets have been replaced with the slightly less destructive drum lines. These drum lines consist of a baited hook suspended under a floating drum. They are quite effective in catching larger, potentially dangerous, sharks without decimating other marine life. In 2014 drum lines were also deployed off Western Australia after a series of shark attacks. However, they didn't remain in place for long, as public protests and a recommendation from the Environment Protection Authority saw them removed.

There have been many reviews and proposals from conservation groups to get beach meshing and drum lines banned, but it continues today as governments fear a backlash from the beach-going, and still shark-paranoid, public.

SHARK FINNING

Sharks have always been captured as bycatch by many net and line fisheries. Seen as little more than a nuisance, they were generally returned to the ocean alive. However, Asian fishers didn't return sharks back to the ocean, as they removed the fins for shark fin soup. Seen as a delicacy by the Chinese, shark fin soup uses the fibrous rays in shark fins, which are actually tasteless and add little more than gelatinous bulk. Taking shark fins was once seen as a very minor fishery by most nations, with little money to be made from the fins and a lot of trouble to remove them.

However in the 1980s, coinciding with the growth of the Asian economies, there was suddenly a demand for shark fin soup. A kilogram of dried shark fin was soon worth over US$100, but the body of the shark was next to worthless. With a lot of quick money to be made, all sharks captured were having their fins sliced off and their bodies dumped into the ocean. This practice, known as finning, often saw the fins removed while the shark was still alive, only to die a slow and agonising death.

Many fishers quickly realised that they could make more money catching sharks than fish, with the bycatch suddenly becoming the main catch. Fishers started to target any shark species they could land. By the end of the 1980s an estimated 100 million sharks a year were being killed around the world, with many of the fins being imported into China. The numbers have since dropped as shark numbers have declined, but the decline has meant that the price of shark fin has risen.

Moves to stop or restrict shark finning in the past have met with resistance from a fishing industry that is already unprofitable. While many countries have placed restrictions on finning, requiring the entire shark to be landed, a large black market exists and many shark populations have decreased by as much as 90 per cent. Some shark species are now protected by the Convention on International Trade in Endangered Species of Wild Fauna and Flora (CITES), but with a high demand and high prices, plus many illegal fishing operations, sharks will continue to be slaughtered until the demand for shark fin soup declines or sharks become extinct.

BELOW - Shark finning is a hideous practise that has seen shark numbers plummet around the world.

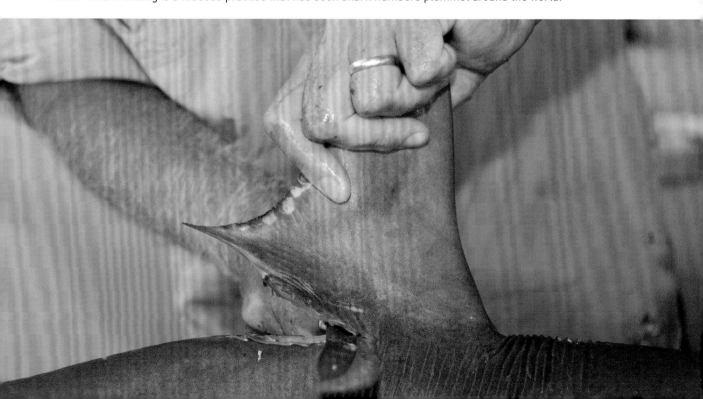

SHARK CONSERVATION

With shark populations plummeting around the planet due to fishing pressures, what can be done to save these vital members of a healthy marine ecosystem?

While some enlightened countries such as the Bahamas, Maldives and Palau have fully protected all sharks in their waters, most nations have done little to protect them, as they are still seen as a danger to the general public. Protecting sharks may seem like the key, but this doesn't work by itself, as those studying the Grey Nurse Shark population off the east coast of Australia will testify.

When the Grey Nurse Shark was protected in New South Wales in 1984 it became the world's first protected shark. This was seen as a victory for common sense, as the shark population had dramatically declined over the previous decades due to fishing pressures. Unfortunately, the government didn't protect the shark's key habitats at the same time, so fishers continued to catch them. While most sharks were released alive, many later died from hooks embedded in their stomachs. Many sharks also continued to be killed by fishers, some even for their fins. In 2002 the New South Wales State Government finally declared ten key Grey Nurse habitats as protected, but strangely still allowing fishers access to the sites, as long as they didn't anchor. So Grey Nurse Sharks in these locations continue to get hooked and die.

This ad hoc protection has been repeated in other countries, especially when it comes to shark finning. While a number of countries, like the USA, have banned shark finning, others allow the finning of certain species as long as the entire shark is landed. Allowing any shark fishing puts all the sharks in the area at risk, whether they are protected or not, as fish hooks don't discriminate, and often the fishers don't as well.

Even when the sharks and their habitats are protected, little is done in most countries to enforce the law. Legal and illegal fishers have been caught fishing in protected waters for sharks, often after they have already decimated the local shark population. Plus many shark species migrate, so once they leave protected waters they are easy prey for fishers.

Obviously more protection for sharks and their habitats is needed, and more importantly the law needs to be enforced. Unfortunately, until the demand for shark fin soup declines, shark numbers will continue to decline.

So what can the average person do to help save sharks? Don't eat shark fin soup and don't patronise restaurants that have it on the menu, and inform them why they will not get your business. Also don't buy shark products such as shark teeth and jaws, and avoid supplements containing shark oil or cartilage. It was once believed that sharks don't get cancer, which is untrue, but this myth is still used to sell these products. Education and knowledge is the key to saving sharks.

There are a number of conservation groups fighting to save sharks, such as Sharks Savers (www.sharksavers.org), Sea Shepherd (www.seashepherd.org), Shark Trust (www.sharktrust.org) and Support Our Sharks (www.supportoursharks.com). They are educating people not to eat shark fin soup and

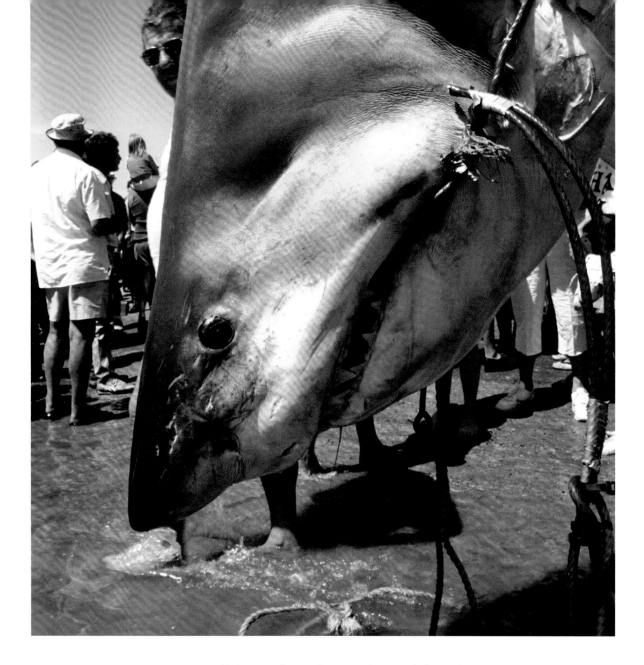

encouraging restaurants not to sell this product. They are also working with governments to get better protection for sharks. These conservation groups have seen many victories, but there is a long way to go in the battle to save sharks.

ABOVE - The Great White Shark is now a protected species in many countries, but this one was unfortunately killed in Australia before the law changed.

FEEDING SHARKS

Most sharks are shy and timid of divers, which makes them difficult to observe, photograph and study. Divers long ago discovered that by feeding sharks they will come in quite close and stay around until the food is gone. However, shark feeding is a touchy subject, with many arguments for and against the practice.

Humans have been directly and indirectly feeding sharks for thousands of years. They feed on the garbage we dump in the sea and follow fishing boats to pick up scraps and bycatch. The whaler sharks are also commonly known as requiem sharks because of their habit of following boats and waiting for discarded food scraps and burials at sea – much like a funeral procession in the eyes of many early sailors. Recreational fishers occasionally wind in their catch to find it bitten in half by a shark and spear-fishers must always be vigilant for sharks looking to steal their catch.

Shark feeds were first conducted by underwater film-makers in order to capture spectacular action of so called 'man-eaters'. Soon, commercial dive operators started to do their own feeds for paying customers. Shark feeds are now popular at many locations around the world, with divers spending thousands of dollars to see sharks feeding up close.

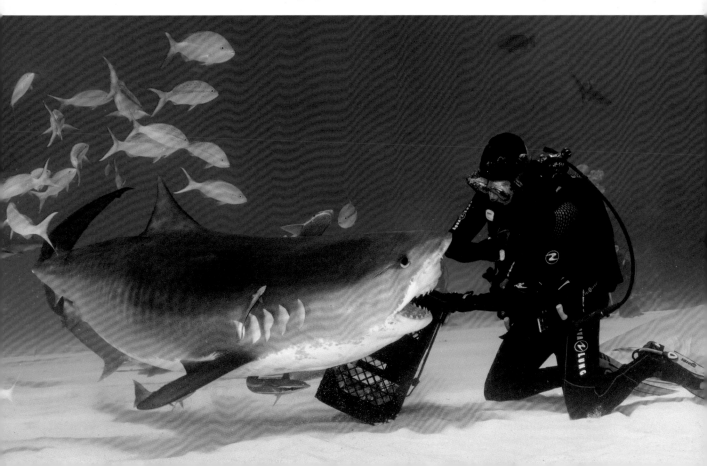

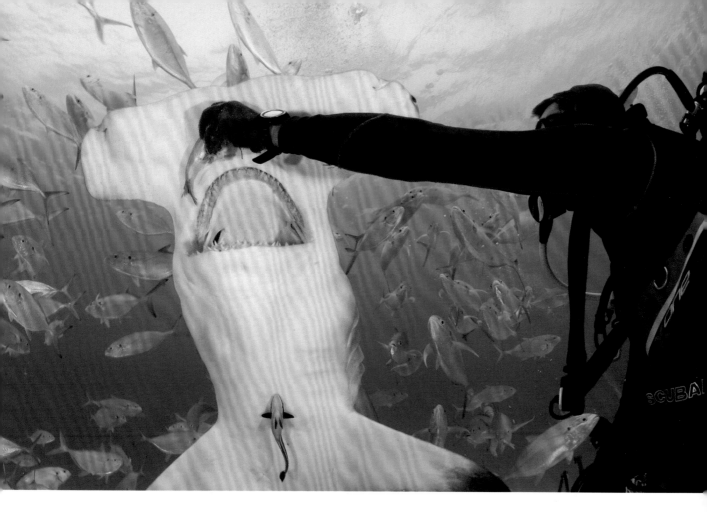

Shark feeding is not simply a process of placing baits in the water and expecting sharks to arrive. There is a real art and science to attracting different species of shark. Reef sharks are the easiest to attract, as most have a small home range and can nearly always be found on the same patch of reef. Once the sharks have been fed a few times they soon learn the routine and await the arrival of the boat and food. However, to attract larger free-swimming sharks they first have to be lured close with chum.

Chum, or berley, which is usually made of fish blood, fish oil and ground-up fish flesh, is ladled from the boat to form a surface slick. This slick spreads with the current and any shark that detects this enticing cocktail follows it back to the source. This method is used to attract Great White Sharks and other open-ocean species. Often these sharks are not fed, as the chum is enough to keep them interested.

OPPOSITE - Tiger Sharks are rarely seen in the wild and are very timid around divers, but are attracted to a number of shark feeds around the world.
ABOVE - Hand-feeding sharks, like this Great Hammerhead, should be left to the professionals, as occasionally they bite the hand that feeds them.

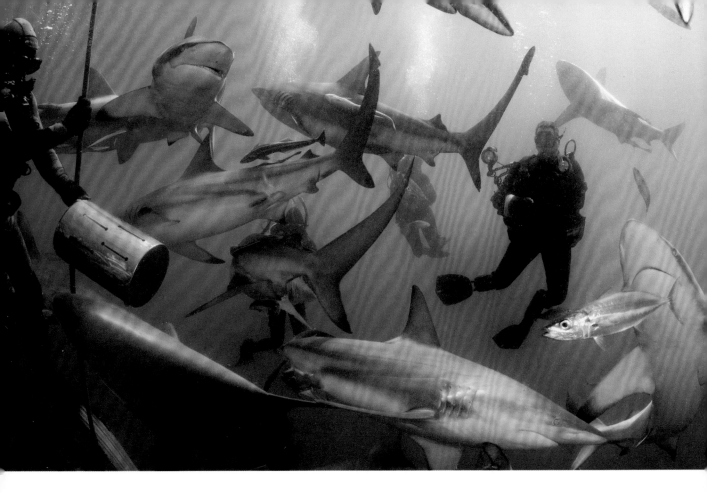

Professional shark feeds are well organised and safe for both the divers and sharks. However, the practice is not popular with some people, and has been banned in a few areas, including parts of Australia and the USA.

Should we be feeding sharks at all, for either study or entertainment? Some people argue that sharks associate humans with food and this has led to more attacks. This is not true as research has shown that sharks are intelligent animals and learn to associate us as a source of food, but not as the food itself. Sharks take advantage of a free hand-out, but rarely bite the hand that feeds them. When the food is finished, the sharks move off to search for their own natural prey. Shark feeds are also conducted in areas well away from swimmers and surfers, so pose no threat to other ocean users. People fishing for sharks pose more of a threat to swimmers and surfers, as they often do this close to popular beaches.

Others have argued that by feeding sharks we are changing their natural behaviour. This is certainly true. At many feeding sites the sharks appear as soon as the boat anchors, these sharks having learnt

ABOVE - Divers surrounded by Blacktip Sharks at a mid-water shark feed at Aliwal Shoal, South Africa.

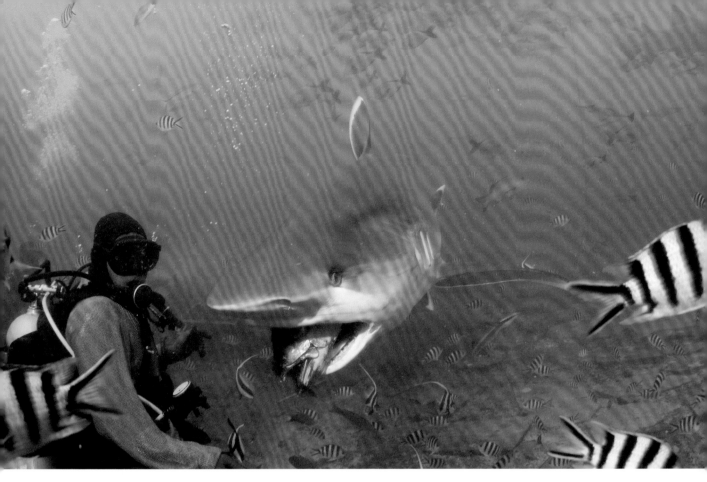

to associate the boat with a free meal. However, the amount of food they receive at a shark feed is little more than a snack. Once the food is gone they generally disperse and go about their normal behaviour.

Sharks also associate trawlers and other fishing boats with free food, taking advantage of bycatch that is wastefully shovelled back into the sea. Far more damage has been done to sharks' behaviour through the relentless overfishing of our oceans, which decimates both fish and shark numbers.

Feeding sharks does have one huge benefit; it puts an economic value on sharks, showing they are worth a lot more alive than dead. A number of countries, such as the Maldives, Palau and the Bahamas, have fully protected all sharks in their waters. Shark feeds in the Bahamas are very popular and are thought to contribute more than US$78 million dollars to the economy annually.

The benefits that have been obtained from shark feeds far outweigh the minor disadvantages. We still know very little about these creatures and we would know even less if it weren't for shark feeds.

ABOVE - A Silvertip Shark takes a fish head at a shark feed at The Bistro, Beqa Lagoon, Fiji.

SHARK ATTACKS

The average person has an unnatural fear of shark attack, imagining millions of mindless killing machines are lurking in the oceans waiting to attack every human they find. Any diver who has encountered sharks knows that this isn't true, and is an unrealistic fear created by movies, the media and ignorance. Sharks are an important part of a natural and healthy marine environment, and have no interest in eating people. The great majority of shark attacks are either the shark biting someone on the surface to see what they are, or biting someone by mistake when after their normal prey.

In reality, shark attacks on humans are extremely rare, with a few dozen bites on people every year and on average five fatalities. Humans have more to fear from dogs, cows, mosquitos, snakes and falling coconuts, as these all kill more people every year than sharks do. But as this is a book about diving with sharks, let's look at the real risks divers face from sharks.

Very few divers are actually bitten by sharks, as most shark attacks happen at the surface on swimmers and surfers, and often in murky shallow water. Most attacks on divers are linked to spear-fishing activities. In most encounters the shark will simply take the speared fish, but if the diver has the fish at hand or close to them, the shark may bite the diver instead.

When no baits are in the water, most encounters between divers and potentially dangerous sharks such as the Great White Shark and Tiger Shark are either very brief or involve little more than the shark swimming around the diver for a quick look. Divers are not prey for these sharks, which view us as another large predator, so they tend to check us out to see what we are and then move on. Each year thousands of divers report close encounters with potentially dangerous sharks, and the main complaint these divers express is that the shark didn't come close enough for a photo!

Of course large sharks are far more dangerous when baits are added to the mix at a shark feed. At professionally organised shark feeds, shark bites are extremely rare, but they do occasionally happen, especially when people get careless and don't follow the rules.

Shark feeds can occur on the seafloor or in open water, and can involve a diver feeding the sharks or the food being in a box or even compacted into a frozen block. Every shark feed is different and has its own risks, and the shark feed organisers will brief divers to ensure they have the best and safest experience possible. In general, divers should wear a full wetsuit, hood and gloves, so no flesh is exposed, and never wave their hands about as a shark may think this is food. And always stick with the group – don't get isolated from other divers.

Shark feeds done on a reef or sandy bottom are generally the safest, as divers can kneel or rest on the bottom. Most of the action happens in front of the divers, but don't forget to always look around. Divers

OPPOSITE - This Great White Shark was killed by a fisher in revenge for the death of a surfer off Brisbane, Australia. Eyewitnesses to the shark attack claimed it was a Tiger Shark, but that didn't stop this poor shark being slaughtered because it was in the area.

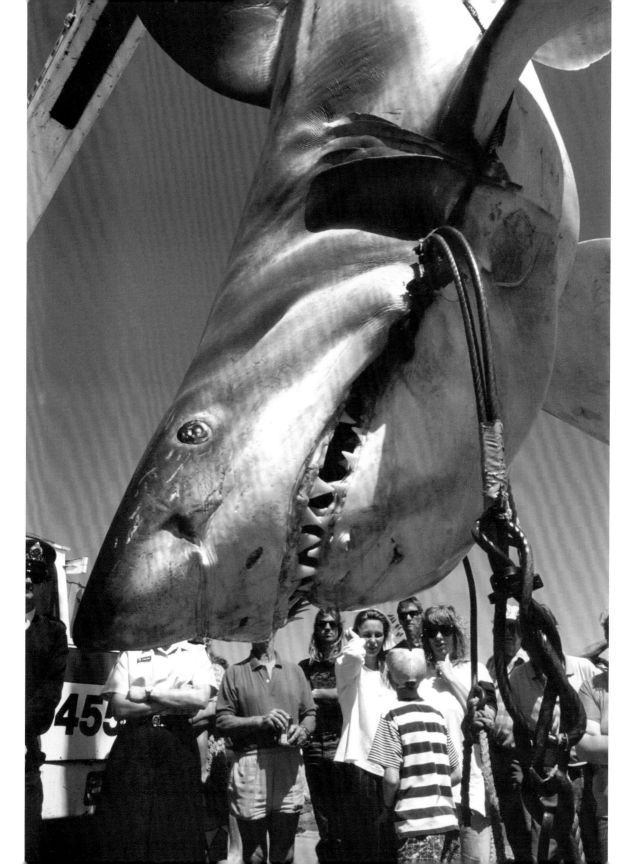

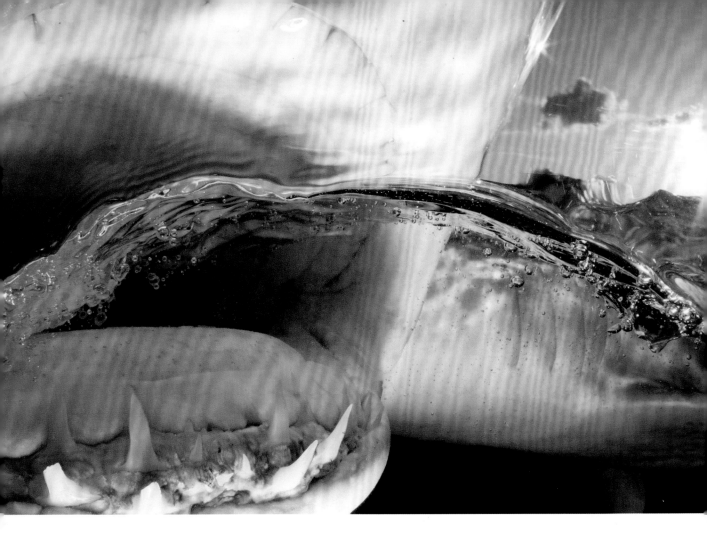

generally don't have to worry about sharks sneaking up from behind, but stray pieces of bait can cause a problem, and divers have been bitten when bait has floated close to them. This rarely happens as most dive staff at shark feeds are watching the baits, the sharks and the guests to ensure nothing goes wrong.

Shark feeds done in open water are much more difficult for dive staff to control, so divers have to be more aware of themselves, the baits and the sharks. For a start divers need good buoyancy control so they don't sink or end up going up and down like a yoyo. Divers should also maintain a vertical position and work with another diver so they are positioned back to back, then they don't have to worry about sharks approaching from behind. In open water the sharks can come from any direction, so always look around, up and down. The sharks are mainly interested in the baits, but some open-ocean species such as Oceanic Whitetip and Blue Sharks are very curious and have been known to take a bite, just to see what a diver is.

The people taking the most risk at any shark feed are the shark feeders. While the sharks are quick to learn the feeding procedure, mistakes do happen, and some sharks get overexcited or confused when grabbing the food. Many shark feeders wear chain-mail suits to ensure they don't get bitten accidentally.

Underwater photographers are slightly more at risk of getting bitten, as many get stuck behind the viewfinder and forget to keep an eye on the action happening elsewhere. Don't get carried away taking photos or video and forget where you are. Lower the camera every now and then and enjoy the experience of having so many wonderful sharks cruising around.

Shark bites at shark feeds are extremely rare, in fact more divers get bitten each year by harmless-looking bottom-dwelling sharks. Most bottom-dwelling sharks have small teeth and are very docile, except for the angel sharks and wobbegongs. Both these families of shark have sharp dagger-like teeth and they are not afraid to use them on divers that harass them. Wobbegongs and angel sharks generally flee from divers when they get too close or pat them, but every now and then one will bite back. While an angel shark will generally give a quick bite and swim off, wobbegongs will sometimes lock their jaws and refuse to let go, so always treat these sharks with respect.

In reality, the chances of a shark biting a diver are so remote that divers have much more to fear from other divers, currents, the bends and seasickness.

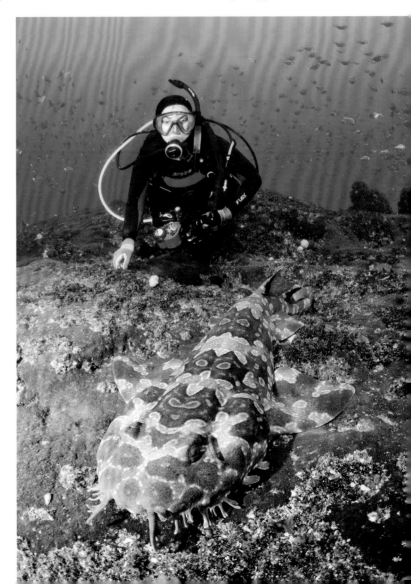

OPPOSITE - The Lemon Shark in this picture might look like it is attacking the underwater photographer, but is actually snapping at baits. The only danger the photographer is facing is scratches to an expensive underwater camera housing.

RIGHT - Spotted Wobbegongs look harmless but have bitten many divers that try to pat them.

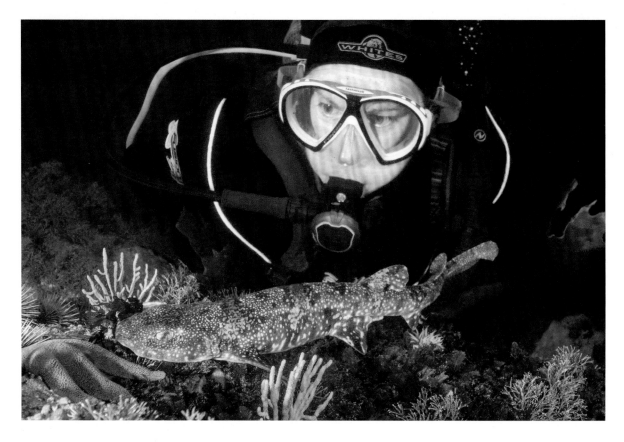

DIVING WITH SHARKS

There is nothing like the thrill of encountering your first shark underwater. For many people it has come after a lifetime of fearing these creatures, but for others it is a desire to see one of these majestic predators of the deep. Either way the encounter is generally very different to what many imaged or feared. In most cases the encounter will be brief, with the shark swimming around the reef going about its daily business. If lucky the shark might even inspect the diver, but as most sharks are shy and wary they generally stay well away from divers unless baits are in the water. Most people, however, can't fail to be thrilled or even changed by the experience of their first shark encounter.

Diving with sharks may not be for everyone, but once a diver has seen one of these streamlined and graceful creatures, and realised it is not trying to eat them, sharks soon become the highlight of many diving adventures. While exploring colourful coral reefs, investigating shipwrecks and seeing turtles, friendly fish and other reef creatures is great fun, there is something extra special about diving with sharks. While some divers are happy to leave their shark encounters to chance, those that get the shark diving bug will find they are planning dives, and booking dive holidays, just to see sharks.

All shark encounters are different, as all sharks are different in their behaviour and habits. Even individual sharks of the same species react differently to divers depending on the situation, their personality and their past experiences with divers. However, for simplicity, sharks can be classified as two types – the free-swimmers and the bottom-dwellers.

The free-swimmers are the species that are mostly seen swimming around the reef or in mid-water. The great majority of these shark species are wary of divers, including many that are considered potentially dangerous. Encounters with most free-swimming sharks are very brief, with the shark keeping its distance and quickly disappearing into the blue. The only way to see many of these free-swimming sharks is to introduce bait, to draw the sharks close and keep them interested.

The free-swimming sharks are generally the species that most divers want to see, including Great White Sharks, Whale Sharks, Tiger Sharks, Bull Sharks, Grey Nurse Sharks, whaler sharks and

OPPOSITE - Even small sharks like the Puffadder Shyshark are fun to dive with.
BELOW - A Great Hammerhead cruises between divers at a shark feed at Bimini Sands, Bahamas.

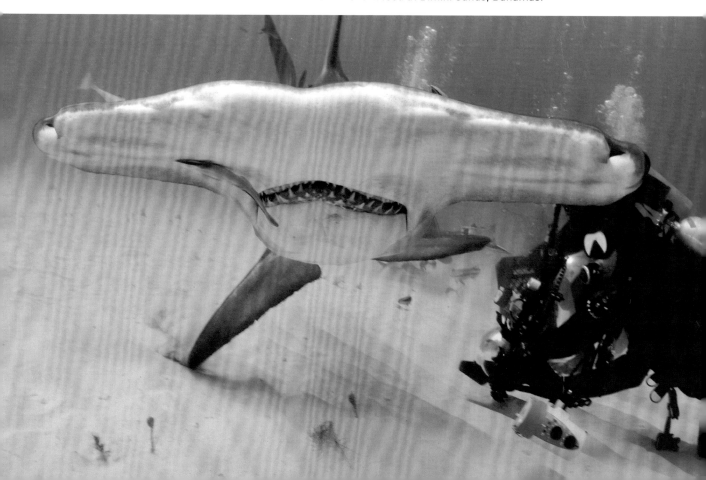

hammerhead sharks. These species are always exciting to dive with, and are guaranteed to get the heart pumping and the adrenaline flowing. Most of these large free-swimming sharks are the star attractions at shark feeds, and because of this they are generally easier to find than their cousins, the shark species that dwell on the bottom.

The bottom-dwellers are the shark species that rest on the bottom, sometimes out in the open, but many of them hide in caves, crevices or even under a layer of sand. These sharks are far easier for divers to approach, even though some are wary of bubble-blowing divers. However, many bottom-dwelling species are difficult to find. Often eaten by larger sharks and other predators, bottom-dwelling sharks are experts at concealing themselves. Many of these sharks have elongated or flattened bodies, and most have camouflaged skin patterns that make them difficult to spot.

Bottom-dwelling sharks are still great fun to dive with. This group including Leopard Sharks, wobbegongs, horn sharks, angel sharks, bamboo sharks and catsharks. While bottom-dwelling shark species might not get the adrenaline flowing as fast as a close encounter with a free-swimming shark, many of these species are much rarer and require much more effort to find, so the encounters can be just as exciting and rewarding.

A final word of warning, shark diving is addictive, as once divers start studying, photographing and sharing the water with these wonderful creatures, they will want to see more and more of them.

BELOW - Grey Nurse Sharks are wonderful sharks to dive with. They look mean and menacing but are in fact docile and harmless.
OPPOSITE - Shortfin Makos can get very excited when baits are in the water, snapping at cameras, boats and divers. Fortunately bites are very rare.

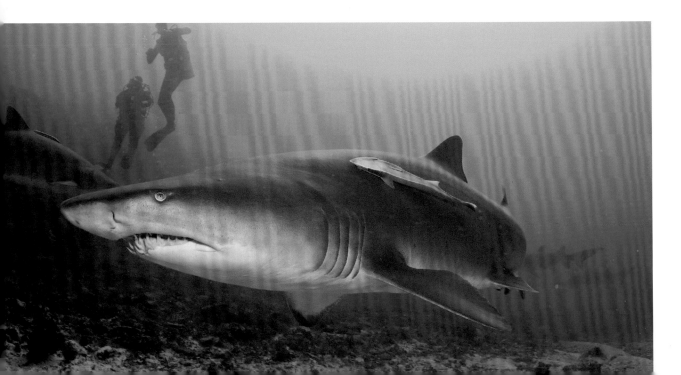

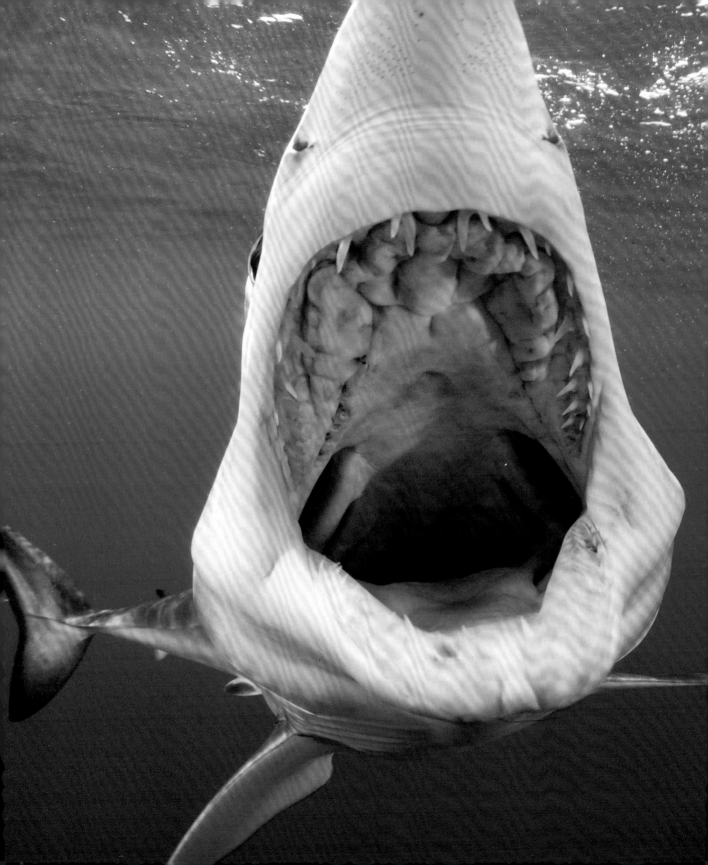

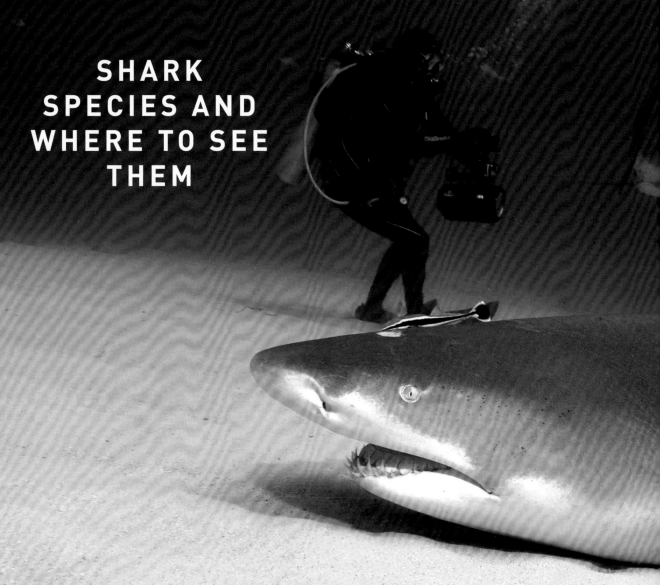

SHARK SPECIES AND WHERE TO SEE THEM

There are currently more than 500 known species of sharks, and many new species still await discovery. However, divers only come into contact with a small proportion of shark species, as most are found in deep water or in turbid estuaries where diving is not possible. The following pages contain a guide to shark species that divers are most likely to encounter. This list is arranged by family, and includes information about each shark's size, description, distribution and also the best dive locations to encounter the species. Information is also provided on diving with each species, including what they are like with divers, how they react to divers, and tips that can help divers get close for the best possible shark encounter.

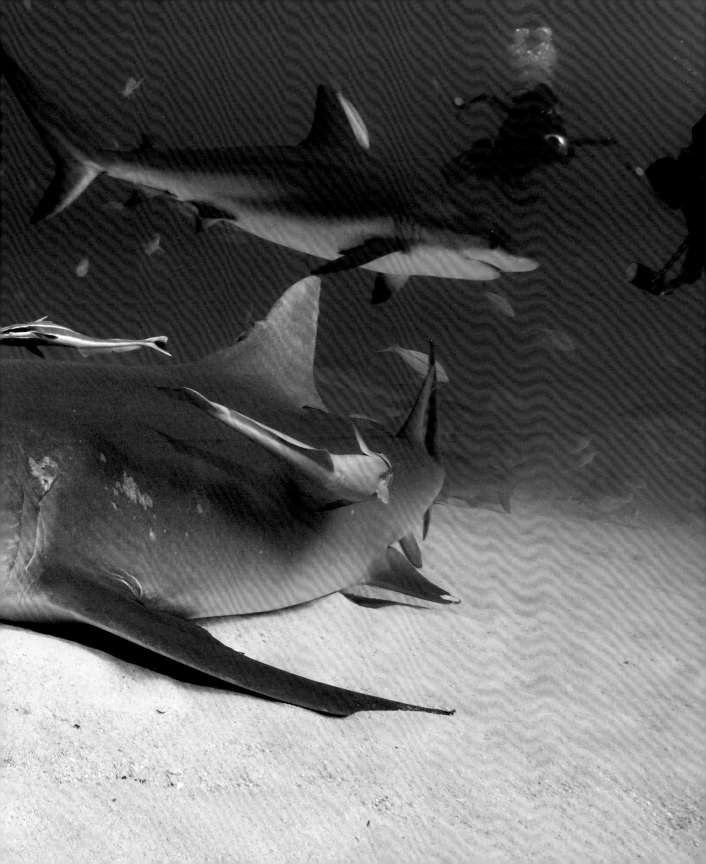

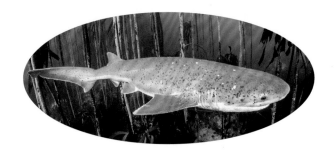

COWSHARKS

FAMILY HEXANCHIDAE

This family of large sharks is considered quite primitive as all species have either six or seven gill slits, unlike all other sharks that have five. From fossil records they seem to have changed little in the last 200 million years. Cowsharks are very distinctive as they have blunt faces and what looks like a permanent smile. Their single dorsal fin is set far back on the body towards the tail. Worldwide four species of cowshark are currently known and are found in both tropical and temperate seas.

Little is known about the biology and behaviour of the sharks in this family, but it is known that the females retain egg cases in the uterus until the young hatch, before giving birth to live young. Litters also appear to be large and can number more than 100. Cowsharks feed on large prey, including sharks, rays, fish, seals and crustaceans, plus they also scavenge for carrion. Most members of this family inhabit deep water and are found in depths from 100–2,000m (330–6,560ft), however two cowshark species venture into shallow water and are encountered by divers.

DIVING WITH COWSHARKS

These large, slow-moving sharks are generally considered harmless to divers, but can become aggressive if baits are in the water, and have even bitten a few divers. Cowsharks are thought to be ambush predators, using an unexpected burst of speed to take prey and surprise divers. Of the two species encountered by divers, the Bluntnose Sixgill Shark is less commonly seen and most encounters are very brief. Broadnose Sevengill Sharks are more common in shallow water. Once they become accustomed to the presence of divers they swim boldly around and closely inspect them, allowing for great photographic opportunities with these strange-looking sharks.

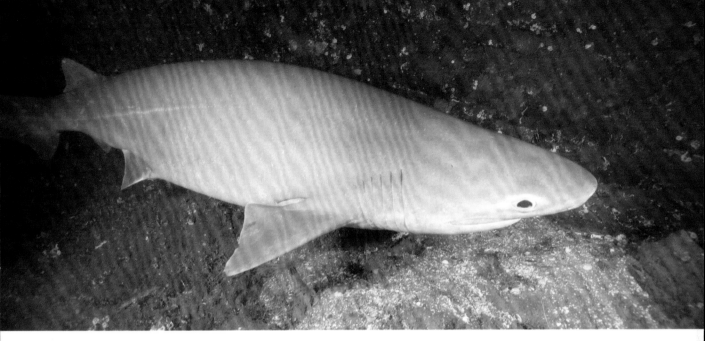

BLUNTNOSE SIXGILL SHARK *Hexanchus griseus*

A very large shark, which grows to a length of 4.8m (15.7ft). As the name suggests, they have six gills and a broad, blunt nose. They also have reflective eyes that are a fluorescent green colour. Found in tropical and temperate waters around the world, they usually live in deep water, on the continental shelf in depths to 2,000m (6,560ft). However, they occasionally venture into shallow water at night, and at a few locations during the day.

WHERE TO SEE

Unless you have a submersible and can drop into the depths, the best place to see a Bluntnose Sixgill Shark is the Pacific Northwest coast of Canada and the USA. There are several locations where divers have encountered these sharks between Washington State and Vancouver Island, but their appearances are unpredictable. Since 2010, they have most commonly been seen during the summer months in Barkley Sound on the west coast of Vancouver Island. They were once regularly seen off Seattle, but that population in Puget Sound seems to have moved on.

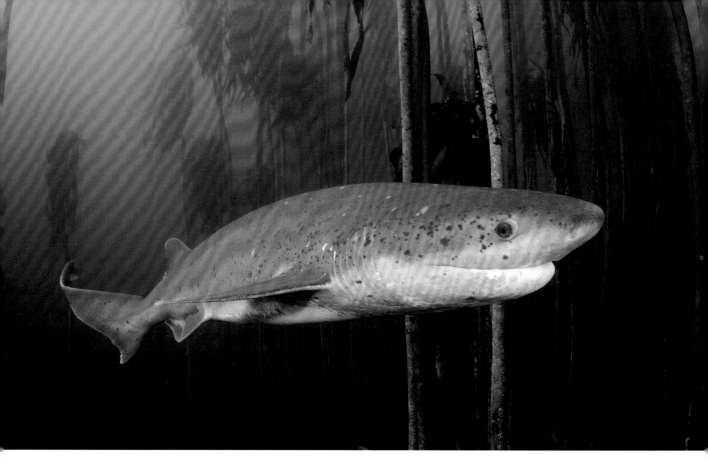

BROADNOSE SEVENGILL SHARK *Notorynchus cepedianus*

Occurs in temperate waters around the world, but has a more limited range than the Bluntnose Sixgill Shark in the Northern Hemisphere. Grows to 3m (9.8ft) in length and covered with a scattering of dark and light spots. Found in depths to 135m (443ft) and will enter shallow bays, especially on the incoming tide when searching for food. These large sharks have a very varied diet and eat everything from octopus to fish and seals to other sharks.

WHERE TO SEE

Encounters with Broadnose Sevengill Sharks used to be rare, but in the last decade a few locations have been discovered where divers can have a close encounter. South Africa is the best place as they gather in False Bay, near Cape Town. While up to a dozen sharks can be seen at this site year-round, False Bay is best dived between November and May, when the water is calmer and clearer. Other sites where they can occasionally be seen include: La Jolla Cove in California, USA; Fiordland, New Zealand; Bahía Bustamante, Argentina; and off Melbourne, Australia.

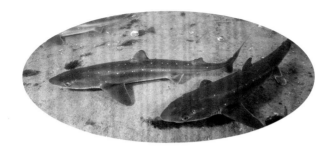

DOGFISH SHARKS

FAMILY SQUALIDAE

The dogfish sharks, or dogfishes, are mainly found in deep water and as such only a handful of species are seen by divers. The dogfish shark family contains more than 30 species, which are found around the planet. These sharks typically have a short snout, large eyes, no anal fin and dorsal fin spines. The spines vary greatly between species, with some large and some very small, but all contain a venom that is mildly toxic to humans. These sharks are generally small, only 1–2m (3.3–6.6ft) long, and feed on a variety of prey, including fish, octopus, squid, crabs, molluscs and worms. Often feed in packs, and have small saw-like teeth.

Dogfish sharks give birth to live young, and have litters that number from 1–30. They have the longest gestation period of any shark, which can vary from 12–24 months. These small sharks are targeted by fisheries, and as such their numbers have declined in many areas. However, being a deep-water species, not a lot is really known about their biology and behaviour.

DIVING WITH DOGFISH SHARKS

Dogfish sharks are great little sharks to dive with, and are often curious of divers. Unbaited encounters are generally brief, with the shark coming in for a quick look and then fleeing. With baits in the water these sharks will swarm around divers, allowing for very close photographs and observations. Dogfish sharks are generally considered harmless, but be mindful of those sharp spines in front of their dorsal fins.

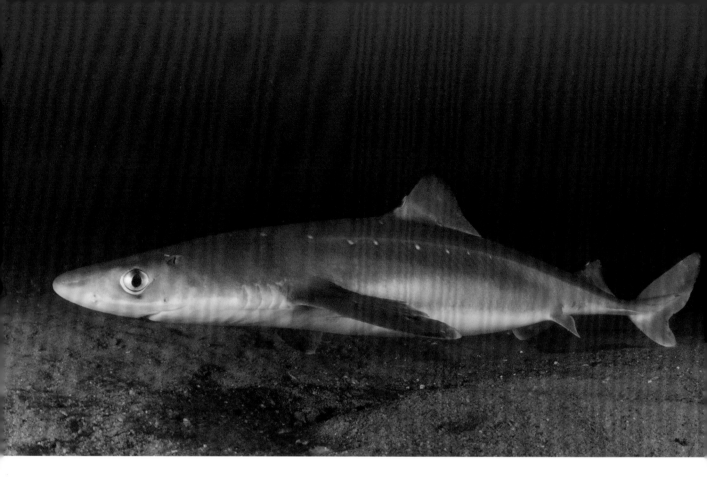

SPINY DOGFISH *Squalus acanthias*

The most common and widespread member of its family. Found in temperate waters around the world, except the North Pacific, from the shallows to 900m, and mostly found over sandy bottoms. Growing to a length of 2m (6.6ft), the Spiny Dogfish is typically grey to brown in colour and has a scattering of small white spots across its back. This species is known to migrate with changes in water temperature, preferring cool temperate waters. Can live for 70 years and thought to be the most abundant shark species in the world.

WHERE TO SEE

Considering how common and widespread this species is, there are few places where divers can see Spiny Dogfish. While divers can have a chance encounter with a Spiny Dogfish anywhere across its range, one place they can be seen is off Rhode Island, USA. Baits are required to lure these small sharks in, and on a good day 50 or more can be seen. The best time of year to see them in this area is during summer.

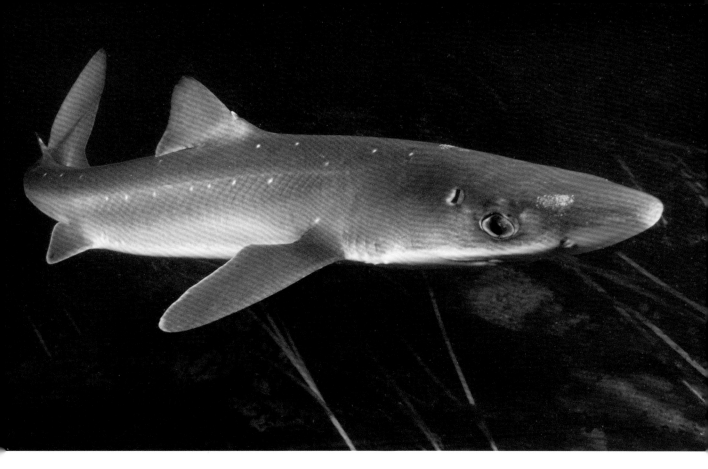

PACIFIC SPINY DOGFISH *Squalus suckleyi*

Looks very similar to the Spiny Dogfish and for a long time the two were considered to be the same species, but recent research has shown that they should be treated separately. The Pacific Spiny Dogfish is another temperate-water species that replaces the Spiny Dogfish in the North Pacific. It reaches a length of 1.6m (5.2ft) and is often found in large schools.

WHERE TO SEE

The Pacific Spiny Dogfish is mostly seen by divers north of Seattle, USA, and off Vancouver Island, Canada, during the summer months. Divers sometimes see them in Saanich Inlet and around Campbell River. While at these sites divers may have a brief encounter, the best way to interact with dozens, and sometimes hundreds, of these little sharks is with the use of baits. Shark feeds to attract Pacific Spiny Dogfish have been very successful at Quadra Island, with large numbers seen in this area in July and August.

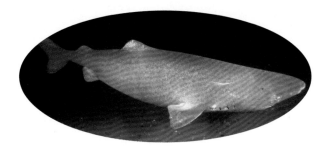

SLEEPER SHARKS

FAMILY SOMNIOSIDAE

The sleeper sharks are closely related to the dogfish sharks, and actually both form part of the large Squaliformes order. These sharks inhabit deep-water areas around the globe, and little is really known about the 18 members of this family. Sleeper sharks have similar body features to the dogfish sharks, such as small fins and no anal fin, but most also have a broad flat head. Some species have small spines before the dorsal fins, but others lack spines. Sleeper sharks give birth to live young, and have litters that range in number from 4–60 pups. These sharks have needle-like teeth in their upper jaw and blade-like teeth in the lower jaw, and feed on fish, sharks, rays, squid, octopus and some take marine mammals. Divers only encounter one member of this family, the very strange Greenland Shark.

DIVING WITH SLEEPER SHARKS

Living in very deep water, divers generally don't encounter sleeper sharks. However, the one member of this family that divers can see, the Greenland Shark, appears to be quite curious of divers. This species takes food when and where it can find it, so when they encounter a diver these sharks are very interested to know what they are and whether they are edible. They have been known to sneak up on divers, especially in places with low visibility, and several Greenland Sharks have been known to converge on a diver from different angles. They may be bold and curious, but Greenland Sharks are easily spooked by divers getting too close and also by lights and strobes. Although this species has never bitten a diver, and many consider them harmless, the Greenland Shark is potentially dangerous and divers should always take care around these large predators. In Canada, the Greenland Shark and Elasmobranch Education

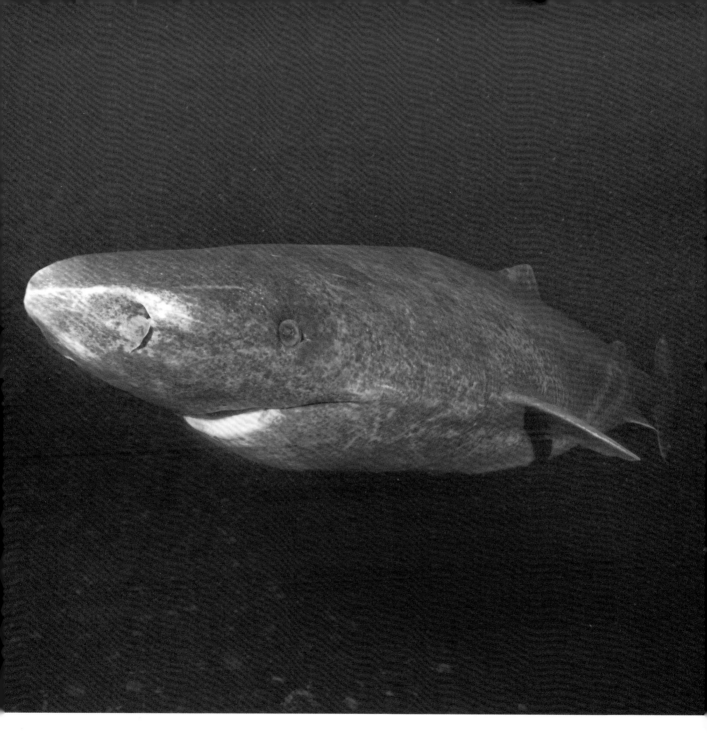

and Research Group (GEERG) have put together a code of conduct for diving with Greenland Sharks to ensure diver safety and the health of these unique sharks.

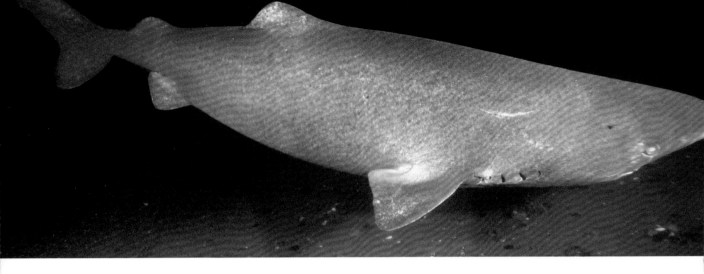

GREENLAND SHARK *Somniosus microcephalus*

One of the largest and strangest shark species of all. Growing to a length of 7.3m (24ft), it is thought that they can live to be more than 400 years old, and they are considered to reach sexual maturity only when 150 years old. Found only in the cold, dark waters of the North Atlantic and Arctic, in depths to 1,200m (3,950ft), and known to come into shallow water to feed. Although a slow swimmer, they are thought to be ambush predators, grabbing fish, rays, sharks and even seals. They also consume carrion and have been found with reindeer, horse, whale, Moose and even Polar Bear flesh in their stomachs. Greenland Sharks are often found with copepods attached to their eyes, and it is thought the sharks may take advantage of the luminescent glow from these parasites in order to attract prey.

WHERE TO SEE

Although occasionally seen off Greenland, Canada is the best place for divers to find Greenland Sharks. While they have been seen in the Saguenay Fjord, the best place for encounters is Baie Comeau, Quebec. During the summer months these sharks sometimes enter small bays in this area. However, encounters are never guaranteed unless divers can hang around for several weeks, as the sharks come and go, and the timings of their arrivals and departures can fluctuate from season to season. Repeatedly tapping two rocks together may encourage these sharks to come in for a closer look.

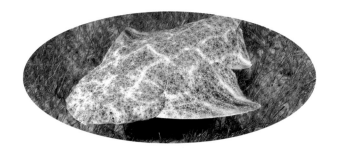

ANGEL SHARKS

FAMILY SQUATINIDAE

Although similar in shape to a ray, angel sharks are true sharks, with distinctive pectoral fins and gills on the side of the head. This unusual family contains 21 members from around the world, with species found in both shallow and deep water. Angel sharks have flattened bodies and bury themselves under the sand to ambush prey, exploding from the bottom to snatch fish, crustaceans, octopus and squid. At night they occasionally emerge from the sand to stalk nearby reefs or to relocate to a new hiding spot.

Angel sharks have sharp dagger-like teeth, and can become aggressive towards divers when disturbed, either accidentally by sitting on one or by trying to uncover one. These sharks are usually solitary, but have been known to aggregate in some areas. They give birth to live young and have litters of up to 13 pups. The five species included in this book are the ones most commonly encountered by divers.

DIVING WITH ANGEL SHARKS

Angel sharks are among the most difficult sharks to find. Hidden under a layer of sand, divers need sharp eyes to detect the outline of a buried animal. It is often best to use the services of an experienced dive guide to find angel sharks, as they are so well camouflaged that many divers swim right past without seeing them. Once discovered, divers will need to fan off a covering of sand, otherwise all they will be looking at is sand. We generally don't recommend disturbing sharks, but unless divers encounter an angel shark resting on top of the sand or swimming around – both rare events – they will need to fan off some sand to observe these strange flattened sharks. Most angel sharks are so confident of their camouflage that they tolerate divers removing a little sand and don't react at all, but others quickly rebury themselves or swim off and settle nearby.

Angel sharks are generally quite docile, but occasionally one will react badly to being uncovered, cornered or accidentally sat on, by swimming around erratically, and sometimes snapping at divers. Angel sharks have bitten divers, and being ambush predators they often bite anything near their mouth, which can include a diver's hand.

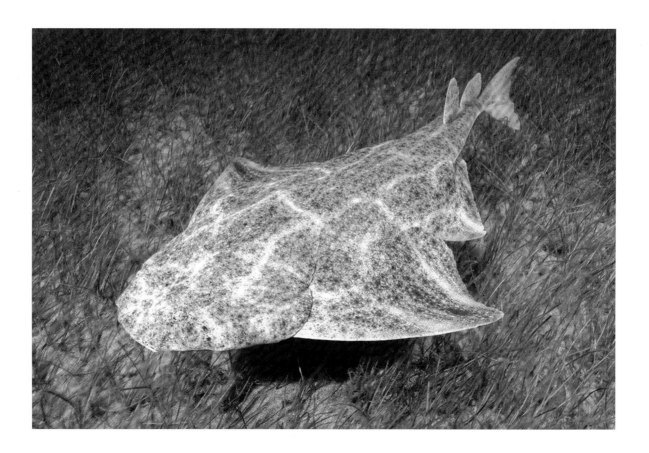

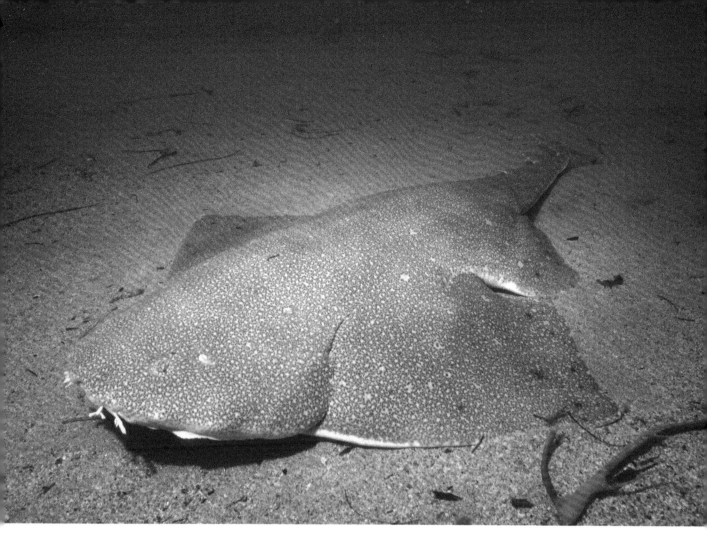

AUSTRALIAN ANGEL SHARK *Squatina australis*

This is probably a very common shark – the only problem is that it is very hard to find. One of several angel shark species found in Australian waters, but the others live in deep water. It occurs in shallow water from central New South Wales throughout the southern states to southern Western Australia. Grows to a maximum length of 1.5m (5ft) and has sandy colouration, which aids in camouflage.

WHERE TO SEE

Best found off the southern coastline of New South Wales, with Jervis Bay a good place. These sharks bury in the sand close to the reef edge, but are also found in sandy areas near seagrass. Divers also occasionally see this species on night dives in Victoria at Melbourne's Port Phillip Bay.

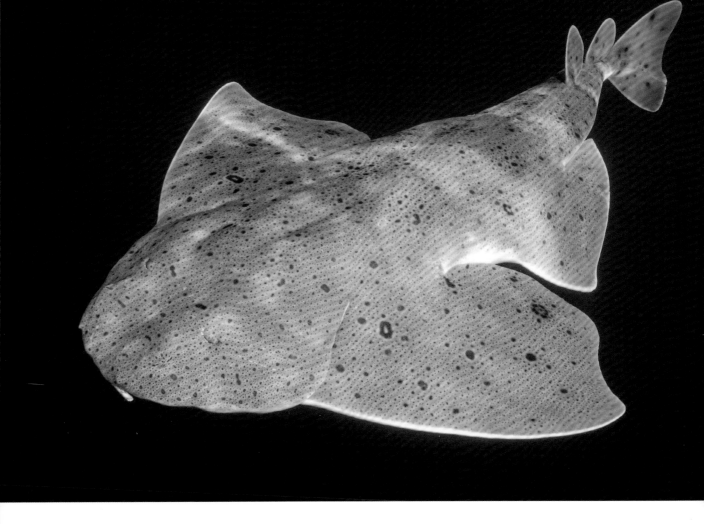

PACIFIC ANGEL SHARK *Squatina californica*

A common angel shark species in the eastern Pacific. Found along the temperate Pacific coastline of North and South America. It is possible that there are several subspecies within this population, or even separate species. Like all angel sharks it hides under a layer of sand, generally close to the reef edge. Grows to a length of 1.5m (5ft) and has a row of small thorns running down its back.

WHERE TO SEE

Best seen off the coast of California, USA, especially around Catalina Island, and also off many local beaches, with Tajiguas Beach near Santa Barbara a reliable location for a sighting.

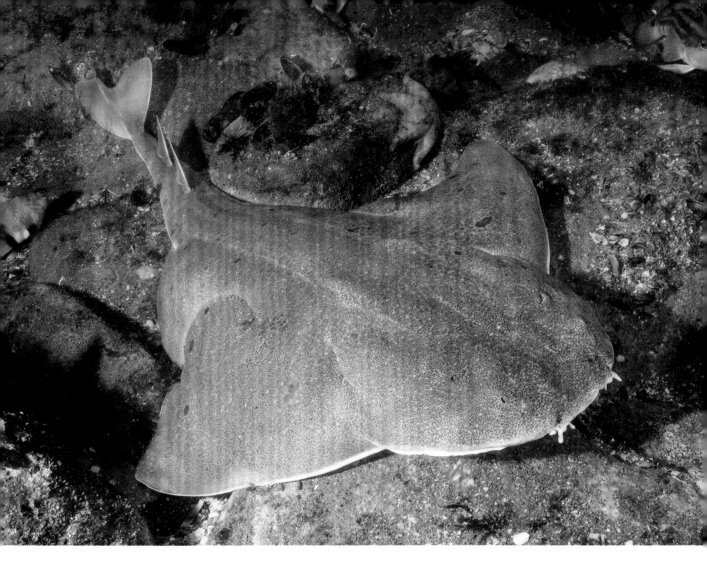

ANGULAR ANGEL SHARK *Squatina guggenheim*

Found on the Atlantic coast of South America from Brazil to Argentina. Although there are a number of very similar angel sharks in this region, the Angular Angel Shark is the only one that is regularly seen by divers. It inhabits sand flats and reef flats from 10–150m (33–500ft), but is most common between 10–80m (33–260ft).

WHERE TO SEE

Rarely encountered by divers along most of its official range. However, it has been seen with some regularity on the offshore reefs near Mar del Plata in northern Argentina.

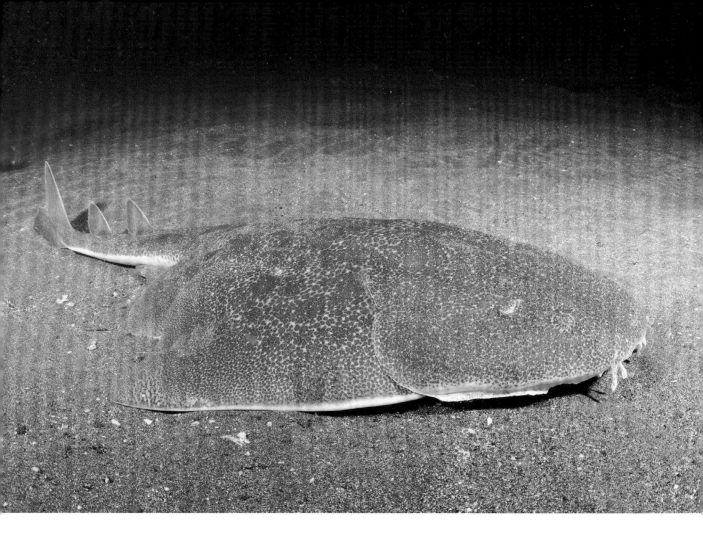

JAPANESE ANGEL SHARK *Squatina japonica*

A number of angel shark species are found in Asian waters, but only the Japanese Angel Shark is encountered by divers. Found in shallow to deep temperate waters off Japan, China and Korea, but generally only seen by divers in Japan. Grows to 2m (6.5ft) in length and is reddish-brown with a row of small thorns down its back.

WHERE TO SEE

Divers looking to encounter Japanese Angel Sharks will have to travel to Japan and dive around the spectacular Izu and Chiba Peninsulas, south of Tokyo. While the sharks are found in this area year-round, they are more common in winter.

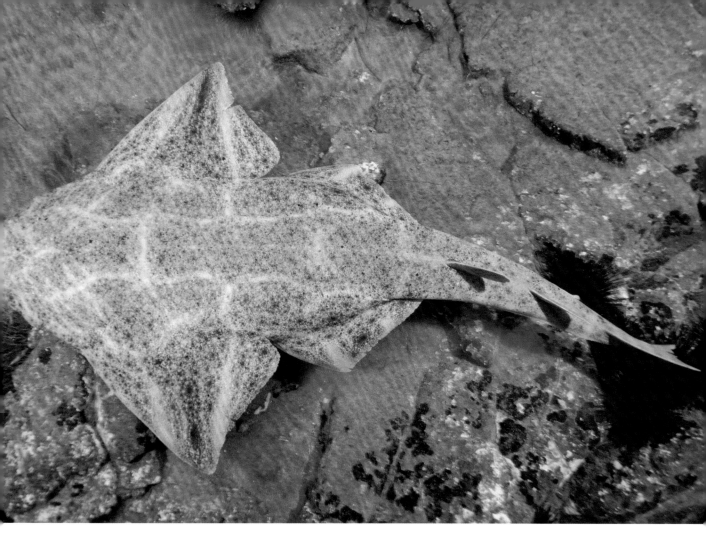

COMMON ANGEL SHARK *Squatina squatina*

The largest member of this family, found in the eastern Atlantic off southern Europe and northern Africa and growing to 2.4m (7.9) in length. This species has been captured for human consumption for thousands of years, resulting in a decline in numbers and a decrease in its range.

WHERE TO SEE

The Common Angel Shark is not very common at all, with the Canary Islands being the only place where it is regularly seen. Found in good numbers around Gran Canaria all year, although appears to be more commonly observed during the winter months.

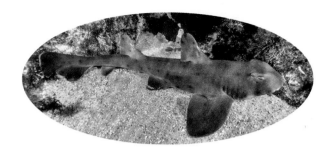

HORN SHARKS

FAMILY HETERODONTIDAE

Horn sharks, also known as bullhead sharks, are easily distinguished from other sharks as they have spines in front of their dorsal fins and ridges over their eyes. Nine species have been identified from around the world and all are quite docile and easily approached by divers. Horn sharks have molariform teeth, known as crushing plates by some, which they use to break up the shells of prey such as molluscs and crustaceans. They actually have the strongest bite force of any shark, relative to their small size.

Most horn sharks lay unusual spiral-shaped egg cases, which are generally wedged between rocks, but some species lay spiral eggs with tendrils, which are attached to sponges or corals. Eggs are laid in winter and spring and take 6–12 months to hatch depending on the species. The horn shark species included in this book are the ones most commonly encountered by divers on shallow reefs.

DIVING WITH HORN SHARKS

Horn sharks are a joy to dive with, as they are easily approached and rarely swim away. They present no danger to divers – even though their dorsal fin spines can be sharp, they don't use them for defence. While lethargic during the day, horn sharks can be seen slowly swimming over rocky reefs and sand at night looking for food, and have been observed blowing sand away to expose prey species.

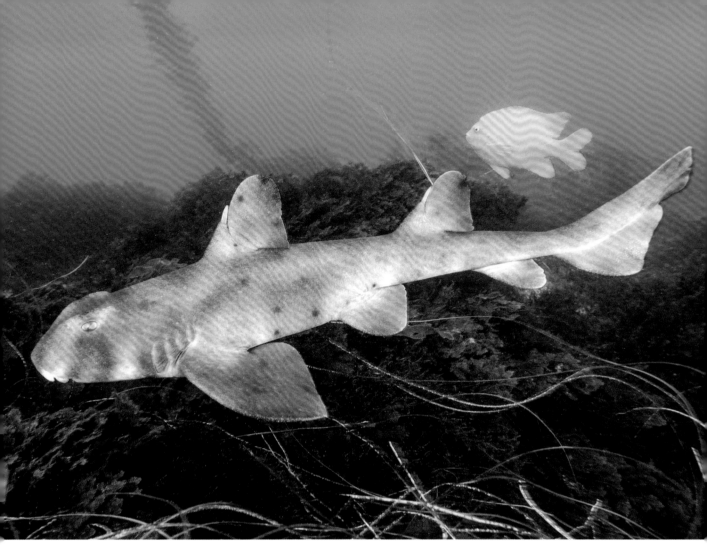

CALIFORNIA HORN SHARK *Heterodontus francisci*

As its name suggests it is found off California, USA, but this small species also occurs off the west coast of Mexico. A pretty shark covered in small dark spots, it grows to 1.2m (4ft) in length and is found on shallow rocky reefs. Like other horn shark species it is nocturnal, spending the day hidden in caves and crevices and emerging at night to feed.

WHERE TO SEE

Regularly seen at dive sites along the California coastline and at offshore islands such as Catalina Island and throughout the other Channel Islands.

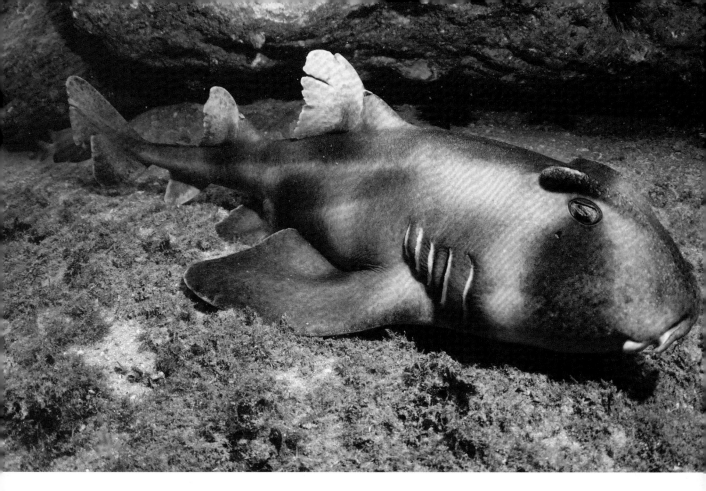

CRESTED HORN SHARK *Heterodontus galeatus*

Found off the east coast of Australia, and often confused with the more common Port Jackson Shark. However, the Crested Horn Shark has a different banded pattern and is generally smaller, only growing to 1.3m (4.3ft). Found only off New South Wales and southern Queensland, it is a solitary animal that is just as likely to be located sheltering under a rocky ledge as sitting out in the open. This species is known to eat molluscs, crustaceans and echinoderms, and has also been observed eating the eggs of Port Jackson Sharks.

WHERE TO SEE

An elusive species and can turn up at almost any dive site across its range. Divers generally have more chance of seeing it during winter and spring, when they venture into shallow water to mate. At these times of year the rocky reefs off Jervis Bay are the best place to see this lovely little shark.

JAPANESE HORN SHARK *Heterodontus japonicus*

One of the most striking members of this family. It has a pretty striped pattern and grows to a length of 1.2m (4ft). Found off Japan, Korea, Taiwan and northern China, this wonderful shark occurs on rocky reefs in depths from 6–40m (20–130ft).

WHERE TO SEE

The Japanese Horn Shark is another species that is difficult to find. It is generally only seen by divers in Japan, usually around the Izu and Chiba Peninsulas, south of Tokyo.

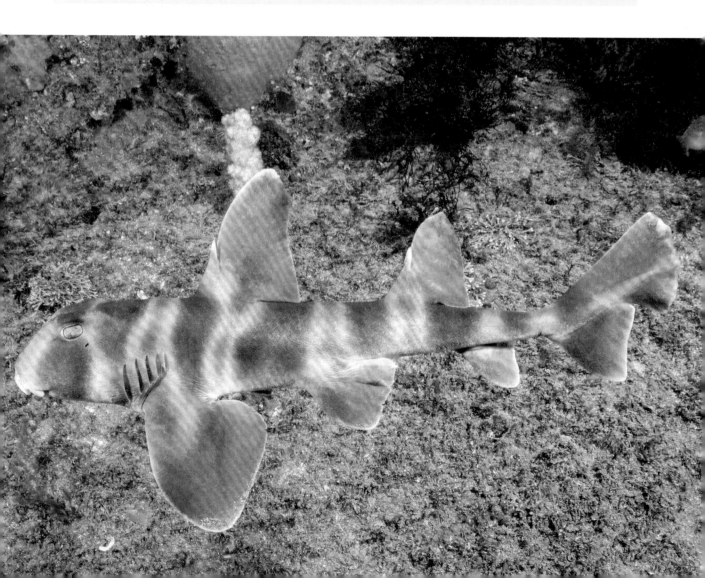

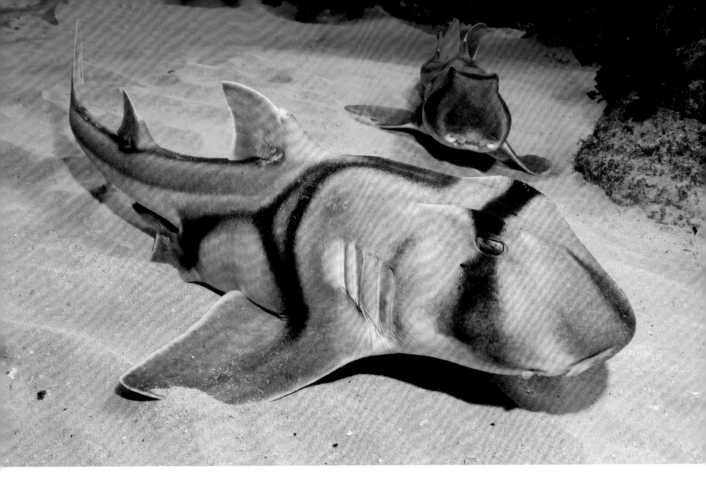

PORT JACKSON SHARK *Heterodontus portusjacksoni*

One of the most common sharks encountered by divers in southern Australia. Growing to a maximum length of 1.6m (5.2ft), it is the largest of all the horn sharks. Found in temperate waters from southern Queensland to central Western Australia. These wonderful sharks migrate in and out of deep water and up and down the coast, and aggregate in large numbers in winter and spring to mate.

WHERE TO SEE

The easiest species of horn shark for divers to see. Can be found almost anywhere in southern Australia, but most commonly observed in New South Wales, especially in winter and spring. At this time of year large numbers gather on shallow reefs to mate, and dozens can be seen on a single dive. The best place to encounter them is on rocky reefs between Forster and Narooma, and they are often abundant at dive sites off Sydney and Jervis Bay.

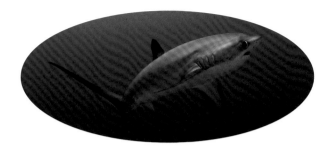

THRESHER SHARKS

FAMILY ALOPIIDAE

A very distinctive family of sharks that has evolved an extremely long tail. This thresher-shaped tail can be longer than the body of the shark and is used to stun prey such as fish, squid and cuttlefish. It was once thought that thresher sharks waved the tail back and forth to stun prey, but recently they have been observed charging at schools of fish and cracking their tail over their head like a whip. Three species of thresher sharks are found around the world in tropical and temperate seas, and recently a fourth species has been identified from DNA samples.

Thresher sharks are generally found in deep water, but do visit shallow water to feed and get cleaned by several species of cleaner fish. It was recently discovered that these sharks have a modified circulatory system, allowing them to have a warmer body temperature than the surrounding water. They give birth to live young, and have small litters of only 2–4 pups. Only one species from this family is generally seen by divers, the Pelagic Thresher Shark.

DIVING WITH THRESHER SHARKS

Thresher sharks are very graceful creatures, even with those long tails, and watching them cruising along a wall, or hovering to get cleaned is a memorable experience. However, they are very wary of bubble-blowing divers, so there are a few things you can do to ensure an unforgettable and extended encounter. At sites where these sharks are seen the dive guides will instruct divers on what to do, which is basically settle on the bottom and watch the sharks. However, a few extra tips include: get down low, slow your breathing, avoid direct eye contact and try to get away from the main pack of divers. The sharks are there to get cleaned, but they are also curious of divers, and if these tips are followed divers will find

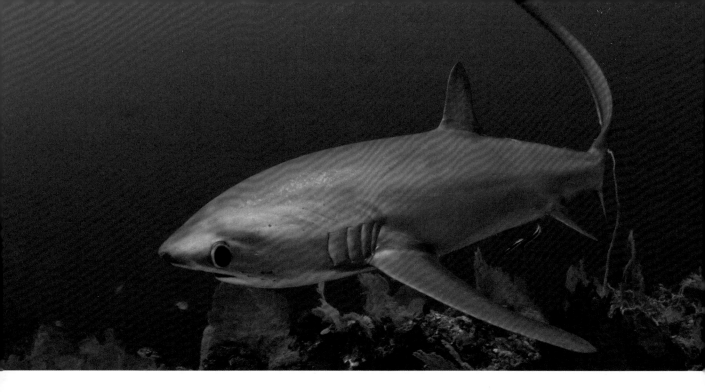

that the sharks come very close to inspect them. Thresher sharks are spectacular to dive with and pose no threat to divers.

PELAGIC THRESHER SHARK *Alopias pelagicus*

Divers rarely see thresher sharks, but this species is encountered at a few locations. Found throughout tropical and subtropical waters of the Indian and Pacific Oceans, the Pelagic Thresher Shark is the smallest member of the family, but still grows to an impressive length of 3.6m (11.8ft). It has large eyes, deep blue body colouration, and is found in depths to 150m (500ft), often venturing into shallow water to feed and get cleaned.

WHERE TO SEE

This species has been seen at many dive sites throughout the Indo-Pacific region, cruising walls and visiting sea mounts at locations such as: Elphinstone Reef and The Brothers, Egypt; Osprey Reef, Queensland, Australia; and Moalboal, the Philippines. However, encounters at these sites are still rare and most of the encounters are very brief. There is only one place in the world where divers can guarantee a close encounter with one of these strange sharks, and that is Monad Shoal, off Malapascua in the Philippines. The dive operators at Malapascua visit the sea mount every morning at dawn, and generally see 2–12 sharks rising from the depths to get cleaned.

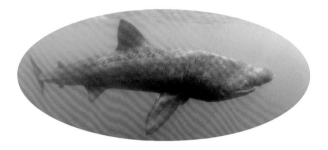

BASKING SHARK

FAMILY CETORHINIDAE

The second-largest of all the sharks is in a family all of its own.

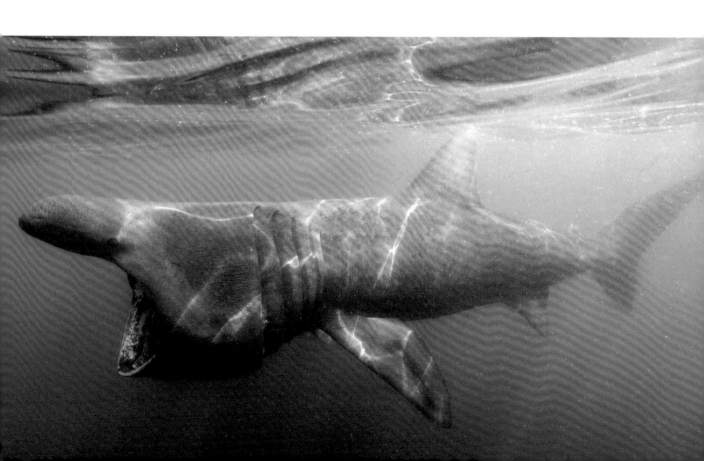

BASKING SHARK *Cetorhinus maximus*

The strange and wonderful Basking Shark is found worldwide in cool temperate waters. It grows to at least 10m (33ft) in length, but possibly even 15m (49ft), and is named because it appears to bask when at the surface. Greyish-brown in colour and often has mottled skin. Although similar in shape to the closely related mackerel sharks, the Basking Shark differs in having huge gill slits, which almost wrap right around the head. A filter-feeder that consumes plankton, these large sharks swim close to the surface with their mouths open wide, funnelling huge volumes of water through their large gill rakers to trap plankton.

Little is really known about these huge sharks. They migrate with the changing seasons, and are only seen close to the surface during summer. In winter they go into deep water and possibly shed their gill rakers. They are thought to give birth to live young, and have small litters of less than six pups. Basking Sharks are often seen in large schools when feeding, and these can sometimes number more than 100 individuals.

DIVING WITH BASKING SHARKS

You would think that such a large shark would be indifferent to a tiny diver in the water with them, but Basking Sharks don't seem to like bubbles and also don't like people getting too close. The only way to swim with them is on snorkel (or possibly a rebreather) and to avoid splashing at the surface. Also keep all movements slow, as sudden movements can startle the sharks. However, this may be difficult when finning very hard to keep up with a shark travelling at three knots! In the UK a code of practice is in place to ensure that snorkelers have minimal of impact on the Basking Sharks.

WHERE TO SEE

Rarely seen in most areas across their range, these large sharks were once hunted for their liver oil and numbers still haven't recovered. The waters around the western United Kingdom are the best place to watch Basking Sharks, with large numbers seen off both Cornwall and Scotland. Off south-west Cornwall they are best seen south of Penzance between May and July, while off Scotland they are seen around the Hebrides from May to September. Other locations where they are occasionally seen include Newquay, north Cornwall, and the Isle of Man. They can also be encountered off the USA during the summer months. Off Cape Cod, Massachusetts, they are seen in June and July, while off Rhode Island they are more common in June.

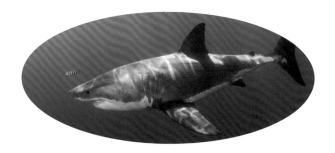

MACKEREL SHARKS

FAMILY LAMNIDAE

One of the only shark families that can maintain their body temperature a few degrees higher than the surrounding water. The advantage of this is that they have a greater metabolism and more powerful muscles, allowing them to swim faster and take larger prey. Mackerel sharks are highly efficient predators that feed on fish, sharks, rays and marine mammals.

There are five members in this family and all have long dagger-like teeth for gripping prey, except for mature Great White Sharks which have triangular-shaped teeth that can saw large chunks out of prey. Mackerel sharks are identified by their conical snout and their half-moon-shaped tail. Little is known about the reproductive strategy of these sharks, but they are thought to have small litters of less than a dozen pups. Only two members of this family are regularly seen by divers, the Great White Shark and Shortfin Mako Shark, but we have also included the Salmon Shark, as they can be seen with a little extra effort.

DIVING WITH MACKEREL SHARKS

Members of this family of sharks are all very different to dive with, and each has its own temperament and personality. Unfortunately, the only way most divers get to see these sharks is when they have been lured close by baits, so their behaviour is often more aggressive than normal.

The member of this family most commonly seen by divers is the Great White Shark. While a shark cage is generally considered the only way to safely view a Great White, many divers have swam with these sharks without a cage and without incident. The sharks are not mindless killing machines and some divers are very disappointed with their cage diving experience when the sharks don't smash the

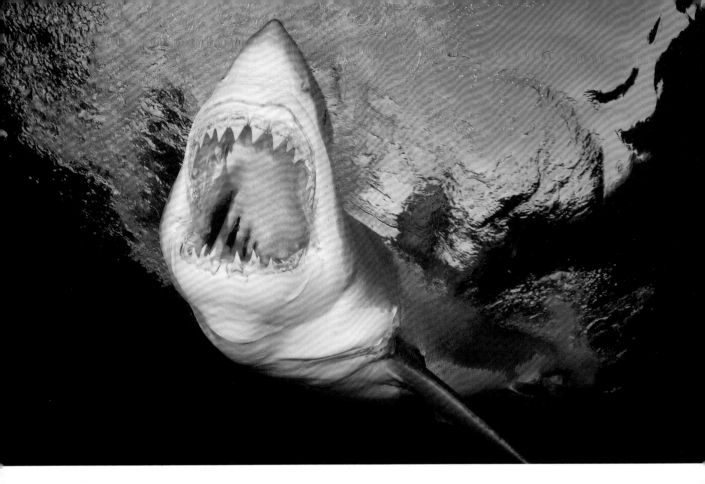

cage and try to eat them, as seen in most documentaries. In reality, Great White Sharks are the same as all other shark species – most are wary of divers, some are curious, and many are just not interested in divers at all.

It is worthwhile doing a cage diving trip over several days, and also at different times of the year, in order to see a variety of Great White Sharks and observe how differently they behave. Most swim slowly around the cage, often at the edge of visibility, and only come in close when lured by baits. Others linger below, unseen until they make a rush to the surface to grab a bait, and then disappear just as quickly. Some Great Whites come in, take one look, and are never seen again, but just seeing one of these incredible sharks underwater is an experience never to be forgotten.

Shortfin Mako Sharks can be viewed without a shark cage, but many dive operators still prefer the safety of a cage, as a few people have been bitten by makos. These hyperactive sharks zoom around divers at lightning speeds, occasionally snapping their jaws, overstimulated by the presence of baits. After the initial rush of blood they settle down and keep their distance from divers.

Even with baits in the water Salmon Sharks are very shy and wary of divers. They can be lured close to divers with baits, but even then encounters are all too brief with these fascinating sharks.

GREAT WHITE SHARK *Carcharodon carcharias*

The most infamous of all the sharks, this master predator reaches a length of 6.5m (21.3ft), but many people claim to have seen larger animals. Young Great Whites are around 1.3m (4.3ft) long at birth and have dagger-like teeth, which they use to catch mainly fish. As the shark grows, these are replaced by large triangular-shaped teeth that are designed to saw through flesh. Mature Great White Sharks feed on sharks, rays, dolphins, seals and whales.

Found in temperate and tropical waters around the globe. From tagging studies Great White Sharks have been found to migrate vast distances, even crossing oceans. However, they seem to return to favourite hunting grounds each year and are most commonly seen around shallow reefs where they find their prey.

WHERE TO SEE

While most divers never want to run into a Great White Shark it does happen, and when it does these sharks generally just swim around the diver for a quick look and then swim off. However, encounters are rare without baits in the water, and when there are baits involved it is best to view them from the safety of a shark cage. While Great Whites are found at numerous places around the world, there are only four locations where divers can almost guarantee an encounter.

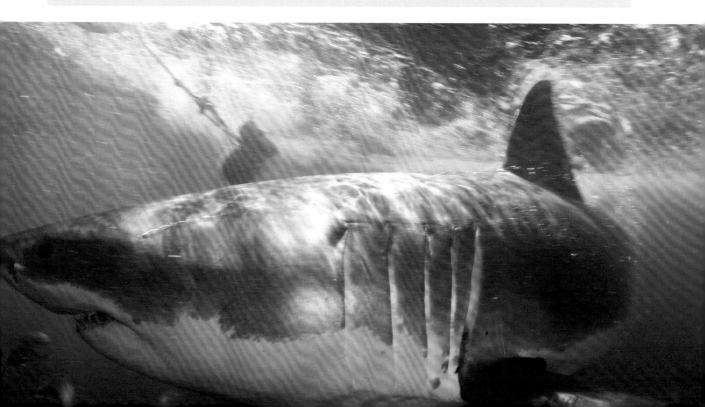

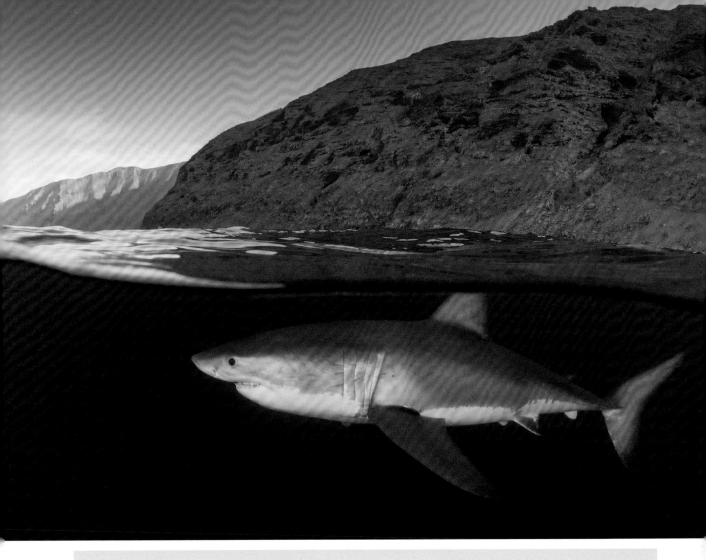

The islands off Port Lincoln, South Australia, were the first place in the world where Great White Sharks were filmed underwater and this destination is still a popular place to view these incredible creatures. Cage diving takes place year-round at the Neptune Islands, with males seen at any time and larger females only observed during the winter months. In New Zealand, Great White Sharks can be viewed from a cage at Stewart Island, at the southern tip of the country. Cage diving trips are offered from December to June.

Great Whites can also be viewed at several locations off South Africa. Cage diving is a year-round activity at Dyer Island off Gansbaai and takes place most of the year at Seal Island off Simon's Town. Both these locations are close to Cape Town, and at both destinations winter is considered the best time to see the sharks. The only other destination where Great White Sharks are seen with regularity is Isla Guadalupe off the west coast of Mexico. A liveaboard destination, trips to Isla Guadalupe only take place between July and November, with male sharks common at any time and the larger females seen from September to November.

SHORTFIN MAKO SHARK *Isurus oxyrinchus*

Considered to be the fastest of all sharks, Shortfin Makos chase and capture powerful billfish, and quite a few have been reported with bills embedded in their body. Grows to 4m (13ft) in length and is a bluish colour that appears to be almost metallic. Found around the world in both tropical and temperate waters, but appears to migrate into warmer waters during the winter months. Wanders the open ocean migrating great distances and rarely seen on inshore reefs.

WHERE TO SEE

Rarely seen when divers are exploring reefs. Being an ocean wanderer the only way to see this species is by using baits. These impressive sharks are only encountered at a handful of destinations around the globe. In the USA, they are seen off San Diego, California, year-round, but the summer months are best. Also seen off Rhode Island between July and October. In Mexico they are occasionally seen off Cancun between March and April, and also off Los Cabos in Baja. In the Azores Shortfin Mako Sharks can be encountered off Pico Island between July and October. South Africa is considered the best place to see this species with charters running out of Simon's Town from October to July, but once again summer is the best time.

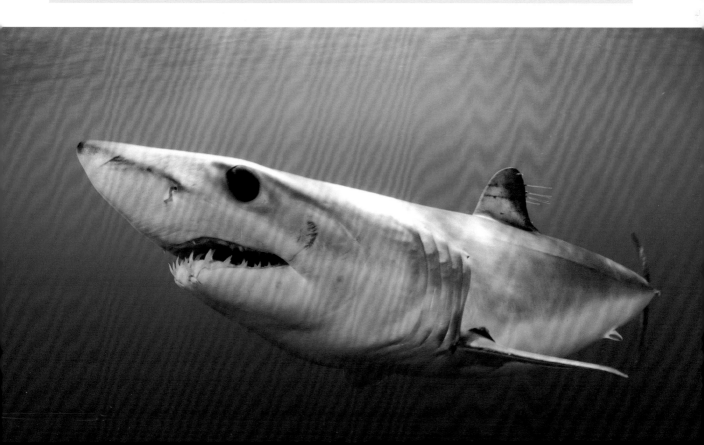

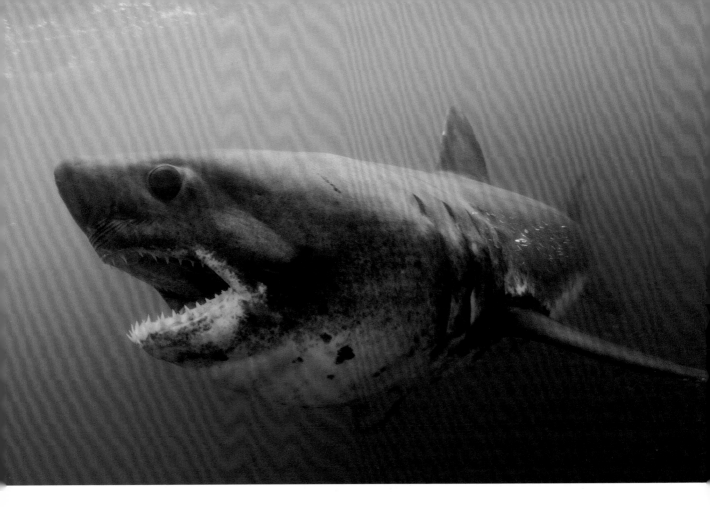

SALMON SHARK *Lamna ditropis*

One of the oddest members of the mackerel shark family. It is found only in the North Pacific and looks similar to the Great White Shark but is smaller, stockier and has dark spots along its side and belly. Little is known about this species. It grows to 3m (10ft) in length and populations are divided by sex, with females more common in the eastern part of the range and males in the west. Mainly found in offshore waters, but will visit shallow bays to feed on salmon and other fish species.

WHERE TO SEE

There is only one destination where it is possible to dive with Salmon Sharks – Port Fidalgo Inlet in Prince William Sound, Alaska, USA. The sharks gather in this area in June and July to feast on spawning salmon. Baits are required to bring the sharks in close to divers, as they are quite shy and wary. Although they have been seen on scuba, it is easiest to lure them in while snorkelling.

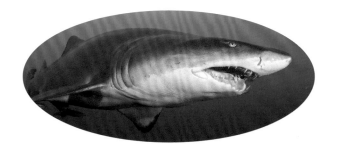

SANDTIGER SHARKS

FAMILY ODONTASPIDIDAE

The sandtiger shark family comprises three species that are found in temperate to tropical waters throughout the world. These sharks are identified by their long upper tail lobes and by their teeth, which are long, sharp and project forwards out of the mouth. These fearsome-looking teeth are used to catch their prey of fish, rays and small sharks, and are designed to grip rather than cut. Sandtiger sharks are generally quite docile and easily approached by divers, but can be aggressive if food is in the water. These sharks give birth to live young and have small litters of generally 1–2 pups. Only two species of sandtiger sharks are encountered by divers – the relatively common Grey Nurse Shark and the much rarer Smalltooth Sandtiger Shark.

DIVING WITH SANDTIGER SHARKS

Diving with sandtiger sharks is one of the best shark diving experiences a diver can have, especially when surrounded by a school. These sharks look mean and aggressive, but are very placid and slow-swimming creatures. They don't like to be cornered or chased, and will swim off with a mighty crack of their tail and often not return. The best way to observe them is to sit on the side of a gutter, on the edge of their territory, and watch them patrol. They often get curious, and if divers remain still the sharks will slowly get closer and closer on each pass. They have also been known to play chicken with humans, swimming straight at a diver's head and only turning away at the last second. These sharks are always more bold when in a group, and tend to be skittish when solitary. In Australia, a code of conduct is in place for diving with Grey Nurse Sharks to ensure divers have minimal impact on this endangered species.

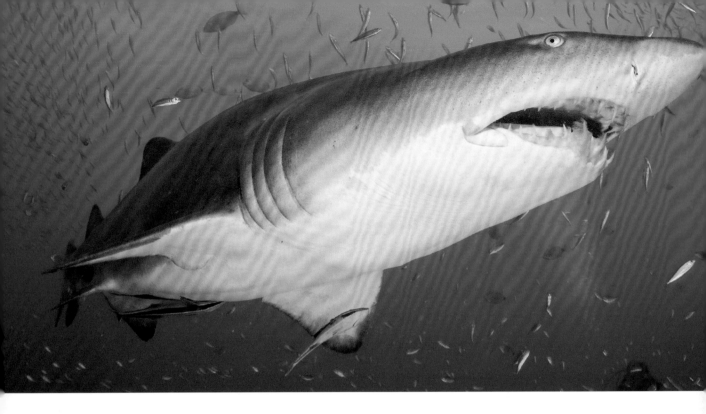

GREY NURSE SHARK *Carcharias taurus*

Found around the world in subtropical and temperate seas, the Grey Nurse Shark is known by many common names. For example, in South Africa it is called the Spotted Ragged-tooth Shark, while in the USA it is known as the Sandtiger Shark. These sharks reach a length of 3.8m (12.5ft) and are typically found around shallow rocky reefs, gathering in gutters where currents allow them to hover. They often form loose aggregations that can number from half a dozen to several hundred. Grey Nurse Sharks seem to prefer waters warmer than 16°C (61°F), and migrate with changes in water temperature. The species is found in subtropical and warm-temperate seas off Australia, Africa, North and South America and East Asia.

WHERE TO SEE

Grey Nurse Sharks migrate and as such are only seen seasonally on most reefs. Off Australia, divers most commonly encounter them from southern Queensland to southern New South Wales. During summer they are seen from Forster south to Merimbula, and off Rainbow Beach in Queensland. In winter they are observed from Forster north to Brisbane. They also occur off Western Australia, with a small number seen off Perth during autumn and off Exmouth in winter.

In the USA these sharks are found off the east coast, from Maine to Florida, and also in the Gulf of Mexico. However, they are mostly observed on shipwrecks off North Carolina. The sharks are present year-round, especially on the shipwrecks off Beaufort and Morehead City, but most diving on this coastline is done during summer.

The east coast of South Africa is another good location, and they occur from Western Cape to southern Mozambique. The two best places to see them are Aliwal Shoal and Protea Banks, near Durban. Another area where they are seen in late summer and autumn is Sodwana Bay, 400km (250 miles) north of Durban.

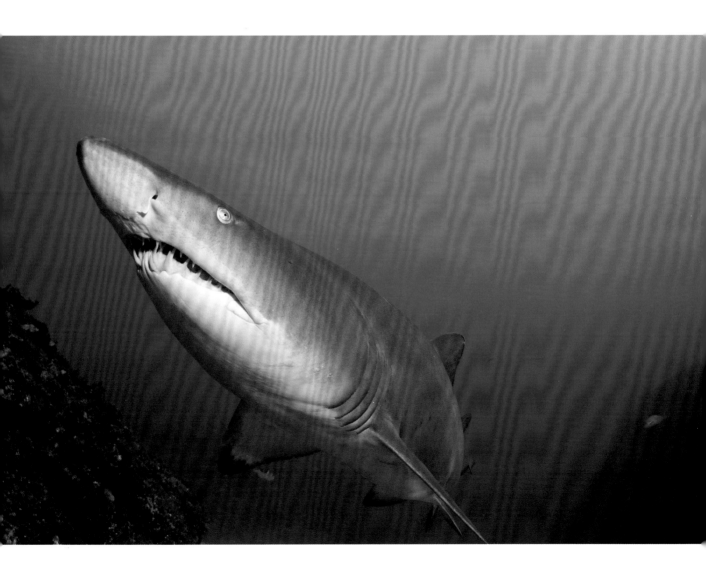

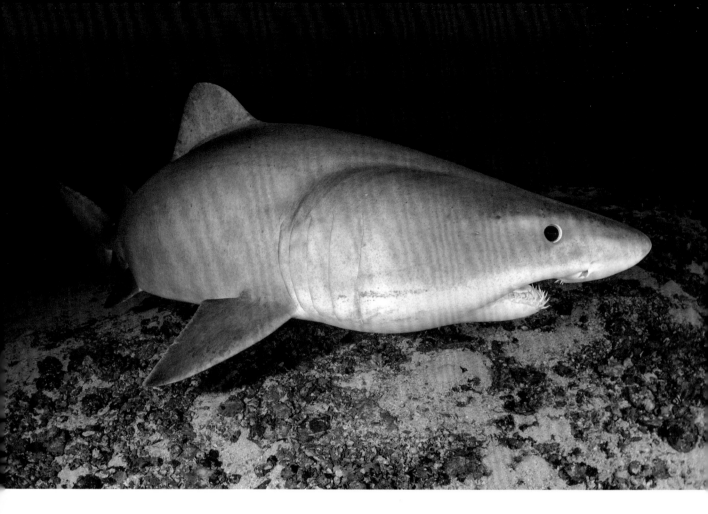

SMALLTOOTH SANDTIGER SHARK *Odontaspis ferox*

A widespread but rare member of this family is the Smalltooth Sandtiger Shark. This species is much bulkier and more heavy-set than the Grey Nurse Shark, and can grow to 3.6m (11.8ft) in length. Found in isolated locations around the world, and has been recorded in depths to 420m (1,380ft). Also ventures into shallow water and has been encountered by divers at a number of locations.

WHERE TO SEE

There are only a handful of sites where divers can encounter this species. During summer they are sometimes seen off El Hierro in the Canary Islands. They are also found at a site called Shark Point off Beirut, Lebanon, between July and October. However, the best location for a sighting is at Isla Malpelo, an island off the Pacific Coast of Panama. Here, up to a dozen gather on a reef slope at a depth of 60m (200ft) at a site called Bajo del Monstruo. They are usually seen between December and April, but encounters are never guaranteed.

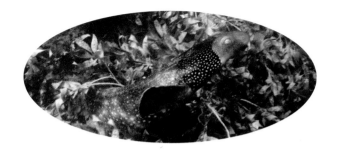

COLLARED CARPET SHARKS

FAMILY PARASCYLLIIDAE

These small nocturnal sharks spend most of the day sheltering in caves or hidden under seaweed. Seven species of collared carpet shark have been identified, of which four are found off southern Australia and the rest are found in deep water in the North-West Pacific. Collared carpet sharks have slender elongated bodies, which allow them to slither in and out of narrow ledges in search of food and shelter. These sharks feed on small fish, worms and crustaceans, but a great deal of research still has to be conducted regarding their behaviour and biology. They lay small rectangular eggs that are attached to the bottom with tendrils. Collared carpet sharks appear similar to many other families of catsharks, but differ in having nasal grooves and their mouth positioned forward of their eyes.

DIVING WITH COLLARED CARPET SHARKS

Collared carpet sharks are small shy sharks that divers will have trouble finding. They are most commonly observed at night, when they emerge to feed, but can be found during the day if divers are prepared to search under ledges and seaweed. They are quite docile, so if a diver finds one they can usually spend a bit of time photographing and observing these cute little sharks.

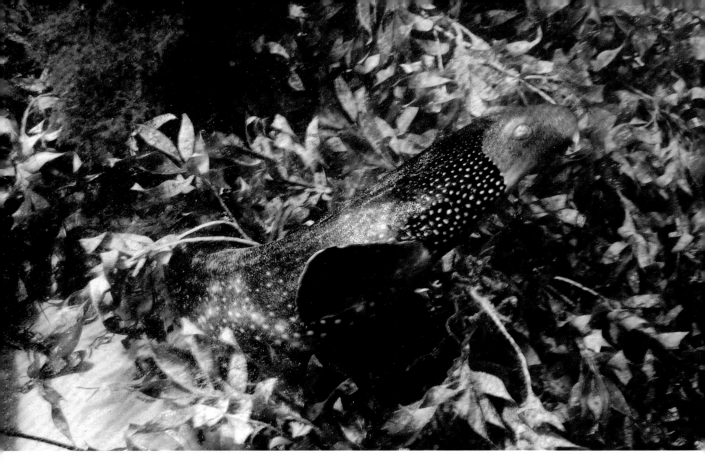

VARIED CARPET SHARK *Parascyllium variolatum*

Australia is the only place where divers can encounter a collared carpet shark. Three of the Australian species live in shallow water, but only one is regularly seen by divers – the Varied Carpet Shark. It grows to 90cm (35in) in length and has dark brown to black bands along its length which are decorated with white spots. It has a very distinctive collar that looks like a studded dog's collar, which has led to another common name of Necklace Carpet Shark.

WHERE TO SEE

Occurs from Victoria to southern Western Australia, and also around the northern coastline of Tasmania. Can be found in depths down to 180m (590ft), but is quite common on shallow rocky reefs with a good covering of kelp, seaweed and algae. While the species can be seen almost anywhere across its range, it is particularly abundant off Melbourne. Often found in the southern reaches of Port Phillip Bay, but more commonly seen off the ocean beaches outside the bay.

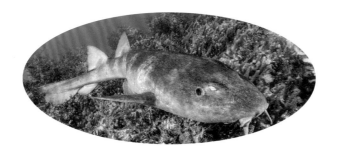

BLIND SHARKS

FAMILY BRACHAELURIDAE

This family is represented by two species from the eastern seaboard of Australia. Blind sharks are small, harmless, bottom-dwelling sharks that feed at night on invertebrates and small fish. They spend most of the day hidden in caves or wedged under rocks, so are rarely seen by most divers. They give birth to live young during the summer months. The young, and occasionally the adults, fall prey to wobbegongs.

DIVING WITH BLIND SHARKS

Often all that divers will see of a blind shark is a tail protruding from a ledge or crevice. They are more active at night, when they emerge from their daytime hiding places to feed. Both members of this family are very shy and wary, so are difficult to observe and photograph. However, occasionally divers will find one resting out in the open or only partially covered, allowing an opportunity to closely study these interesting little sharks.

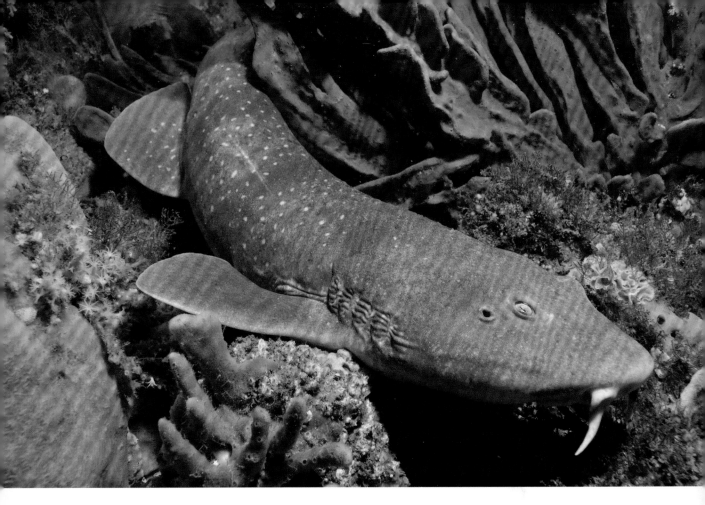

BLIND SHARK *Brachaelurus waddi*

The most common member of this family is simply called the Blind Shark. It was given this name when first discovered, because of its habit of closing its eyes when removed from the water. Grows to a maximum length of 1.2m (4ft), although specimens measuring in excess of 1m (3.3ft) are rarely seen. Colour varies from pale brown to almost black, and most individuals exhibit darker bands and a scattering of white spots.

WHERE TO SEE

Occurs off New South Wales and also into southern Queensland. Although common, can be difficult to find. Divers are most likely to encounter them on rocky reefs that have a good covering of kelp and seaweed, where there is plenty of food and places to hide. Seems to be most abundant in northern New South Wales, from Sydney north to Tweed Heads, with one of the best locations to see them being Port Stephens.

COLCLOUGH'S SHARK *Brachaelurus colcloughi*

The second member of this family is quite rare and only occasionally encountered by divers. Very little is known about the behaviour and biology of the Colclough's Shark. It is similar to the Blind Shark in size and appearance, being ash-grey to grey-brown, sometimes with faint bands. This species is easily mistaken for the more common Brown-banded Bamboo Shark as both are greyish and a similar size. Colclough's Shark can be identified by its rounded fins and by the position of the spiracle behind the eye.

WHERE TO SEE

Has a very limited range and is only found on rocky reefs off southern Queensland and northern New South Wales, from Gladstone to Byron Bay. An encounter is a very rare event and divers wishing to see this species are recommended to search dive sites off Brisbane, the Gold Coast and Byron Bay. This species is just as shy as the Blind Shark, hiding under ledges and caves during the day.

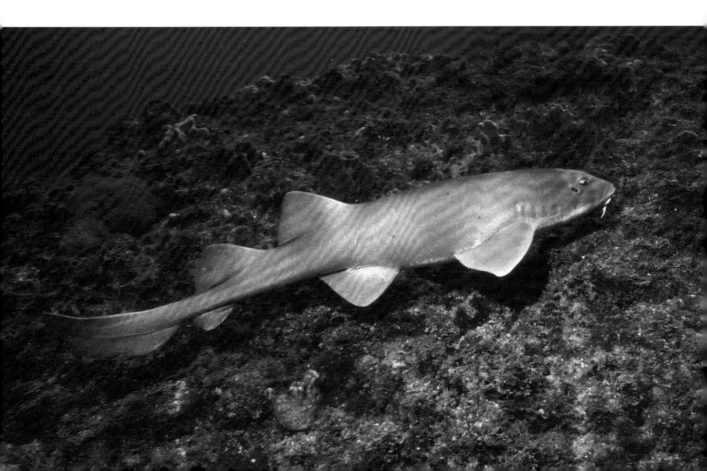

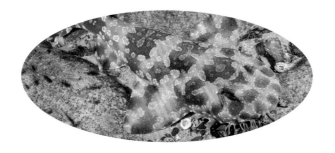

WOBBEGONGS

FAMILY ORECTOLOBIDAE

The name wobbegong comes from an Australian Aboriginal word meaning 'shaggy beard', which is a great description of one of the most unique sharks a diver will encounter. The wobbegong family, or 'wobbies', are represented by 12 described species and several undescribed species. These sharks are easily identified by their flattened bodies, colourful camouflaged skin-patterns, and by their dermal lobes – those shaggy beards around their heads. All species have a wide mouth and long sharp teeth, which they use to great effect to catch their preferred prey of fish, crustaceans, rays, octopus, squid and even other sharks.

Ambush predators, wobbies laze on the bottom during the day, ready to snatch anything edible that comes within range of their mouth. They give birth to live young. Gestation is about one year and litters can vary in number from 1–40. Wobbies are very common in Australian waters, with ten of the known species coming from this region, including the six species described in this book.

DIVING WITH WOBBEGONGS

Many divers in Australia have a love-hate relationship with wobbies, as unlike most sharks, large wobbies are unafraid of divers and rarely move when a diver gets close. They are responsible for more non-fatal shark bites in Australia than any other shark, as they will bite if harassed or accidentally sat on. Once they bite they often don't let go, meaning a number of divers have exited the water with a wobby still attached to an arm, leg or buttock. If bitten the best action is to relax and don't struggle – the shark will eventually realise that it can't swallow you, and let go. Wobbies sometimes give a warning 'bark', a quick snap of the jaw at divers who get too close.

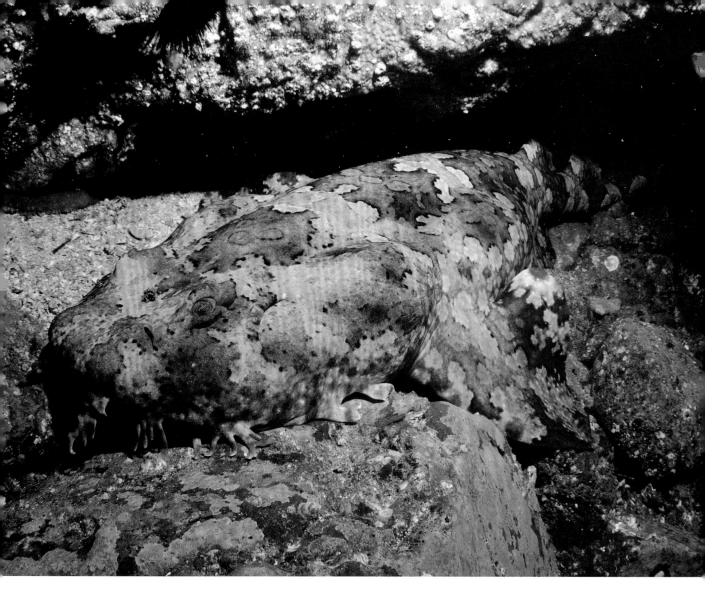

In reality, wobbies are wonderful sharks to dive with and most divers never have a problem with them. They tolerate people getting close to take photos, and will usually swim away rather than bite if a diver encroaches too close. Divers should be careful when wobbies are surrounded by schools of fish and have their head held off the bottom. This is a sign that they are in feeding mode and ready to grab a fish, or a diver's hand, that comes too close. In some locations, wobbies are difficult to find because they hide in caves and under ledges, but in other areas they litter the bottom, confidently sitting out in the open.

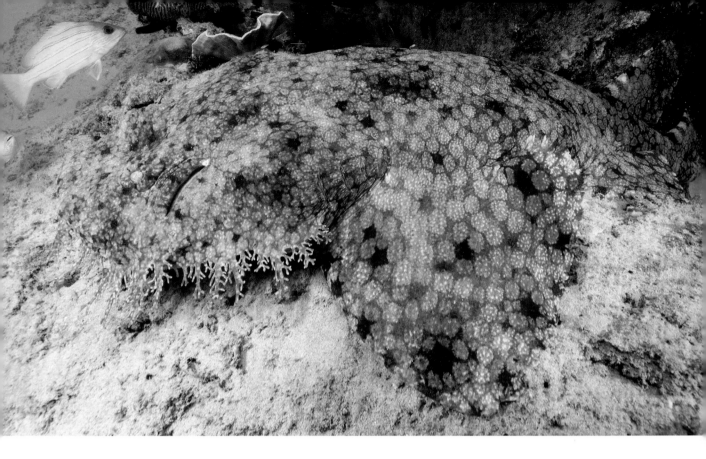

TASSELLED WOBBEGONG *Eucrossorhinus dasypogon*

Of all the wobbies, this species has the most cryptic camouflage. It has a more flattened body than any other species, and its sandy colour allows it to blend in perfectly against coral rubble or between hard corals. An ambush predator like all wobbies, but also uses its tail as a lure, flicking it back and forth to attract potential prey. Grows to 1.8m (6ft) in length, although many books incorrectly report them reaching a maximum length of 3m (10ft). Found in the tropical waters of Australia, and also off Papua New Guinea and eastern Indonesia.

WHERE TO SEE

Can be found almost anywhere on the Great Barrier Reef, but the only area where divers can guarantee an encounter is around the reefs of the Capricorn and Bunker Groups, especially Heron Island and Lady Elliot Island. Off Western Australia, divers will see the species at Ningaloo Reef, with quite a few residing under the famous Navy Pier dive site at Exmouth. Encounters are a little hit and miss throughout Papua New Guinea, with these sharks occasionally seen off Port Moresby and Milne Bay. This species is also common in the Indonesian province of West Papua, and divers regularly see them on reefs in the Raja Ampat area.

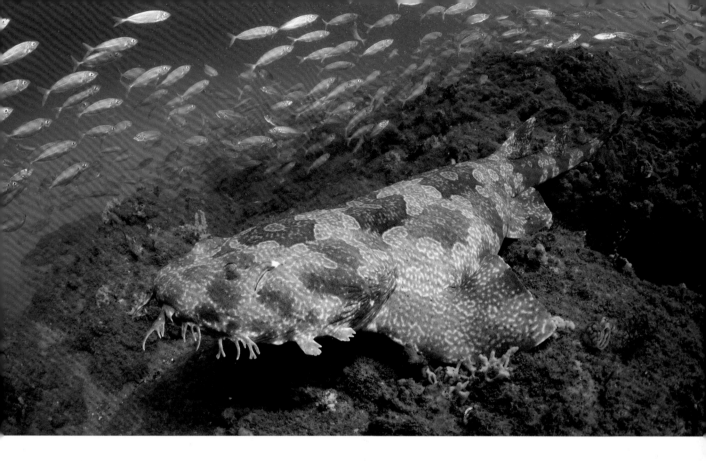

SPOTTED WOBBEGONG *Orectolobus maculatus*

Growing to maximum length of 3.2m (10.5ft), this shark is one of the top predators on the rocky reefs of southern Australia. It is found from southern Western Australia eastwards to southern Queensland, but does not occur off Tasmania. Varies in colour from sandy-brown to dark chocolate-brown and has a covering of paler rings and white spots. Easily the most social member of the family, often found in groups lying on the bottom or packed into caves.

WHERE TO SEE

Although this species is found over a large area of southern Australia, it is most commonly seen off southern Queensland and northern New South Wales. Common at dive sites from Brisbane to Forster, with large populations especially encountered off Byron Bay and South West Rocks.

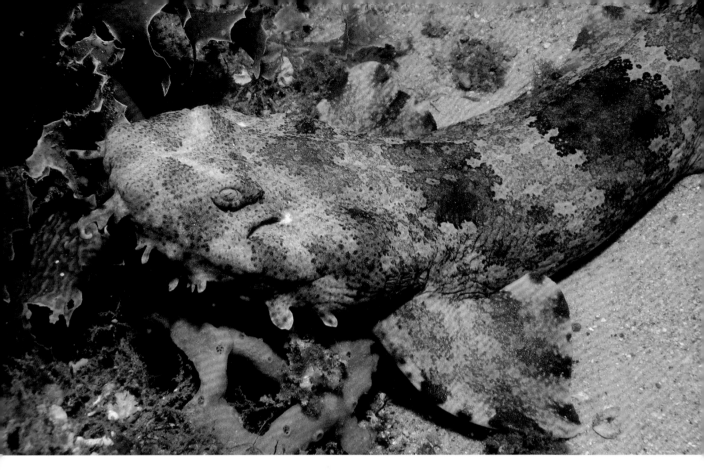

ORNATE WOBBEGONG *Orectolobus ornatus*

For many years two wobbegong species were confused as one, with the smaller Ornate Wobbegong thought to be the juvenile form of the larger Banded Wobbegong. Divers had for a long time suspected that they were two distinct species, but this wasn't confirmed until DNA testing was done. The Ornate Wobbegong reaches a maximum length of 1.2m (4ft) and is found off the east coast of Australia, from Sydney north along the Queensland coastline.

WHERE TO SEE

Often shelters in caves, on ledges and under corals, so frequently overlooked in many areas. Like its cousin the Spotted Wobbegong, the best area to see this species is southern Queensland and northern New South Wales. At Byron Bay and South West Rocks, Ornate Wobbegongs are often found sitting on plate corals waiting to ambush prey.

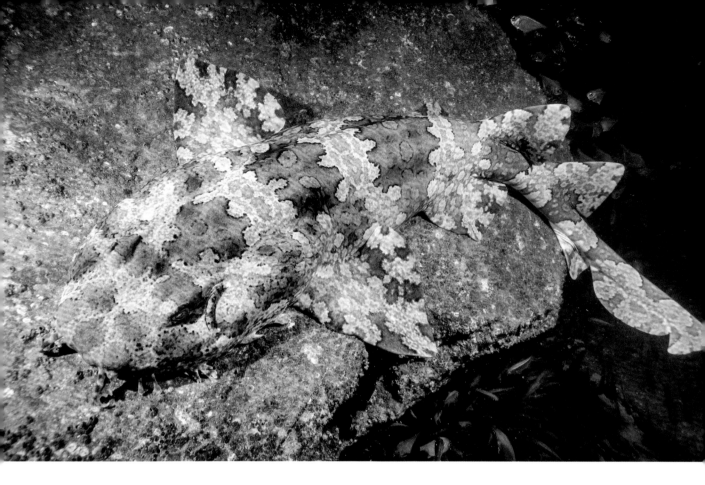

BANDED WOBBEGONG *Orectolobus halei*

As mentioned, this species was once confused with the Ornate Wobbegong, even though they look different and are found in different areas. The Banded Wobbegong grows to 2.9m (9.5ft) in length and is found in temperate and subtropical waters around Australia's southern coastline, from Brisbane, Queensland, to Coral Bay, Western Australia, and also off Flinders Island in the Bass Strait. Identifying Ornate and Banded Wobbegongs is not too difficult. The Banded is pale brown in colour with darker brown bands which are undulated on the edges. It also has a sparse covering of greyish cloud-like spots. The Ornate Wobbegong has a more elaborate skin pattern, with much finer detail.

WHERE TO SEE

The Banded Wobbegong is not a common species, and is generally found sheltering in caves. In southern Australia, encounters with this species are quite rare. Divers have the best chance of locating one off southern Queensland and northern New South Wales. They are most commonly seen from Brisbane south to Forster, with Byron Bay and South West Rocks once again the best locations.

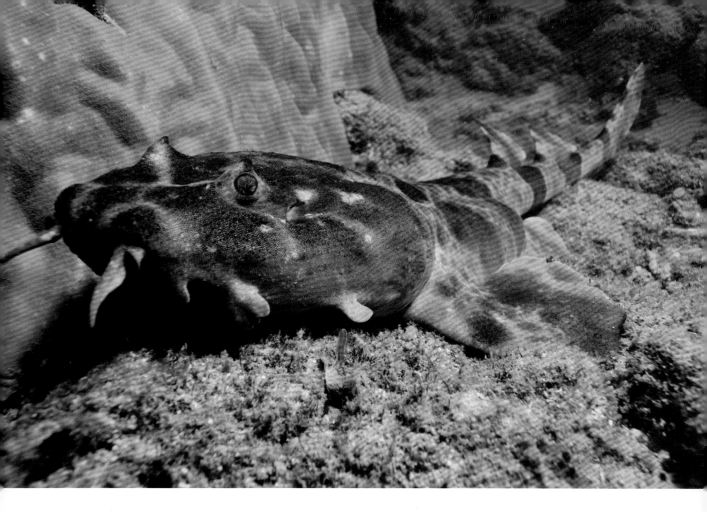

NORTHERN WOBBEGONG *Orectolobus wardi*

One of Australia's lesser-known species, found in tropical waters off Western Australia and a few localities off the Northern Territory and Queensland. Reaches a maximum length of 1m (3.3ft), and is easily identified by its small size and by the limited number of dermal lobes on its head. Its colouration is the least elaborate of this family, being a mottled brownish with darker bands.

WHERE TO SEE

Divers rarely enter the water in most areas where the Northern Wobbegong is found, as Saltwater Crocodiles are a concern in northern Australia. But this species is relatively common at the southern end of its range off Ningaloo Reef, the Muiron Islands and the Mackerel Islands in Western Australia. Divers also find this species hiding under limestone rocks at the Navy Pier dive site at Exmouth.

COBBLER WOBBEGONG *Sutorectus tentaculatus*

The strangest member of the wobbegong family, this species may look similar to other wobbies with its dermal lobes and patterned skin, but it also has warty tubercles across its back. Grows to 1m (3.3ft) in length and has ornate colouration, with a pale brown base colour and darker bands and blotches. Also has distinctive black spots scattered randomly across the body and fins. Found only off South Australia and southern Western Australia, occurring on rocky reefs from Adelaide to Geraldton.

WHERE TO SEE

In Australia's southern waters the Cobbler Wobbegong is a rare species, but divers have found them hiding under ledges off Whyalla in South Australia, and also off Perth, Bremer Bay and Albany in Western Australia.

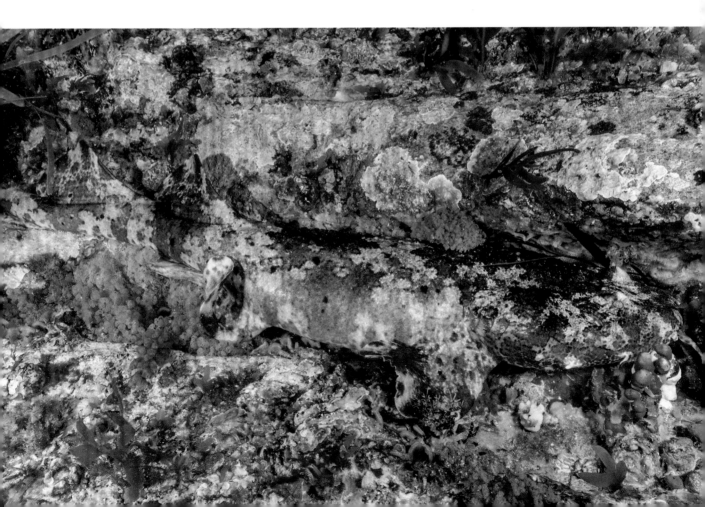

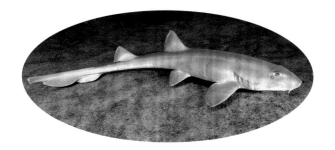

BAMBOO AND EPAULETTE SHARKS

FAMILY HEMISCYLLIIDAE

Bamboo and epaulette sharks are only found in the Indo-West Pacific region, with 16 species so far described and several undescribed species. Members of this family all have long slender bodies, which allow them to wedge tightly into crevices during the day. Epaulette sharks are generally smaller than bamboo sharks, and have the ability to slowly walk along the bottom on their pectoral fins when looking for prey or a place to hide. These sharks can be identified by their rounded fins, long tails and by the location of the spiracle behind and below the eye. Bamboo and epaulette sharks lay small eggs and feed at night on crustaceans, small fish and worms. Many sharks within this family are seen by divers on shallow reefs, and the species included in this book are the ones most commonly encountered by the authors.

DIVING WITH BAMBOO AND EPAULETTE SHARKS

These pretty, small sharks often leave divers, and especially underwater photographers, very frustrated, as they are shy and difficult to approach and often impossible to photograph. During the day, all a diver usually sees of these sharks is part of the body wedged under a ledge. At night, divers generally have a better chance of observing them out in the open as they hunt for food, but even after dark they are wary of divers and torch light and most will quickly dart off into the night. However, every now and then divers are lucky enough to find one of these attractive sharks that is content to sit still on the bottom and pose for photos.

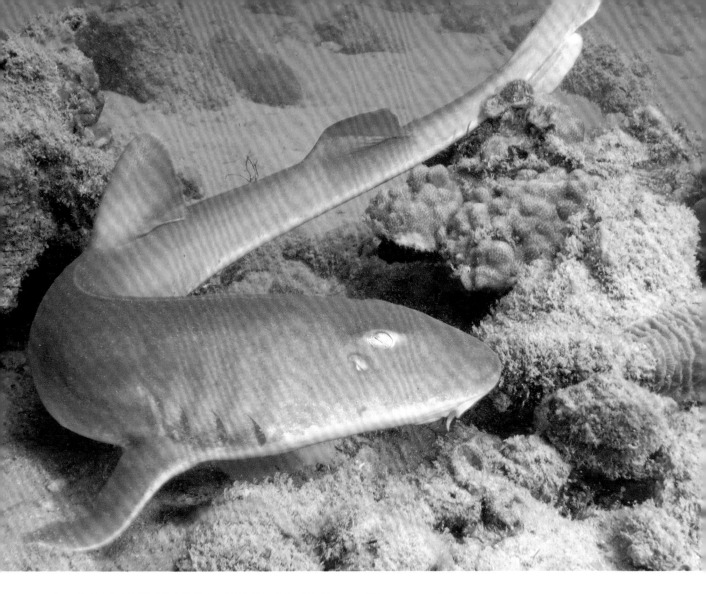

ARABIAN BAMBOO SHARK *Chiloscyllium arabicum*

Looks quite similar to a number of other greyish-brown members of this family. Occurs from the Persian Gulf to southern India. Grows to a length of 70cm (27.5in) and is generally found in shallow water on coral reefs.

WHERE TO SEE

Most commonly seen by divers exploring reefs off the United Arab Emirates. Off Abu Dhabi it is encountered on the local reefs and also on shipwrecks.

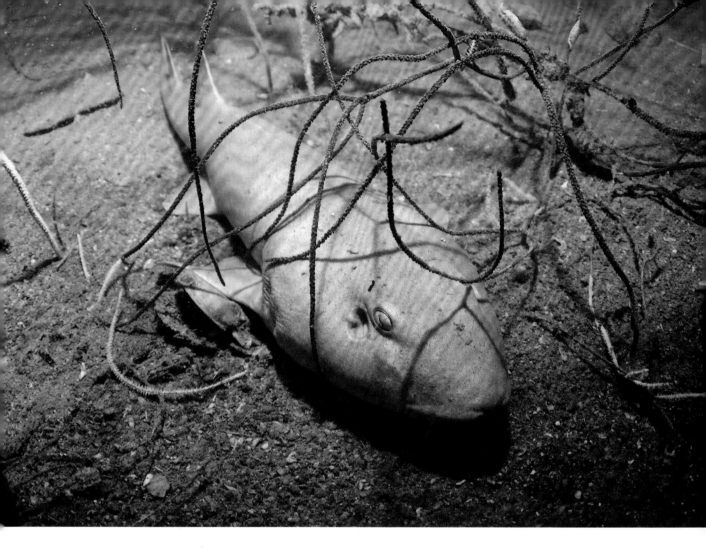

GREY BAMBOO SHARK *Chiloscyllium griseum*

A wide-ranging species, found throughout South-East Asia and west to the Persian Gulf. Its range overlaps with a number of similar-looking species, such as the Arabian Bamboo Shark. Although called the Grey Bamboo Shark, this species is generally a brown colour and grows to 80cm (31.5in) in length.

WHERE TO SEE

Most likely to be seen by divers exploring the east coast of Malaysia. Abundant on the shipwrecks scattered around the Perhentian Islands, with dozens often found sheltering together.

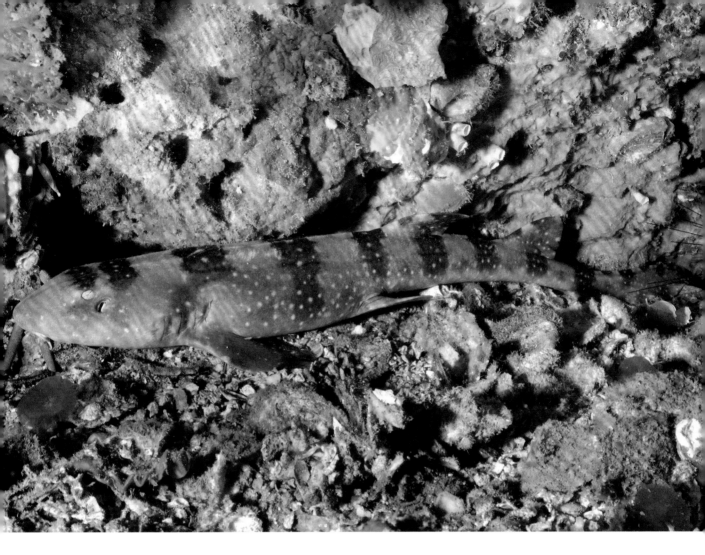

WHITESPOTTED BAMBOO SHARK *Chiloscyllium plagiosum*

Found over much the same range as the Grey Bamboo Shark, this species is very distinctive with its dark bands and pale spots. Like other bamboo sharks it spends the day hidden away, which makes it a difficult species to find. Grows to a length of 95cm (37in).

WHERE TO SEE

One of the best places to find this species is at Gato Island, near Malapascua in the Philippines. These sharks shelter in the many ledges and caves at this site. Unfortunately all a diver may see is a tail hanging out of a hole.

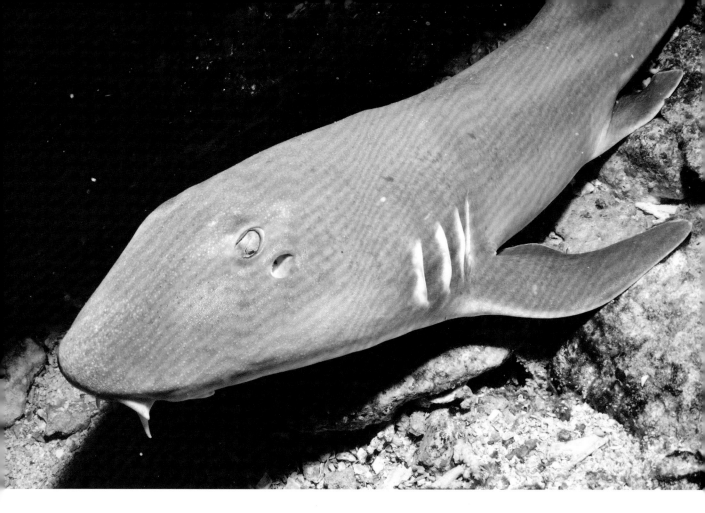

BROWN-BANDED BAMBOO SHARK *Chiloscyllium punctatum*

The common name of Brown-banded Bamboo Shark is very misleading, as these sharks are generally grey or beige in colour and may have very subtle bands. Juveniles have much more distinctive bands but these fade as the shark matures. Occurs across a vast area of the Indo-West Pacific region, from Australia north to Japan and west to India. This species is reported to grow to 1m (3.3ft) in length, but the ones found off southern Queensland may be a separate species or subspecies as these sharks reach a length of 1.5m (5ft) and have a slightly different body shape.

WHERE TO SEE

Can be seen almost anywhere across their range, but divers are guaranteed an encounter in Australia off Brisbane and the Gold Coast. In this area the sharks are often seen at dive sites with plenty of ledges, such as Shag Rock and the *Scottish Prince* shipwreck, and on some dives dozens can be seen.

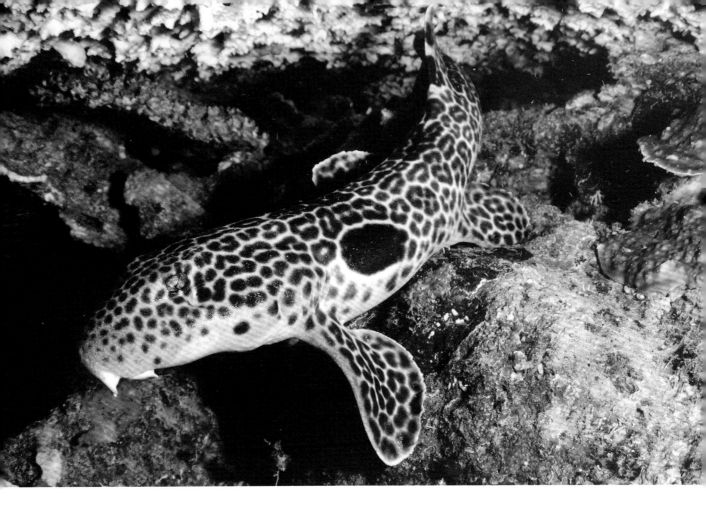

LEOPARD EPAULETTE SHARK *Hemiscyllium michaeli*

All epaulette sharks have very pretty body patterns of spots, dots and bands, and one of the most attractive members of the family is the lovely Leopard Epaulette Shark. It is only found off eastern Papua New Guinea and grows to a length of 70cm (27.5in). There are actually a number of epaulette shark species found off Papua New Guinea, and this species was for a long time confused with several similar-looking sharks.

WHERE TO SEE

Can be seen at numerous dive sites in eastern Papua New Guinea, such as Milne Bay, Tufi and Port Moresby. Mostly seen at night when they emerge to feed.

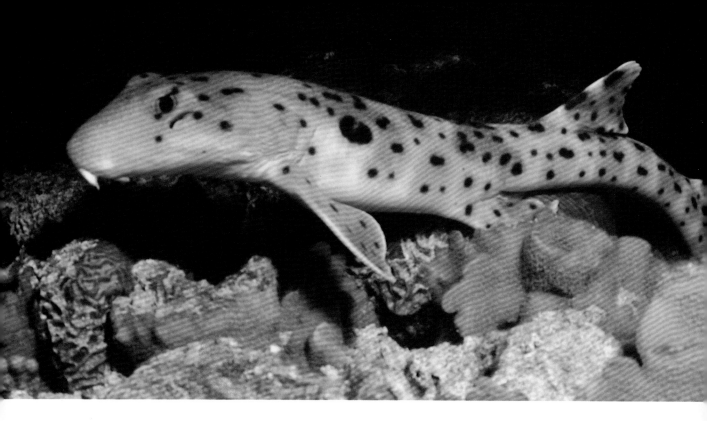

EPAULETTE SHARK *Hemiscyllium ocellatum*

Found in tropical waters in northern Australia, Papua New Guinea and eastern Indonesia, the Epaulette Shark is easily identified by its sparse covering of spots and by its large epaulette spot behind the eye. Growing to 107cm (42in) in length, these sharks are amazing in their ability to wedge themselves into tight crevices and amongst sharp, hard coral. Most commonly found on shallow reef flats, and can survive out of water for several hours if trapped by the falling tide.

WHERE TO SEE

Best observed on Australia's Great Barrier Reef. These lovely little sharks are generally not found when diving, as they prefer shallow reef flats. However, snorkelers find them quite regularly at Heron Island and Lady Elliot Island.

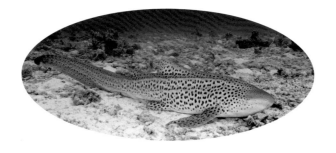

LEOPARD SHARK

FAMILY STEGASTOMATIDAE

A family with only one member that is found throughout the tropical Indo-West Pacific region.

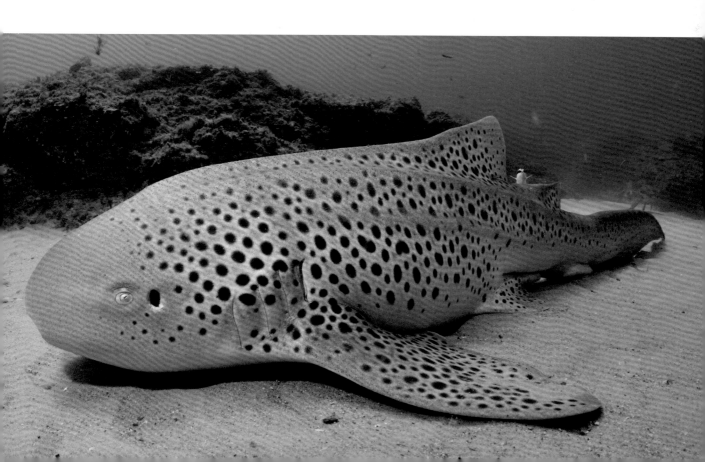

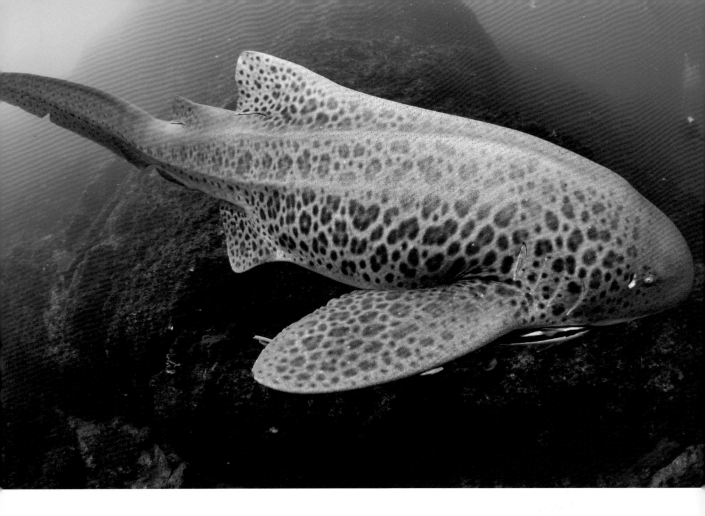

LEOPARD SHARK *Stegastoma fasciatum*

This species is also known as the Zebra Shark, but this name is best applied to the young which have dark zebra-like stripes. Leopard Sharks are very docile creatures and during the day are usually observed lazing on sand or coral, only moving when a diver gets too close. They have a small mouth and tiny teeth, and feed at night on small fish, shrimps, worms, crabs and molluscs.

These sharks lay large eggs, 20cm (8in) long, during the summer months. The young are 25cm (10in) long when they emerge from the eggs six months later and are rarely seen by divers. Adults grow to a maximum length of 2.5m (8ft), and not 3.5m (11.5ft) as noted in many books. Like many shark species, they migrate with the changing seasons. This migration is more obvious in subtropical waters, as they seem to prefer a water temperature above 22°C (72°F). When the water cools, they disappear. Tagging studies of a large population of Leopard Sharks off Brisbane, Australia, found that they head north during winter and can travel 1,300km (800 miles).

DIVING WITH LEOPARD SHARKS

Diving with Leopard Sharks is a real pleasure. These large docile sharks are easy to approach when resting, as long as divers slowly creep up on them from the side. Some are wary of humans and swim off when a diver gets close, but others are quite content to allow divers to photograph and study them. These sharks are mostly observed resting on the bottom during the day, but when breeding they are far more active, swimming around the reef, with a group of males often following a female.

WHERE TO SEE

While the odd Leopard Shark can be encountered by divers on any reef within their range, there are only two locations where they are seen in large numbers. Thailand is a good destination to see Leopard Sharks, especially around the Similan Islands, Koh Phi Phi and Phuket. At many dive sites in this area divers will generally see a few Leopard Sharks in a week-long stay. However, the best location to see them is Australia, off southern Queensland and northern New South Wales. Each summer hundreds of Leopard Sharks invade the reefs from Gladstone south to Coffs Harbour. But individual reefs seem to have higher concentrations, especially off Rainbow Beach, Brisbane, Tweed Heads and Byron Bay. At these sites, divers can see a dozen or more sharks on a good dive. Unfortunately the sharks are only seen for six months in this area, between November and April, and they migrate to the warmer waters of the Great Barrier Reef during the winter months.

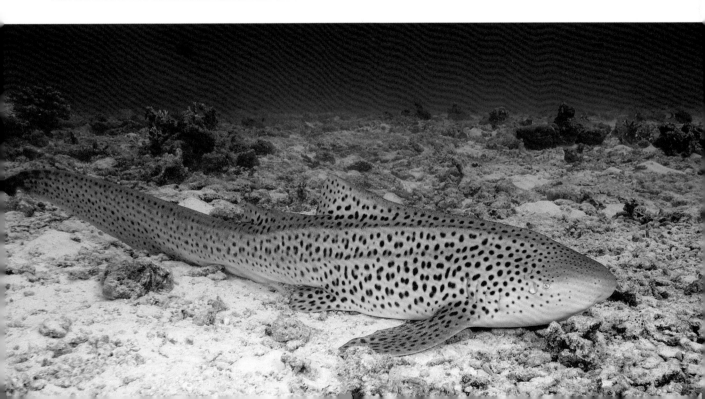

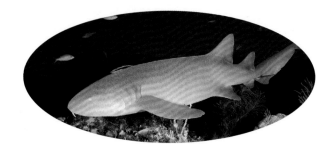

NURSE SHARKS

FAMILY GINGLYMOSTOMATIDAE

Four species of nurse sharks inhabit the tropical waters of the world, but only two are commonly seen by divers. These are among the largest sharks a diver will encounter while exploring reefs, and are mostly found resting on the bottom during the day. Nurse sharks give birth to live young and have litters numbering from 8–30.

Although regular visitors to shark feeds, nurse sharks usually only feed at night on fish, octopus, squid, crabs, molluscs and crayfish. They have one of the most unique feeding methods of any shark as they suck their prey into their mouth using a vacuum action. This suction is so great that it is said to be able to suck fish out of ledges and even clams out of their shells. They are also very determined feeders, known to lift heavy coral heads in order to obtain prey. While nurse sharks have small teeth, a number of divers have been bitten by them. They also have a tendency to hold on when they bite, so treat these large sharks with respect.

Nurse sharks inhabit coral reefs in depths from 10–100m (33–330ft), and are also found in shallow lagoons and mangroves. They are often found sleeping in caves, gutters and shipwrecks during the day, and are happy to share a resting place with fellow nurse sharks or other species such as turtles, wobbegongs and gropers.

DIVING WITH NURSE SHARKS

These large, docile sharks are fun to dive with, but they are often shy of divers, and will swim off if surprised or suddenly woken. If a diver approaches a sleeping nurse shark quietly, by slowing their breathing and pace, they can usually get up right beside one to take photographs. But divers need to take care if they startle one in a cave, as nurse sharks often flee in panic and have been known to knock over divers as they desperately try to escape. So try not to corner them, and always give them an escape route. At shark feeds nurse sharks are very friendly and curious, and will swim up close to divers looking for food.

NURSE SHARK *Ginglymostoma cirratum*

The most common member of this family, found in the tropical waters of the Atlantic Ocean, is the plainly named Nurse Shark. Growing to a length of 3m (10ft), it is hard to confuse with any other species found in the same area. It was also thought to reside along the Pacific coast of Central America, but the nurse sharks in this area were recently found to be genetically different and described as a separate species, the Pacific Nurse Shark (*Ginglymostoma unami*).

WHERE TO SEE

The Nurse Shark is abundant throughout southern Florida, the Bahamas and the Caribbean. Divers are likely to encounter one when exploring any reef in this region. In the Caribbean, a particularly good place where divers can guarantee an encounter is Sail Rock in the Grenadines. In Florida, USA, they are common from Fort Lauderdale to the Florida Keys; often resting on the many shipwrecks and under reef ledges in the area. Perhaps the best place to encounter numerous Nurse Sharks is at Bimini in the Bahamas, with up to 20 turning out for the free food distributed during hammerhead shark feeds.

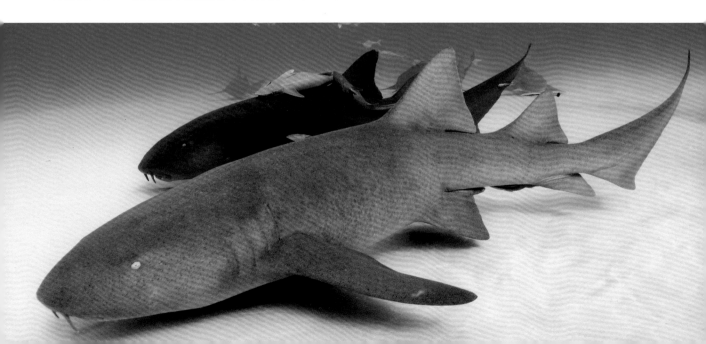

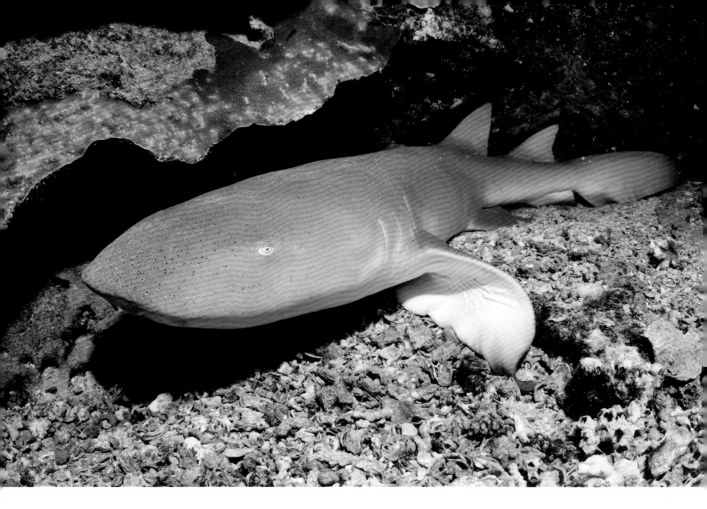

TAWNY NURSE SHARK *Nebrius ferrugineus*

Usually the first part of this shark a diver will see is its tail hanging out of a cave or ledge. This large species grows to 3.2m (10.5ft) in length and is pale brown to greyish-brown in colour. The young are only 40cm (16in) long at birth and have a covering of small spots, but are rarely seen. Found in the tropical waters of the Indo-West Pacific and parts of the central Pacific.

WHERE TO SEE

Can be seen just about anywhere across its range, and encountering one is often a matter of being in the right place at the right time. In Australia, this species is seen on the Great Barrier Reef and Ningaloo Reef, with Lady Elliot Island the best place to see several. In Fiji, they make a regular appearance at the shark feeds at The Bistro, Shark Reef and The Cathedral in Beqa Lagoon. Another great way to see numerous Tawny Nurse Sharks is to do a night dive at Alimatha, Vaavu Atoll, in the Maldives.

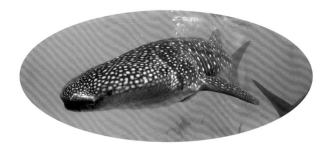

WHALE SHARK

FAMILY RHINCODONTIDAE

The only member of this family is unforgettable and unmistakable.

WHALE SHARK *Rhincodon typus*

This huge animal, which grows to 14m (46ft) in length, has a broad flat head, a wide transverse mouth, small eyes and long gill openings. The colouring is quite surreal, with the base grey to brown and rows of pale spots and stripes. Whale Sharks also have body ridges that are similar to those of the Leopard Shark, and at one time these two species were placed in the same family. For all their immense size, Whale Sharks have tiny teeth and feed on plankton and schools of small fish. They generally feed close to the surface, swimming slowly with their huge mouth open wide. Enormous quantities of water are taken in and their prey is collected on spongy tissues that cover their gills. They have also been observed hovering motionless, with their head near the surface gulping or sucking down concentrations of prey.

Whale Sharks are found in tropical to warm temperate waters around the globe, and are known to migrate vast distances. They are usually observed in the open ocean, but often feed close to shore. Little is known about their reproductive strategy, but it is assumed that they give birth to live young and litters can number more than 300. Until recently, these sharks were rarely seen by divers, but in the past two decades a number of aggregation sites have been discovered around the planet.

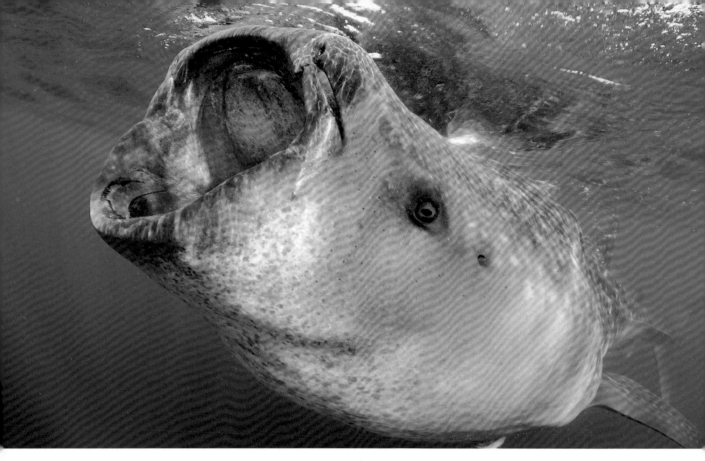

DIVING WITH WHALE SHARKS

Whale Shark encounters are often sadly very brief, as these giants are more interested in feeding than looking at a diver or snorkeler. While there are numerous dive sites where scuba divers can encounter Whale Sharks, most interactions with these giant creatures takes place on snorkel. At most of the destinations listed below, charter boats take out only snorkelers to swim with the sharks. When a shark is sighted they drop the snorkelers in front of the shark so it will swim by the group. In most of these encounters, the Whale Shark sails past very quickly, and snorkelers have to fin extremely hard to keep up. However, occasionally a shark will stop to feed, allowing for a very close interaction. Every now and then, a Whale Shark will become curious and closely inspect the snorkelers or boat. At most of these destinations strict rules are in place to avoid snorkelers harassing the sharks, with no camera flash allowed and also snorkelers have to stay 4m (13ft) away from the shark.

At locations where Whale Sharks are fed, the encounters are very different, as the sharks stay in the one spot. Feeding these creatures is quite controversial, but it does make the encounter a lot easier and last a lot longer. At these sites divers can hover beside the Whale Sharks, while on scuba, and take their time to appreciate these incredible creatures.

WHERE TO SEE

Only a few decades ago encounters with Whale Sharks were very rare, and it became big news in the dive community when the first aggregation site was discovered off Australia in the 1980s. Since then, more than a dozen locations have been found around the planet where these ocean giants gather to feed and possibly breed. As mentioned, Australia was the first place where divers regularly encountered Whale Sharks, and Ningaloo Reef is still a popular destination. The sharks gather off this reef from March to August. Christmas Island is another location off Australia where they can be seen from November to April.

There are many other places around the world where divers can encounter Whale Sharks, but some of these locations are a little hit and miss. The following is a list of destinations where divers can guarantee an encounter with one of these gentle giants. In Indonesia, Whale Sharks are seen in Cenderawasih Bay year-round, and suck small fish out of the nets of fishermen. In the Philippines, Oslob is the best place to see them year-round, as they are hand-fed, which has caused a bit of controversy. They are also seen at Donsal and Sogod Bay from November to May.

In Mozambique, Whale Sharks are seen at Tofo Beach from October to March. In Honduras these sharks are seen year-round off Utila, while in Belize they are seen in April and May off Gladden Spit.

By far the largest accessible gathering of Whale Sharks occurs off Isla Holbox and Isla Mujeres in Mexico between June and September. The peak time is July and August, and on some days hundreds can be seen feeding on tuna eggs at the surface. A similarly sized aggregation occurs during the summer off the coast of Qatar in the Arabian Gulf but the event has yet to be opened up to divers.

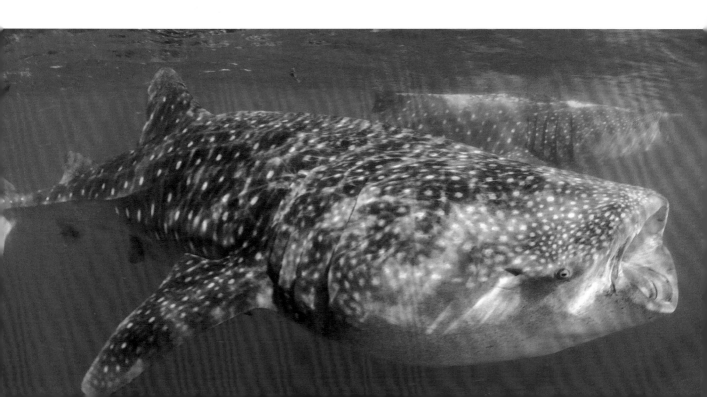

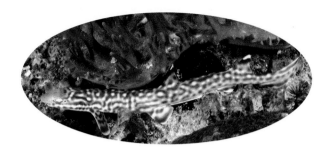

CATSHARKS

FAMILY SCYLIORHINIDAE

The largest shark family with 160 species so far described. These small sharks inhabit all the oceans of the world and are found in shallow to very deep water. However, only a few species are seen by divers, as most are found beyond the range of recreational diving. Catsharks can be easily confused with other small sharks as they have a similar body shape, but differ by having their pectoral fin right above the pelvic fin and their mouth below their eye. These small sharks mainly lay eggs with tendrils, and attach them to the bottom substrate. However, a few catshark species retain the egg cases in the oviducts to hatch in relative safety.

Most catsharks are rarely seen during daylight hours as they are nocturnal and spend the day hidden in caves and crevices. After dark they emerge to feed on a variety of fish, crustaceans and molluscs. A number of catsharks have the ability to swell their stomachs by swallowing water – this allows them to appear larger to frighten predators or wedge themselves tightly into crevices. The catshark species detailed below constitute a representative sample of species that divers may encounter.

DIVING WITH CATSHARKS

Catsharks are great small sharks to dive with, as many species seem to be very sluggish, or just lazy, and will sit on the bottom and allow divers to observe and photograph them very closely. The main problem is finding them in the first place, as they are nocturnal and most spend the day hidden away on rocky reefs. Once a diver finds one, if it is not wedged deep in a cave, they can usually study it without a problem. A few catshark species are surprisingly active during the day, and these species are often more

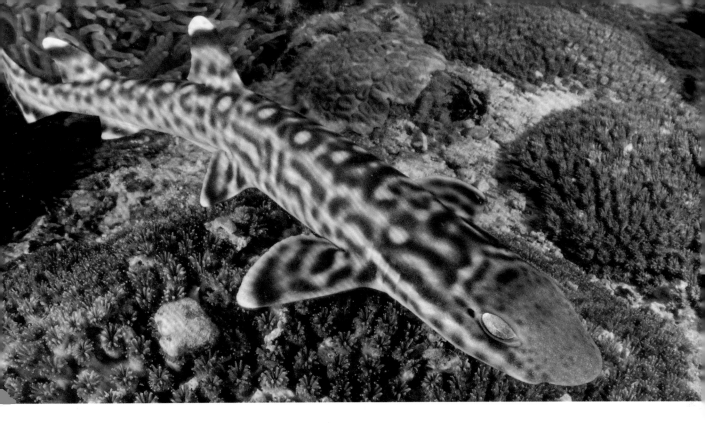

skittish. At night catsharks are far more active, searching the reef for prey, but they are more wary of divers as well.

CORAL CATSHARK *Atelomycterus marmoratus*

The most common member of the catshark family found in tropical seas is the lovely Coral Catshark. Found in the Indo-West Pacific, from Papua New Guinea to Pakistan, it has a grey body covered in striking black and white spots, dots and bands. Grows to a length of 70cm (28in) and has a very slender body. Often found in shallow water, but being a nocturnal species spends the day hidden away in caves and ledges.

WHERE TO SEE

Occasionally encountered on night dives throughout the Indo-West Pacific. Although sometimes found at popular dive destinations in Indonesia and the Philippines, the best place to see this species is off the east coast of Malaysia. Around the Perhentian Islands, they are commonly seen resting in crevices on reefs and shipwrecks by day, while at night groups emerge to feed.

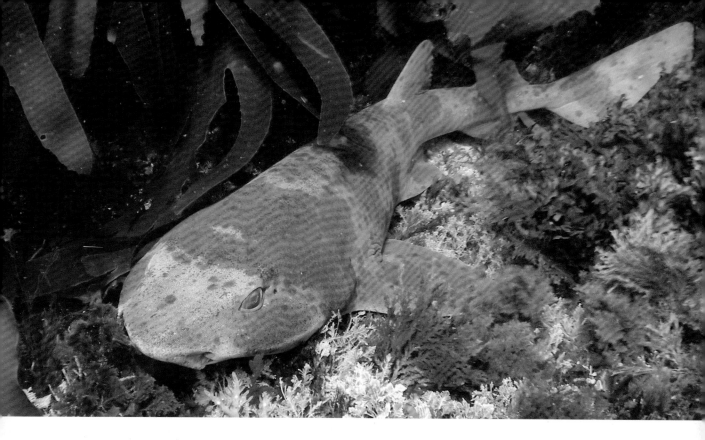

DRAUGHTBOARD SHARK *Cephaloscyllium laticeps*

The most common catshark seen by divers in Australia. Found in shallow water from southern New South Wales through to South Australia, but most often encountered in the cooler waters of Victoria and Tasmania. Brown to grey in colour with darker blotches and small spots, and grows to 1.5m (4.9ft) in length. Like several other members of the catshark family, the Draughtboard Shark has the ability to swell its body, by swallowing water to inflate its stomach. During the day often found resting on the bottom in caves or under kelp, but far more active at night when hunting for prey. Research has found that they spend a lot of time in the same spot, sometimes days, and tagging has revealed that they migrate, with some travelling 300km (185 miles).

WHERE TO SEE

Regularly encountered by divers in the waters off Victoria and Tasmania. Melbourne and Wilsons Promontory are two spots in Victoria where these sharks are occasionally seen. To guarantee an encounter a trip to Tasmania is recommended, with Draughtboard Sharks often seen off the two best dive destinations in the state – Bicheno and Eaglehawk Neck.

BLOTCHY SWELL SHARK *Cephaloscyllium umbratile*

The most common catshark seen off Japan and also known as the Japanese Swell Shark. Grows to 1m (3.3ft) in length and has a pale brown colouration with a dark mottled pattern. Mainly found off the east coast of Japan, but its range extends to Taiwan and possibly parts of China. Like other swell sharks, this species has small, sharp teeth and feeds at night on small fish, crabs, shrimps, squid and octopus.

WHERE TO SEE

Divers only see this species off the east coast of Japan, but it is not common and may be more abundant in deeper water. Best seen off the Chiba and Izu Peninsulas, south of Tokyo, which are a hot-spot for numerous Japanese shark species.

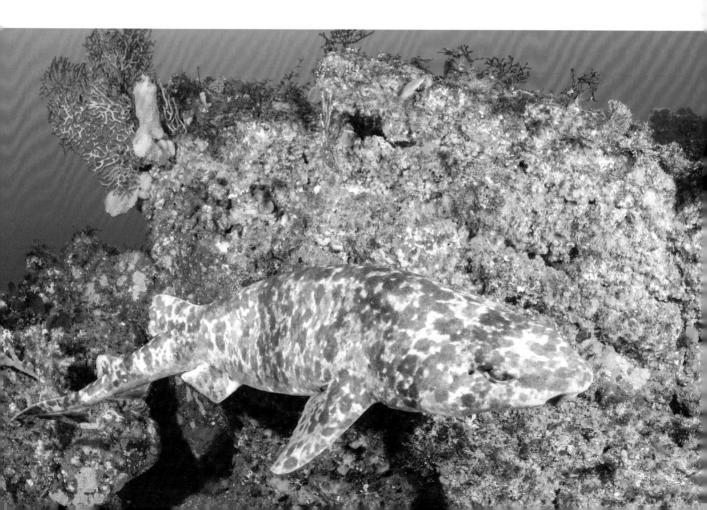

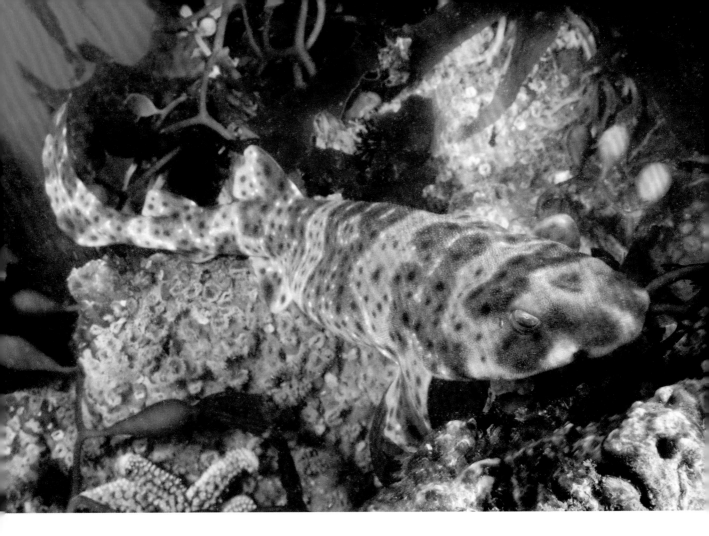

CALIFORNIA SWELL SHARK *Cephaloscyllium ventriosum*

Often known simply as the Swellshark, as it is the best-known member of the catshark family that can swell its body. Growing to 1m (3.3ft) in length, this species is found in the eastern Pacific, from California, USA, south to central Chile. A very pretty shark with brown blotches and dark and light spots. Found on shallow rocky reefs with plenty of places to hide. These sharks inhale water to swell their size, which is thought to deter predators or help them to wedge into crevices.

WHERE TO SEE

As its name suggests, California in the USA is the best place to see this small shark. It is not as abundant as it once was, but divers still encounter them on rocky reefs close to shore and around offshore islands such as Catalina Island. One of the best places to see them is on the rocky reefs off Refugio Beach near Santa Barbara.

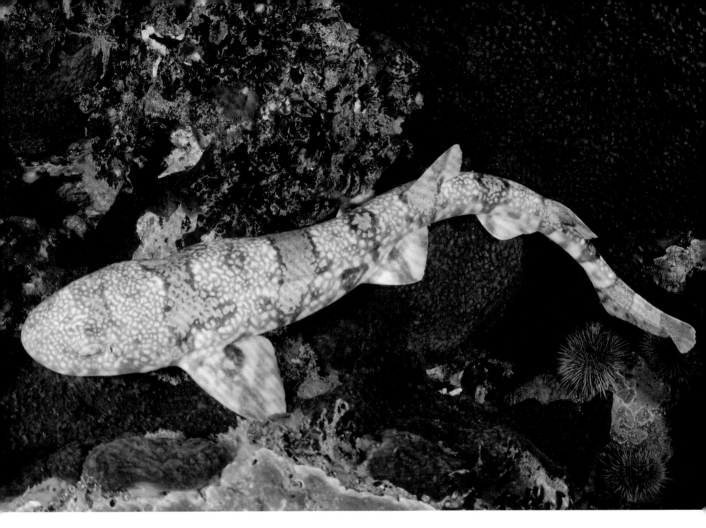

PUFFADDER SHYSHARK *Haploblepharus edwardsii*

One of several species of catsharks found in shallow water off South Africa. Growing to a length of 70cm (28in), this pretty small shark has a brilliant body pattern – pale brown with white spots and golden bands. Endemic to South Africa and found on rocky reefs from Cape Agulhas to Natal.

WHERE TO SEE

This lovely little shark is seen on many rocky reefs off South Africa, and is quite common in the area around Cape Town. Simon's Town is a popular location to find it, with divers exploring Miller's Point likely to locate a few.

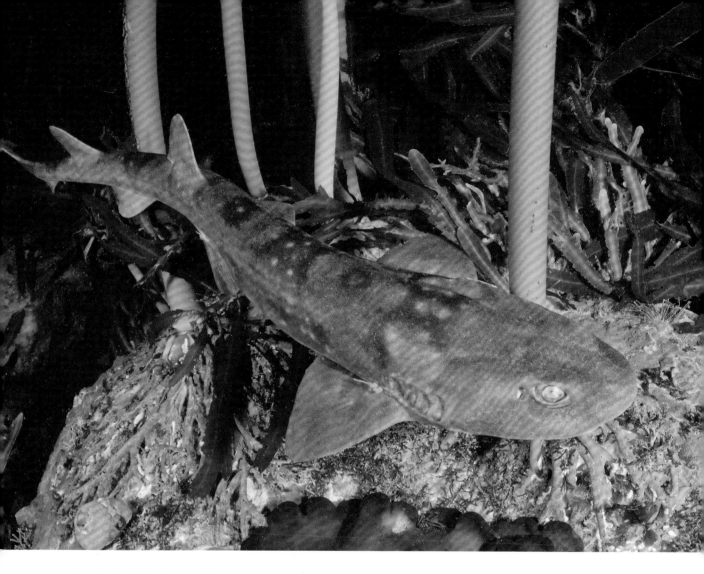

DARK SHYSHARK *Haploblepharus pictus*

Another wonderful small catshark commonly seen off South Africa. Slightly smaller and not as pretty as the Puffadder Shyshark, the Dark Shyshark reaches a length of 60cm (24in) and is a brown colour with darker bands and a covering of paler spots. This species is found from East London to Namibia, but is more common at the southern end of its range.

WHERE TO SEE

Occurs on shallow rocky reefs throughout its range, and is often seen swimming about during the day. The best place to see this species is around Cape Town, with a good population off Miller's Point at Simon's Town.

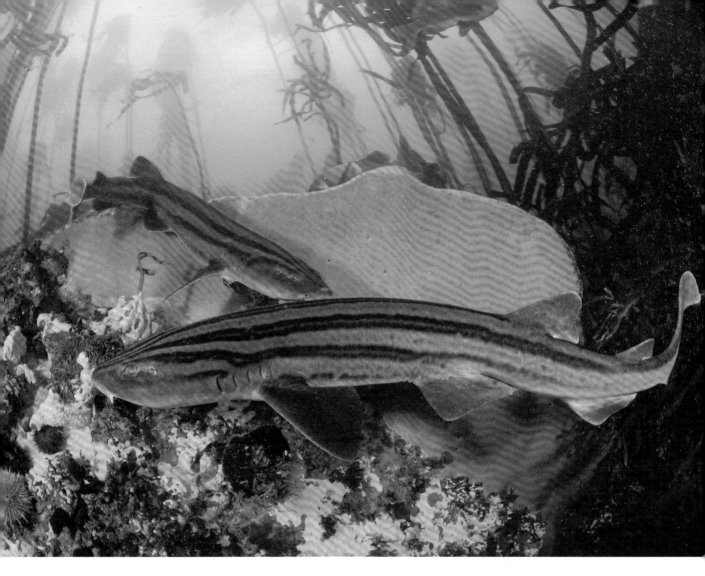

PYJAMA CATSHARK *Poroderma africanum*

South Africa is the place to see catsharks, with the Pyjama Catshark another common local species. Growing to a length of 95cm (37in), this attractive small shark has distinctive dark stripes. It is endemic to South Africa and found from the Western Cape to KwaZulu-Natal. Occasionally active by day, but more commonly found resting in caves.

WHERE TO SEE

Most commonly seen in the same areas around Cape Town as South Africa's other catsharks. This is another species that divers can encounter while exploring the rocky reefs off Miller's Point at Simon's Town.

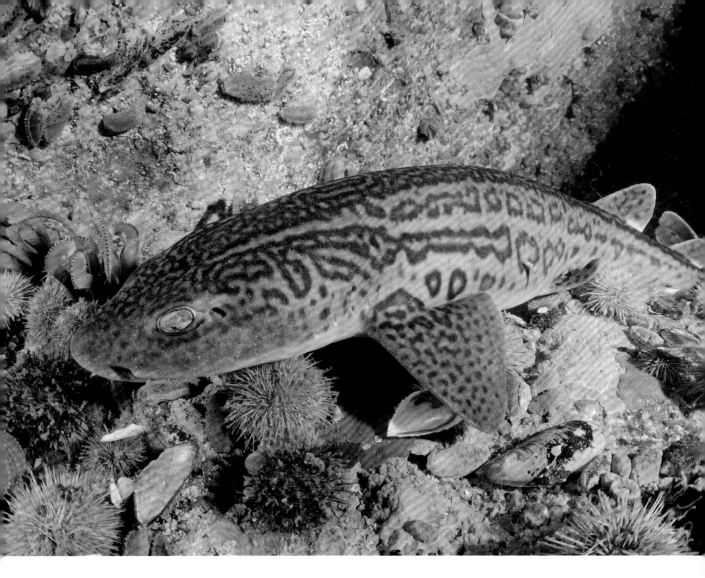

LEOPARD CATSHARK *Poroderma pantherinum*

Looks very similar to its close cousin the Pyjama Catshark, but has a leopard-like covering of black spots. Only found off South Africa, from Saldanha Bay to Sodwana Bay, and reaches a length of 74cm (29in). This species is not as common as its cousin and is harder to find, spending the day hidden in crevices and caves.

WHERE TO SEE

Another species of catshark that divers mainly see around Cape Town. Once again Miller's Point at Simon's Town is a good place to find one hiding under a ledge.

REDSPOTTED CATSHARK *Schroederichthys chilensis*

The most common catshark species seen off Chile and also commonly called the Chilean Catshark. Growing to a length of 62cm (24in), this lovely small shark is a pale brown colour with dark brown bands and a covering of dark and light spots, but strangely no red spots. Found from Peru to central Chile, it spends the day hidden in crevices or under a covering of kelp.

WHERE TO SEE

Quite common in the temperate waters off Chile. Divers often encounter these small sharks between Santiago and Coquimbo, with the rocky reefs off Las Tacas a good place to see several.

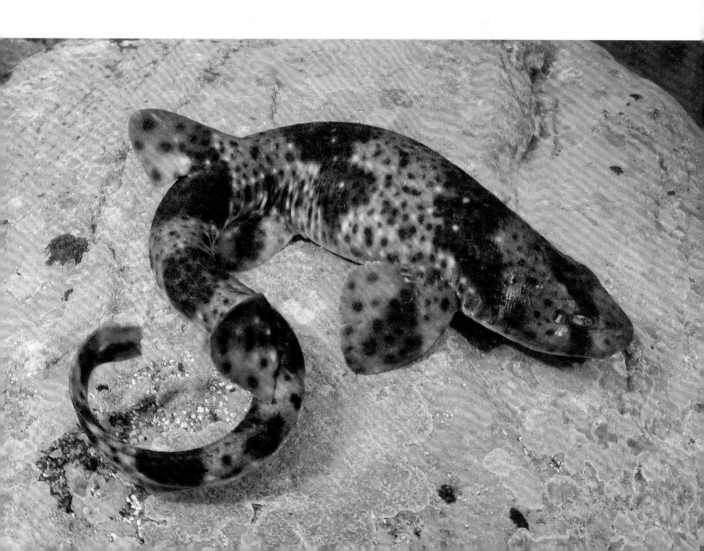

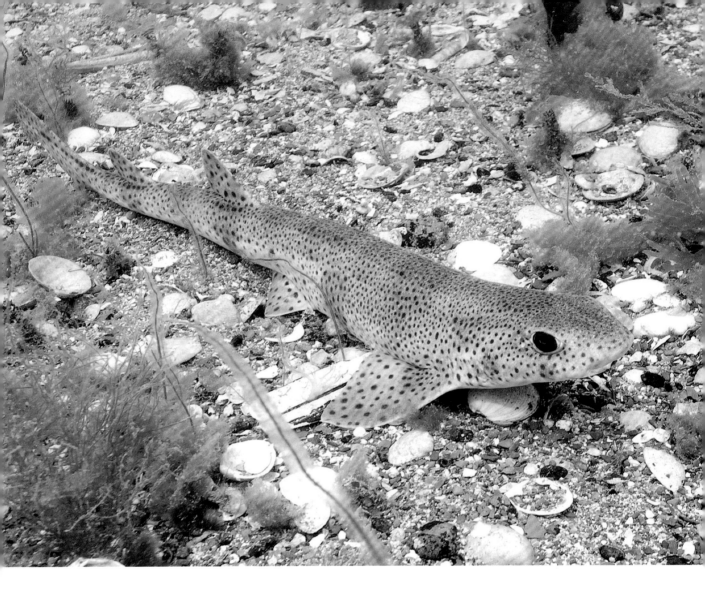

LESSER SPOTTED CATSHARK *Scyliorhinus canicula*

One of the most common catsharks seen off Europe. Covered in small black spots, this species grows to 1m (3.3ft) in length and is found on sandy bottoms from the shallows to depths of 400m (1,310ft). Occurs in the east Atlantic from Norway to the Ivory Coast, and also throughout the Mediterranean.

WHERE TO SEE

Most commonly seen around the United Kingdom. Appears to be abundant on the west coast, especially off Wales and Cornwall. Waters off the island of Skomer, Pembrokeshire, are a reliable location for seeing them.

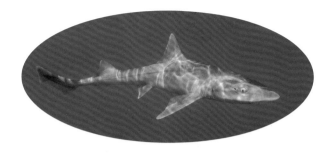

HOUNDSHARKS

FAMILY TRIAKIDAE

The houndsharks are probably best described as looking like a cute and friendly version of a whaler shark. These sharks are usually small, most are less than one metre long, and have two almost equal-sized dorsal fins, large oval eyes, a short snout and nasal barbels (fleshy tentacles hanging from the nostril). Houndsharks are found in temperate and tropical waters worldwide, and many species are captured for human consumption. This family contains 40 species, and most are found in shallow coastal waters.

Houndsharks have small, sharp teeth and feed on fish, octopus, cuttlefish, squid and crabs. They spend most of their time close to the bottom and have a preference for sandy and muddy bottom habitats, often being found in areas of seagrass. They mainly feed at night, and some species are commonly found in large schools. Houndsharks give birth to live young, and litters vary in size from 1–50.

DIVING WITH HOUNDSHARKS

Most houndsharks are not easy to see or get close to for photographs. All members of this family are very wary of divers, and people generally have more chance of getting close on snorkel. Many houndsharks also like shallow bays and estuaries, so many of the best locations to see them have poor visibility. Often the only way to locate one of these sharks is by stealth, by quietly dropping to the bottom and hiding behind rocks or seaweed and waiting for a shark to swim past. Even baits don't seem to entice most houndsharks, the only exception being the Banded Houndsharks in Japan.

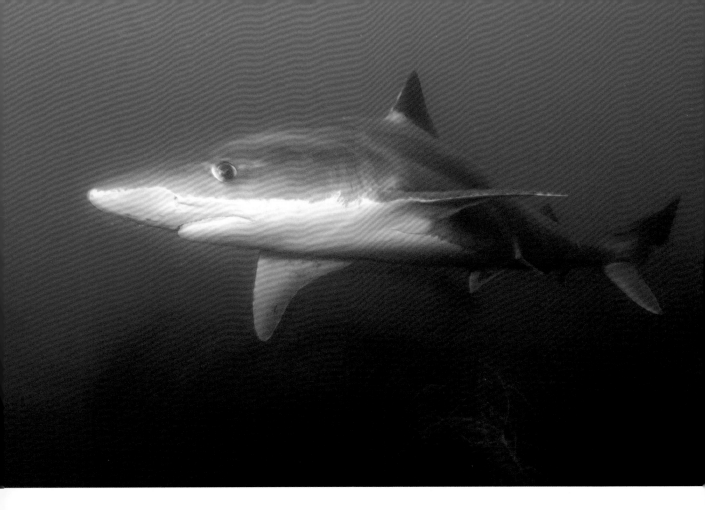

SCHOOL SHARK *Galeorhinus galeus*

Named because it is generally found in small schools, but this species is also commonly known as the Tope Shark and Soupfin Shark. Grey to tan in colour, it has a slender body and can grow to 2m (6.6ft) in length, but the maximum length appears to vary between regions. This species is found in temperate and subtropical waters around the world, apart from east Asia. Occurs in shallow waters to depths of 470m (1,540ft), and while very common, they are wary of divers and rarely seen.

WHERE TO SEE

A species that divers occasionally see in shallow water off Melbourne, Australia, and a few other places. The best place to encounter this shark is La Jolla Shores, California, USA, where it is commonly seen during the summer months, although getting close to one is always a challenge.

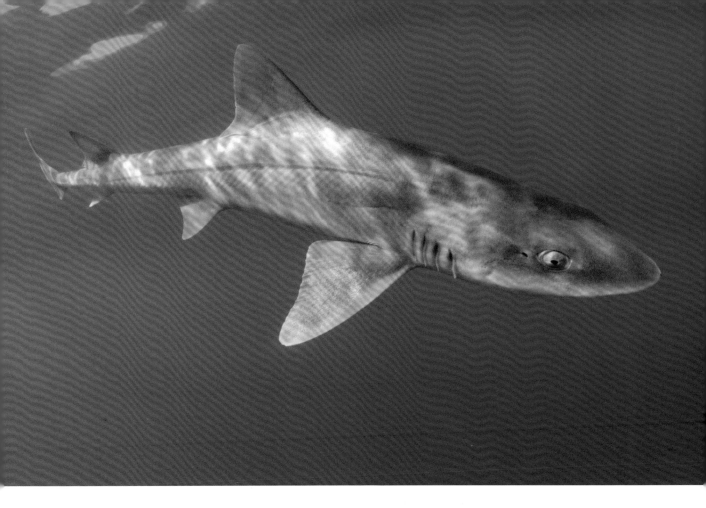

GREY SMOOTHHOUND SHARK *Mustelus californicus*

Found only in the eastern Pacific, off California, USA, and parts of Mexico. Reaches a length of 1.2m (4ft) and is a uniform grey colour. Generally found on sandy bottom environments, it has small blunt teeth and feeds on crustaceans and other invertebrates.

WHERE TO SEE

A species that few divers have seen. The best location to see one is La Jolla Shores, near San Diego, California, USA. During the summer months Grey Smoothhound Sharks, and several other shark species, gather in the shallow bays at this site.

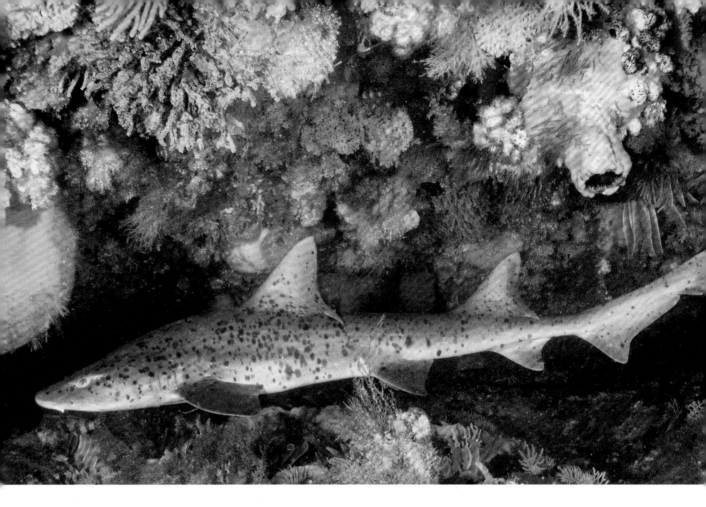

SPOTTED GULLY SHARK *Triakis megalopterus*

Only found off southern Africa, with its range stretching from southern Angola to South Africa. Growing to a length of 1.7m (5.6ft), this species is grey to dark brown in colour and covered in small black spots. Easily identified by its two equal-sized dorsal fins. These sharks are generally found in small schools, and often shelter in caves on rocky reefs.

WHERE TO SEE

Another species that can be seen at the shark diving hot-spot of Miller's Point at Simon's Town, South Africa. These sharks are quite wary of divers, but are often found at this site sheltering in large caves.

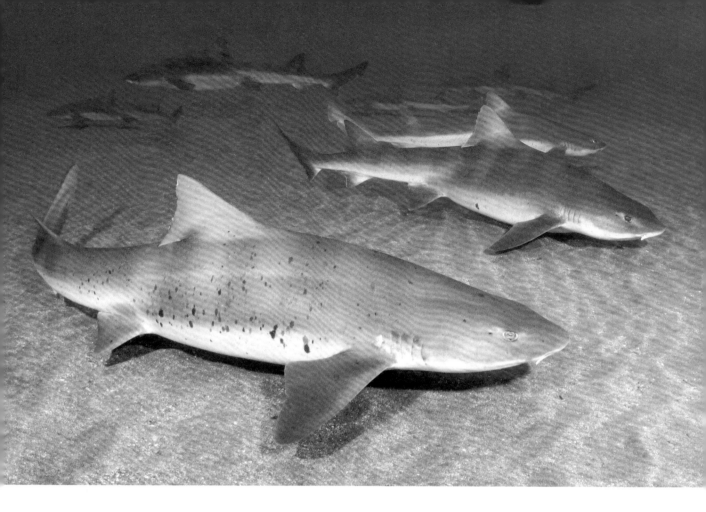

BANDED HOUNDSHARK *Triakis scyllium*

The Asian cousin of the Spotted Gully Shark, with a very similar shape and colouration. Grows to 1.5m (5ft) in length and is a grey to tan colour with subtle bands and a covering of small black spots. Only found in the Northwest Pacific, from Taiwan north to southern Siberia. Generally occurs in shallow water, often in estuaries and bays. Has small, sharp teeth and feeds on small fish and invertebrates.

WHERE TO SEE

Divers will find Japan the best place to encounter a Banded Houndshark. Although usually a shy species, divers can see dozens and possible hundreds of these sharks at Tateyama, on the Chiba Peninsula. This location, south of Tokyo, is where a shark feed is organised that attracts hundreds of Banded Houndsharks that are accustomed to divers.

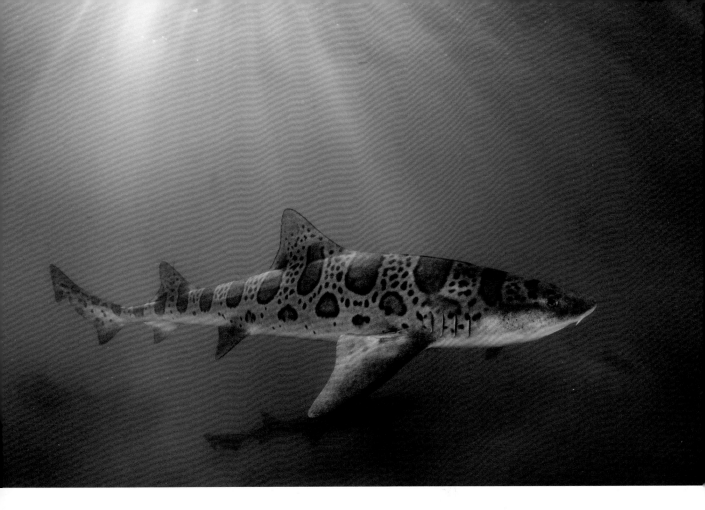

LEOPARD HOUNDSHARK *Triakis semifasciata*

How some sharks get their common name is often a mystery, and this is the case with the Leopard Houndshark which has a bold pattern of large dark saddles rather than spots. Often just called the Leopard Shark, this species grows to a length of 1.8m (5.9ft) and is found in the Northwest Pacific, off the USA and parts of Mexico. Regularly found in large schools, and often seen in shallow bays with other small shark species.

WHERE TO SEE

The coast of California, USA, is the best place to see Leopard Houndsharks, especially during the summer months when they gather in shallow bays. The most reliable location to find them, and other houndsharks, is La Jolla Shores, near San Diego. This popular diving and snorkelling site seems to attract a good variety of shark species, and fortunately the area is protected.

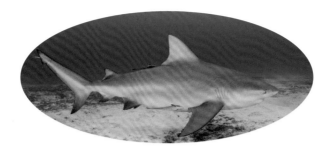

WHALER SHARKS

FAMILY CARCHARHINIDAE

Large family containing about 60 species. Also commonly known as requiem sharks. Whaler sharks typically have two dorsal fins, which vary in size, with their anal fin below the second dorsal fin and their pelvic fin aligned between the dorsal fins. Differentiation between the species can be quite difficult as most have a similar shape, colour and features, with quite a few having dark tips to their fins.

Whaler sharks feed by day and night on fish, rays, sharks, crustaceans and molluscs, with larger members of this family also preying on dolphins, turtles, birds and seals. They give birth to live young and litter sizes vary greatly. Most whalers have less than 10, but some species can have litters of 80–100 pups. Although most of these sharks are timid, quite a few are potentially dangerous and have been responsible for numerous bites on humans. All members of this family can become agitated if food is in the water.

Whaler sharks are more commonly found in shallow tropical waters, but a few species venture into temperate seas, and some are ocean wanderers. The 17 species detailed are the ones most regularly encountered by divers.

DIVING WITH WHALER SHARKS

While many species of whaler sharks are considered to be potentially dangerous, the great majority of species in this family are very wary of divers and hard to approach. Whaler sharks found on coral reefs are generally timid of divers, so most encounters are very brief or the sharks keep their distance. However, the species that roam ocean waters are often more curious of divers, as their meals are often few and far between, so anything new in their environment is inspected as potential prey.

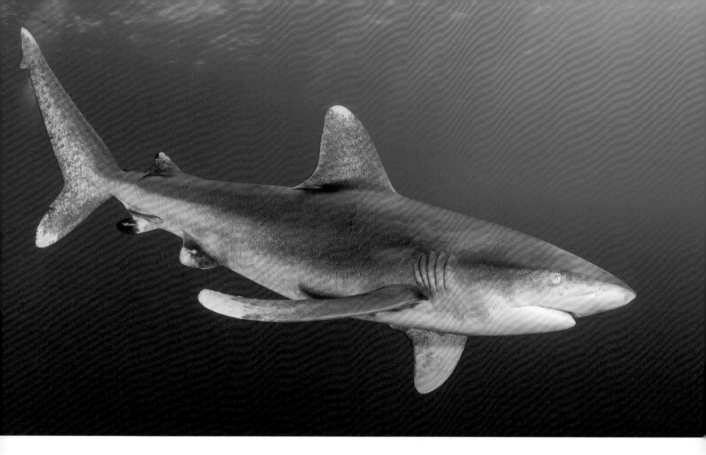

The only way to get close to most species of whaler sharks is to introduce baits into the equation. Sharks within this family are the star attraction at many shark feeds around the world. The baits make the sharks more curious and aggressive, and sometimes unpredictable. In general, the sharks are only interested in the baits, so mostly swarm around the bait box or feeder. However, they will also check out the assembled divers, allowing people to photograph and closely study these sleek and streamlined predators.

While shark bites at shark feeds are extremely rare, whaler sharks are the only family of sharks that appear to be territorial, and several species have been known to bite divers that encroach on their perceived territory. They display when threatened with slow and exaggerated swimming, twisting of the head and body, back arching and dropping of the pectoral fins. This behaviour is still not understood, and it may have nothing to do with territory. If you ever observe this threat display, back away. Don't try to photograph the shark as divers have been bitten seconds after firing their flash. Most of these displays may be just bluff, but it is better to be safe than bitten.

BLACKNOSE SHARK *Carcharhinus acronotus*

Of all the whaler species included in this book, the Blacknose Shark is probably the least known and the least commonly encountered. It occurs in the west Atlantic, from the southern USA to southern Brazil. Grows to 1.4m (4.6ft) in length and has quite small fins and sometimes a black tip on the underside of the snout. Rarely seen by divers, but does turn up at shark feeds in the Bahamas and the Caribbean.

WHERE TO SEE

While divers may accidentally run into a Blacknose Shark while exploring any reef in the Caribbean, this species is most commonly seen at shark feeds. One reliable location where they are regularly seen is at Honeymoon Harbour on Gun Key and Triangle Rocks; both near South Bimini in the Bahamas.

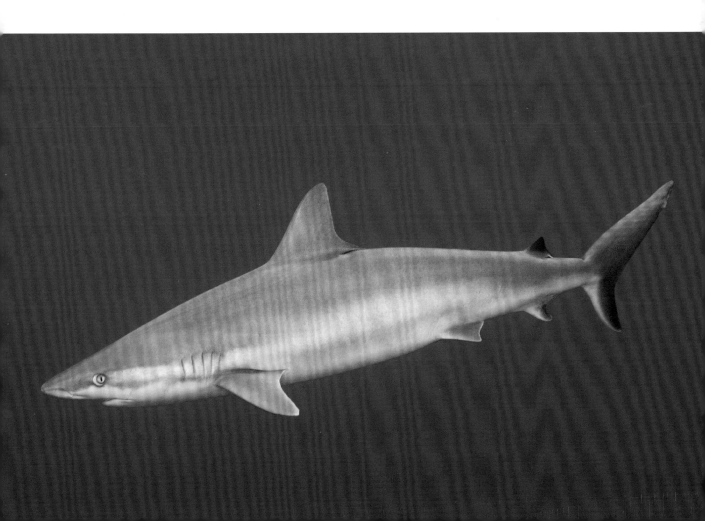

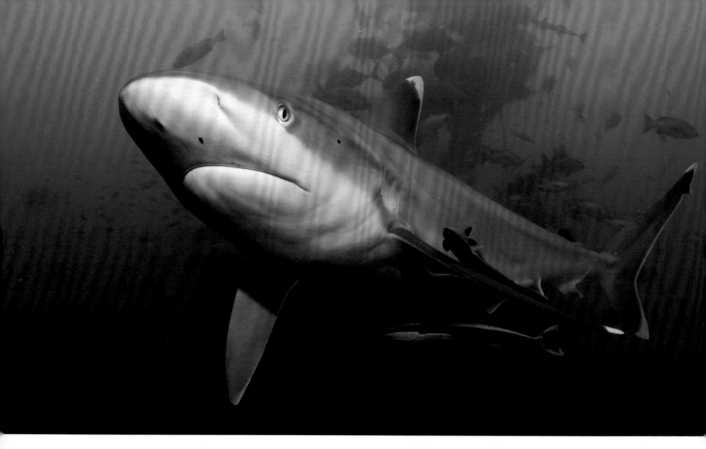

SILVERTIP SHARK *Carcharhinus albimarginatus*

Several whaler shark species have white tips on their fins, but they are easy to tell apart as all have different body shapes and fins. The Silvertip Shark reaches a length of 3m (9.8ft) and has been recorded in tropical waters throughout the Indo-Pacific area. Usually found around deep-water reefs or near drop offs. Tagging studies in the Indian Ocean found that they patrol a small home range; this is apparent at shark feeds, as the same few sharks almost always show up.

WHERE TO SEE

Found at many locations, but there are only a handful of destinations where divers can guarantee an encounter. Off Australia, Silvertip Sharks are mostly seen at Osprey Reef and Lady Elliot Island. In Fiji, these sharks often turn up to the shark feeds at The Bistro, Shark Reef and The Cathedral in Beqa Lagoon. Off Papua New Guinea, the best place to see one is at Fathers Reef near Walindi. In French Polynesia, they are seen at Fakarava Atoll and Rangiroa. Off Mexico these sharks occur around the Socorro Islands. They are also commonly seen off Malpelo Island, Colombia.

GREY REEF SHARK *Carcharhinus amblyrhynchos*

A very territorial shark which has bitten quite a number of divers and should always be treated with respect. Has a grey back and fins, and a dark margin around the back of the tail. Grows to 2.3m (7.5ft) in length and is a tropical species, recorded from the Indo-Pacific region. Seen along drop offs, shallow reefs and also reef lagoons. They are usually quite shy, until baits are produced, but divers should always approach these sharks with caution as they can start to display when threatened.

WHERE TO SEE

Common throughout its range and divers often have brief encounters with these sharks, especially near reef drop offs. However, there are spots where large numbers can be seen. Off Australia this species is common on the Great Barrier Reef and Ningaloo Reef, but the best place to see dozens is North Horn at Osprey Reef. In Fiji, numerous Grey Reef Sharks turn up at the shark feeds at The Bistro, Shark Reef and The Cathedral in Beqa Lagoon. This species is also common on reefs around Papua New Guinea, the Solomon Islands and Vanuatu. In French Polynesia they are often seen in their hundreds, especially around lagoon entrances. Fakarava Atoll is considered the best place to see this species, but divers will also see them off Moorea, Rangiroa and Tahiti. In Palau, Grey Reef Sharks are common at Blue Corner and many other sites. They are also seen in large numbers at Yap, Truk Lagoon and Bikini Atoll. In the Maldives, they are common on all reefs with the local variety having white tips on their fins. In the Red Sea, divers encounter this species at The Brothers and Elphinstone Reef off Egypt.

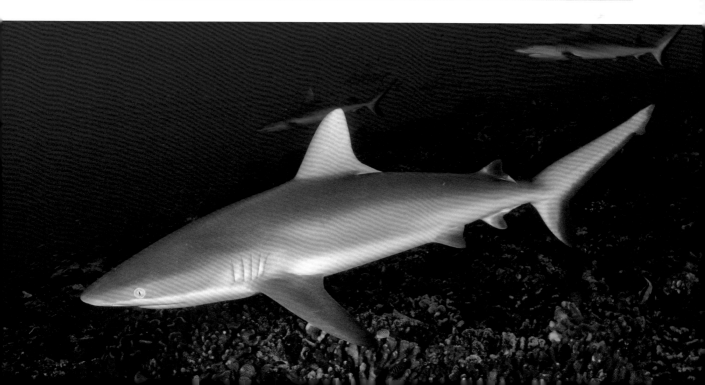

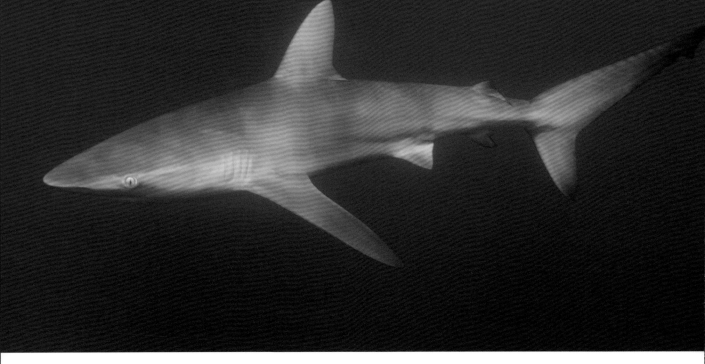

BRONZE WHALER SHARK *Carcharhinus brachyurus*

Also known as the Bronzie, and so-named because of its distinctive brownish-bronze dorsal surface. Attains a length of 2.9m (9.5ft) and has a quite pointed and flattened head. Found in temperate and subtropical waters throughout the world. Not a lot is known about this species, but it occurs around shallow- and deep-water reefs. Thought to migrate into warmer water during winter and often aggregates in packs to feed on schooling fish.

WHERE TO SEE

Most encounters are very brief. More commonly found near deep water and often buzzes divers doing safety stops after diving deep reefs and shipwrecks in temperate waters. Divers have brief encounters with this species off the Poor Knights Islands in New Zealand, off the New South Wales coast in Australia, and also while exploring reefs off South Africa. The best place to see Bronze Whaler Sharks, however, is at the annual Sardine Run off the east coast of South Africa each June and July. The sharks, known locally as Copper Sharks, gather in large numbers to feast on the sardines. They are often so engrossed in grabbing their prey that they completely ignore divers. The species is also seen at Aliwal Shoal, off Durban, South Africa.

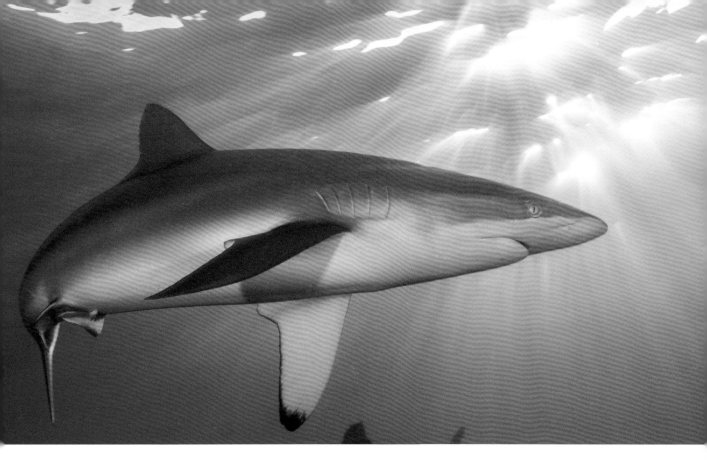

SILKY SHARK *Carcharhinus falciformis*

A graceful ocean wanderer that is often seen near sea mounts and walls that drop into deep water. Regularly found in large schools, the Silky Shark is a slender species with a small dorsal fin. It can grow to 3.3m (10.8ft) in length and is found worldwide in tropical waters. While generally considered to be shy, larger Silky Sharks can be quite bold and curious, and have been known to bump and bite divers.

WHERE TO SEE

Although an open-ocean species, Silky Sharks are relatively common near reefs in the tropical western Atlantic and eastern Pacific. Often seen around oil rigs in the Gulf of Mexico, where they show up in their hundreds during shark feeds. On the west coast of Florida, USA, they are common visitors to feeds near Jupiter Inlet. They are commonly seen off the coast of Baja and at Socorro Island, both Mexico, at dive sites around Cocos Island off Costa Rica, at Malpelo Island off Colombia, and at Darwin Island and Wolf Island in the Galápagos, off Ecuador. They are also seen at shark feeds in southern Cuba, at the Gardens of the Queen.

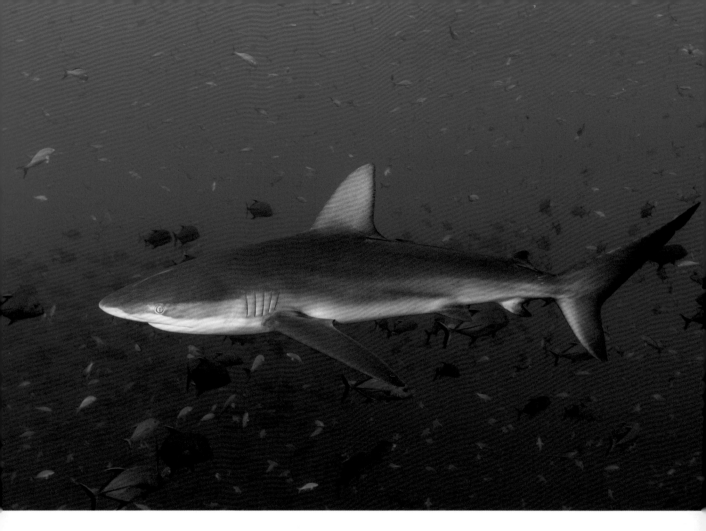

GALÁPAGOS SHARK *Carcharhinus galapagensis*

Found around tropical oceanic islands and reefs throughout the world. Easily confused with the Grey Reef Shark, but lacks the darker tail margin and has a more rounded head. Reaches a length of 3m (9.8ft) and has a grey to greyish-brown back. May be territorial as they have been observed making threat displays, with slow exaggerated swimming and head-swinging similar to that of the Grey Reef Shark.

WHERE TO SEE

Encountered by divers in only a limited number of locations. As their name suggests these sharks are common around the Galápagos Islands, off Ecuador. They are also common at Socorro off Mexico, Malpelo Island off Colombia, Cocos Island off Costa Rica, and Lord Howe Island off Australia.

BULL SHARK *Carcharhinus leucas*

Considered to be the most dangerous shark of all and has been responsible for numerous bites on humans. Tends to inhabit murky inshore waters, such as estuaries, canals, harbours and bays, and even ranges into freshwater rivers, being recorded 4,000km (2,500 miles) up the Amazon. Most bites occur in dirty water, so many bites may simply be a case of mistaken identity. Growing to 3.4m (11.2ft) in length, the Bull Shark is quite a stocky animal. They are best distinguished by their short rounded snout and well-rounded body. Common around the world in subtropical to tropical waters.

WHERE TO SEE

While very common in rivers and canals, where few divers venture, Bull Sharks are also seen on coral reefs. The only way to guarantee an encounter with one of these stocky sharks is to partake in a shark feed at a handful of destinations around the world. In Fiji, Bull Sharks are the star attraction at The Bistro, Shark Reef and The Cathedral in Beqa Lagoon, and are best seen from February to October. In South Africa they are commonly attracted to the shark feeds at the Protea Banks near Durban. In Mexico, Bull Sharks are attracted to a shark feed off Playa del Carmen from November to March. The species is an unwelcome guest at shark feeds off Bimini in the Bahamas, where the target species is Great Hammerhead Shark. These shark feeds only take place from January to March, but the Bull Sharks are probably there year-round.

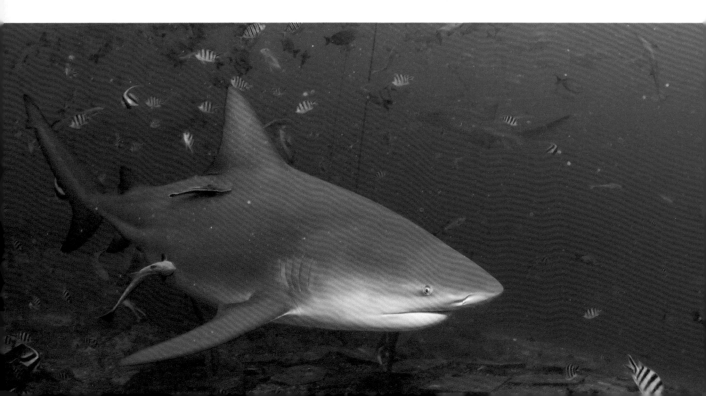

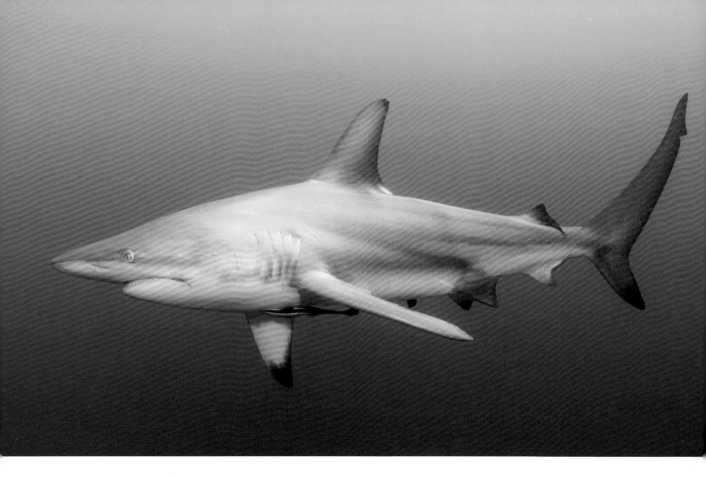

BLACKTIP SHARK *Carcharhinus limbatus*

Found in tropical waters around the planet. This slender, muscular shark has a pointed snout, a distinctive white band on its flank and small black tips on the ends of its fins. Grows to 2.5m (8.2ft) in length, often found in large schools, and is known to migrate. A timid species, especially when larger sharks are nearby, the Blacktip Shark is very difficult to get close to without baits in the water.

WHERE TO SEE

Not often seen by divers, and are more likely to approach a snorkeler than a scuba diver. Off Australia, seen at a few locations on the Great Barrier Reef, but most common at Lady Elliot Island. Off the Bahamas this species is attracted to shark feeds off Walker's Cay at a site called Shark Rodeo. In French Polynesia it is often found among schooling Grey Reef Sharks. However, the best location to see lots of these sharks is at Aliwal Shoal off Durban in South Africa, where dozens of Blacktip Sharks are attracted to organised Tiger Shark feeds, and are often very bold until the larger Tiger Sharks arrive.

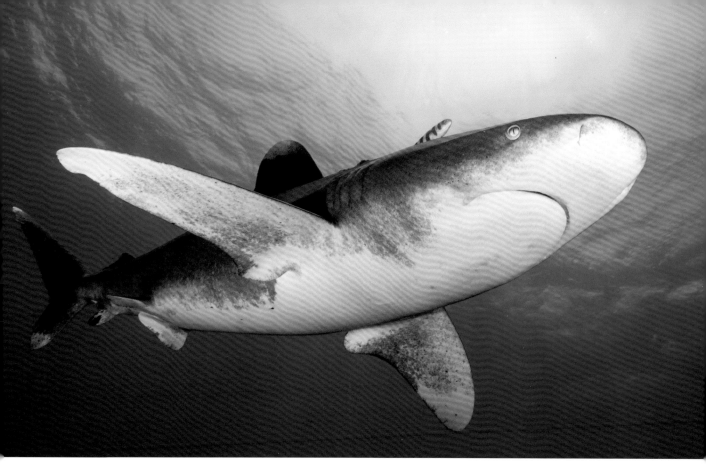

OCEANIC WHITETIP SHARK *Carcharhinus longimanus*

Once considered to be the most abundant large animal on the planet, the Oceanic Whitetip Shark has drastically declined in numbers due to overfishing. Found around the world in tropical and warm-temperate seas, it is a pelagic species that rarely comes close to land. Very distinctive with its long pectoral fins and rounded fin tips. Can grow to 4m (13ft) in length. This species is often curious of divers, and can become aggressive when baits are in the water.

WHERE TO SEE

Oceanic Whitetip Sharks cruise the oceans of the world and rarely come close to reefs or land, but a few locations have been discovered where divers can have close encounters with one of these majestic sharks. Off Egypt, there are a number of isolated reefs in the Red Sea where divers regularly see this species, the best being The Brothers and Elphinstone Reef. At Cat Island in the Bahamas, they can be encountered at special shark feeds in April and May.

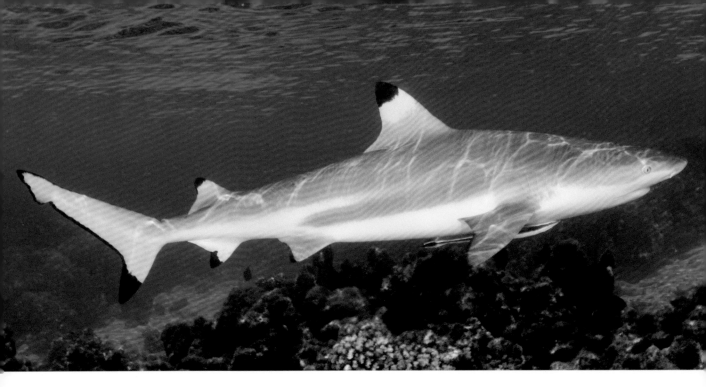

BLACKTIP REEF SHARK *Carcharhinus melanopterus*

A number of whaler sharks have black fin tips, but the most common of these species is the Blacktip Reef Shark. These sharks are pale grey and have black tips on all their fins and a black margin around the tail and pectoral fins. Can grow to 1.8m (5.9ft) in length, but are rarely bigger than 1.2m (3.9ft). Common throughout the tropical waters of the Indo-Pacific region, and usually found in quite shallow water. Commonly feed on reef flats and congregate along reef edges at low tide, waiting for the turn of the tide so they can grab trapped fish. Tagging studies have shown them to have a small home range of only a few square kilometres.

WHERE TO SEE

These shy little reef sharks are commonly seen by divers throughout their range, but only come close to humans at shark feeds. French Polynesia is a great location to see them as they populate the local reefs and are common at shark feeds at Bora Bora, Moorea and Tahiti. They are also common at the shark feeds at The Bistro, Shark Reef and The Cathedral in Beqa Lagoon, Fiji. In the Solomon Islands this species is common at Uepi. In Australia they are common on the Great Barrier Reef and Ningaloo Reef, with the reef flats at Heron Island and Lady Elliot Island great places to see this species. Blacktip Reef Sharks are also commonly seen around Yap and Palau in Micronesia. While in the Indian Ocean, divers regularly see them on many of the dive sites in the Maldives.

DUSKY SHARK *Carcharhinus obscurus*

Easily confused with many other whaler species, as it is grey in colour and has a similar snout and fins to many related sharks, although the Dusky Shark does have a subtle white band on its flank. Occurs in temperate and warm-temperate seas worldwide and grows to 4m (13ft) in length. Found on shallow reefs and in offshore waters, and has been recorded to a depth of 400m (1,310ft).

WHERE TO SEE

A rarely seen member of the whaler family, Dusky Sharks can turn up to shark feeds almost anywhere, but there are few locations where they are regularly seen. In the USA, they occur around offshore sea mounts and oil rigs off Venice, Louisiana. They also show up at shark feeds off Jupiter in Florida. The only other location where Dusky Sharks are regularly seen is off Sydney, Australia, where every year from January to June divers can see numerous juveniles gather in a shallow bay at Manly.

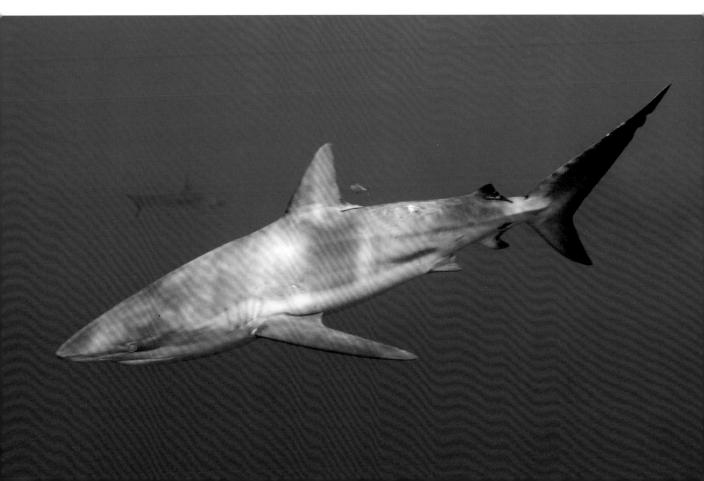

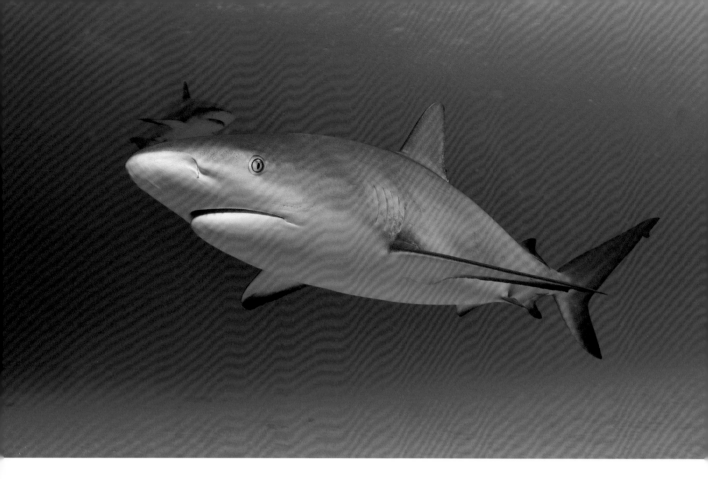

CARIBBEAN REEF SHARK *Carcharhinus perezi*

The most common whaler shark species seen by divers in the warm waters of the Caribbean is the appropriately named Caribbean Reef Shark. Found on reefs from the southern USA to Brazil, it grows to a length of 3m (9.8ft). Quite stocky and dark grey to grey-brown in colour with a short, rounded snout. While most encounters with this species are very brief on coral reefs, it is a popular participant at most shark feeds in the Caribbean.

WHERE TO SEE

The Bahamas is the best place to see lots of Caribbean Reef Sharks, especially at the many well-organised shark feeds around the island nation. Off Grand Bahama, they are common at shark feeds at Fish Tales and Shark Alley. Off Nassau, famous shark feeds at Shark Arena and The Runway attract numerous Caribbean Reef Sharks. Off Long Island these sharks are seen at Shark Reef, while off Walker's Cay another shark feed at Shark Rodeo brings in lots of Caribbean Reef Sharks. Other locations where divers will encounter them include Big Mama's Reef off St Maarten, Roatan Island in Honduras, and numerous sites off Jardines de la Reina off Cuba.

TIGER SHARK *Galeocerdo cuvier*

The largest member of the whaler shark family, growing to 5.5m (18ft) in length and easily identified by its rounded blunt snout and by the dark vertical bars along its body, although these fade with age. Found in tropical to warm-temperate waters around the world. They may migrate with changes in water temperature, but very little is really known about this species.

Tiger Sharks are found in a variety of different environments; on reefs, in bays and in the open ocean, and feed on almost anything they can find, be it edible or not. While these sharks are considered dangerous, and have been responsible for numerous attacks on humans, they are usually shy and wary of divers unless baits are in the water. They should always be treated with respect because although they are slow swimmers and often look docile, they can quickly turn and bump or bite a diver without warning.

WHERE TO SEE

Encounters with Tiger Sharks are very rare unless baits are added to the equation. While they can turn up at almost any shark feed, there are a few dedicated shark-feeding sites where these large lumbering sharks are guaranteed most of the time. The best locations to see numerous Tiger Sharks are two dive sites in the Bahamas – Tiger Beach and Fish Tales. These two dive sites are very close together off Grand Bahama, and while the Tiger Sharks are seen year-round, they can disappear in July and August. Tiger Sharks are also attracted to a shark feed at the Protea Banks and Aliwal Shoal near Durban. Although the sharks can be seen year-round, March to June is considered the best time. Beqa Lagoon in Fiji is another location where Tiger Sharks make a regular appearance, being seen at shark feeds at The Bistro, Shark Reef and The Cathedral.

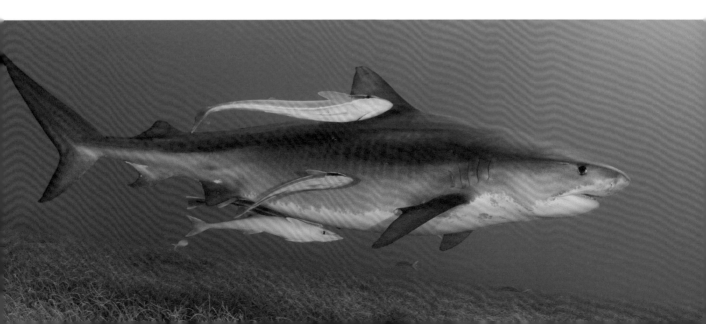

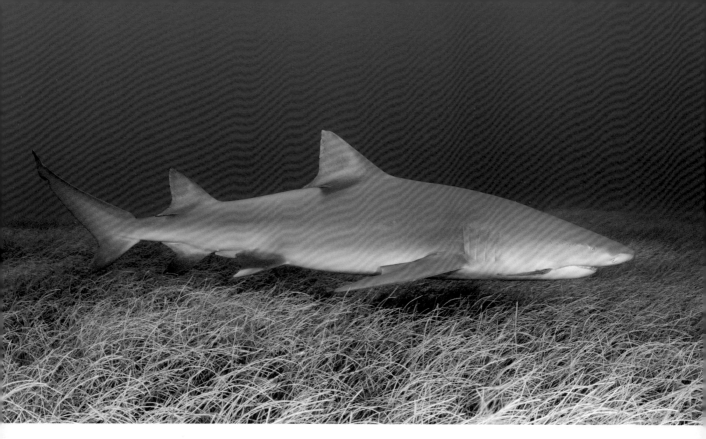

LEMON SHARK *Negaprion brevirostris*

One of the easiest members of the whaler family to identify as their dorsal fins are of almost equal size. Named after its yellowish-brown skin, the Lemon Shark grows to a length of 3.4m (11.2ft) and is found in tropical waters of the Atlantic Ocean and eastern Pacific. Inhabits shallow coral reefs, lagoons and mangroves, and known to gather in large schools. One of the only members of the whaler family that rests on the bottom. Only occasionally seen by divers on coral reefs, but are common visitors at some shark feeds.

WHERE TO SEE

Lemon Sharks were once rarely seen by divers, as they prefer very shallow water where divers don't venture, but they can be seen in large numbers at shark-feeding sites north of Grand Bahama. These two sites are Tiger Beach and Fish Tales, and while they may be more famous for Tiger Sharks, dozens of very friendly Lemon Sharks are often the highlight of the experience. These sharks are a joy to dive with at these sites as they cruise at the surface at the back of the boat, in mid-water and across the bottom. They will also suddenly stop and rest on the bottom beside a diver. The only other location where Lemon Sharks are regularly encountered by divers is in the USA on the reefs and wrecks off Jupiter, Florida.

SICKLEFIN LEMON SHARK *Negaprion acutidens*

Looks very much like its cousin the Lemon Shark, but is smaller and found over a different range. This species reaches a length of 3.1m (10.2ft) and is found in the tropical waters of the Indian Ocean to the central Pacific Ocean. Rarely seen by divers exploring coral reefs, as it seems to prefer shallow bays, lagoons and reef flats. However, it does like a free feed and will frequent shark feeds.

WHERE TO SEE

Divers are more likely to encounter a Sicklefin Lemon Shark on a shallow reef flat than on a coral reef. In Australia, this species is regularly seen by snorkelers on the reef flats at Heron Island. In French Polynesia, they are seen at shark feeds off Bora Bora, Moorea and Tahiti. This species is also seen at the shark feeds at The Bistro, Shark Reef and The Cathedral in Beqa Lagoon, Fiji.

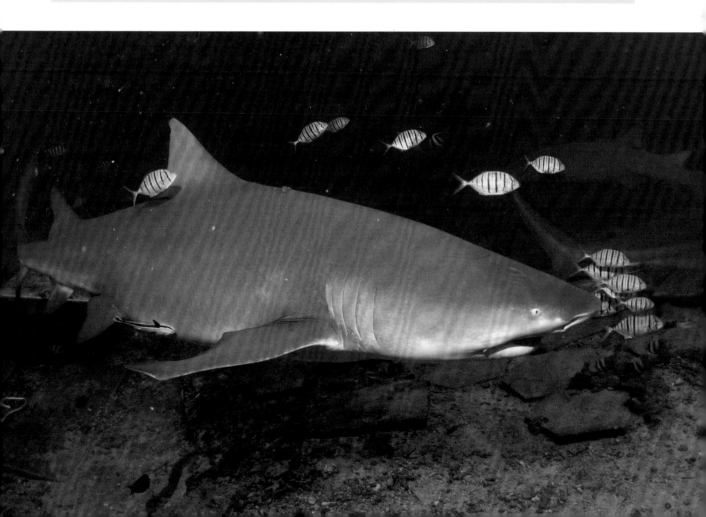

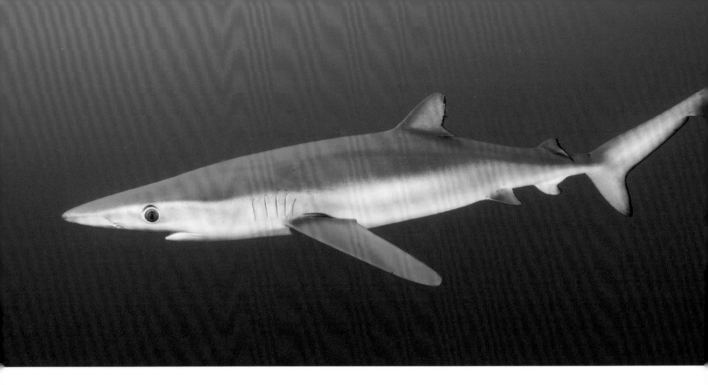

BLUE SHARK *Prionace glauca*

An elegant pelagic species that is found in all tropical and temperate waters. It has a bluish dorsal surface and grows to 3.8m (12.5ft) in length. Can be identified by its slender body, long nose, elongated pectoral fins and large eyes. Used to be abundant, but numbers have drastically declined around the planet due to long-line fishing for shark fins. Known to migrate long distances; for example, one captured off Java, Indonesia, had originally been tagged off Tasmania, Australia. Blue Sharks spend most of their time in deep water, but sometimes feed in shallow inshore waters at night.

WHERE TO SEE

Blue Sharks are very curious creatures and will closely inspect a diver once encountered. However, being pelagic wanderers they are rarely seen on reefs and the only way to attract them to divers is with baits in the water. In South Africa, Blue Sharks are attracted to offshore shark feeds around Cape Point near Cape Town. The sharks are seen in this area from October to July. Another location to see them is Pico Island in the Azores from July to October. They are also seen off both coasts of the USA, year-round off San Diego, California, and between July and October off Rhode Island. Summer is also the best time to see these sharks off the United Kingdom, on trips running out of Newquay, Cornwall. Blue Sharks are also seen off Los Cabos, Mexico. At all these sites, Shortfin Mako Sharks are also seen at the same time.

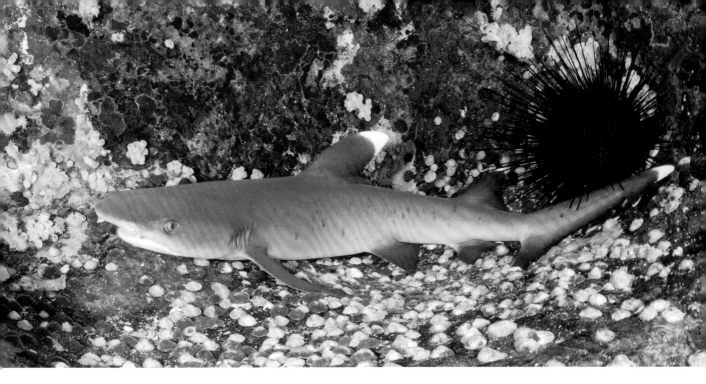

WHITETIP REEF SHARK *Triaenodon obesus*

The most commonly observed shark on coral reefs throughout the Indo-Pacific region. Easily identified by the white tips on its dorsal fin and tail, and by its short rounded snout. Has a greyish-brown dorsal surface and reaches a length of 2.1m (6.9ft), while most have dark spots scattered across their backs. Whitetip Reef Sharks feed at night, and are very determined hunters, often squirming under ledges and wriggling through hard coral to reach their prey. By day they are observed slowly patrolling the reef, resting on the bottom and even sheltering in caves. These sharks are seen in groups or singly, and from studies appear to have a limited home range.

WHERE TO SEE

A very common species, Whitetip Reef Sharks are seen on reefs throughout their range. They are wary of people, but divers can often get close to them when they rest on the bottom or in caves. Common at shark feeds, and often very cheeky, sneaking up on feeders from behind, even coming between their legs. The best locations to see lots of Whitetip Reef Sharks are: Osprey Reef in Australia; at the numerous shark-feeding sites in Beqa Lagoon, Fiji; any shark feed in French Polynesia; Socorro off Mexico; Darwin and Wolf Island at the Galápagos Islands; Malpelo Island off Colombia; and at any dive site at Cocos Island off Costa Rica. At Cocos Island, divers can have a very special Whitetip Reef Shark experience at night, when dozens and sometimes hundreds of these sharks swarm over the reef in search of prey.

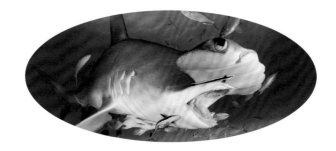

HAMMERHEAD SHARKS

FAMILY SPHYRNIDAE

With their bizarre hammer-shaped heads, hammerhead sharks are unmistakable and amazing sharks to see underwater. This family is closely related to the whaler sharks, having a similar body shape and fins, but they have larger dorsal fins and obviously quite distinctive heads. Hammerheads are thought to be one of the most recently evolved sharks, their wide head enhancing their senses of sight, smell and their electro-receptive abilities by spreading them over a wider area. Their wide heads are also thought to aid swimming, acting as a bow plane. Another advantage of the head comes to the fore when feeding, as they can pin prey to the bottom while they take a bite. There are ten species of hammerhead sharks found worldwide, and each species seems to feed on different prey. Larger members of the family feed on sharks, large fish, crustaceans, octopus, squid and especially rays, while smaller species feed on crustaceans, small fish and molluscs.

Hammerheads give birth to live young and have quite large litters of up to 40. The young sharks have quite flexible heads with the hammer folded back at birth. These sharks are usually solitary, but some species do school in large numbers. Why they school is still a mystery, but mating and feeding have been observed when the sharks are in schooling formations.

Hammerheads are considered to be potentially dangerous, but most are shy unless bait is in the water. These sharks visit shallow reefs to feed and breed, but only three species are seen by divers.

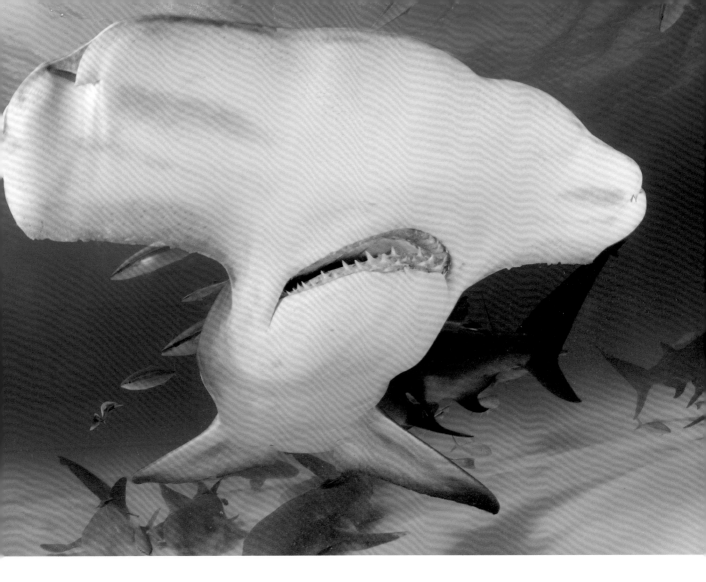

DIVING WITH HAMMERHEAD SHARKS

Hammerhead sharks are very wary of divers and generally veer away when they see a cloud of bubbles. Divers with rebreathers can generally get closer to these animals, but if a diver slows their breathing, stays low and hides behind a rock, they may find the sharks come quite close. Fortunately, when they are in vast schools divers don't have to get too close to watch the spectacle of hundreds of hammerheads swimming overhead in formation. The Great Hammerhead Shark is the boldest member of the family, but it is not generally seen unless baits are in the water. Having several Great Hammerheads cruising around a diver is quite unnerving at first, but they are not aggressive sharks and ignore all the assembled divers, except for the one with the bait.

SCALLOPED HAMMERHEAD SHARK *Sphyrna lewini*

Found in tropical to warm temperate waters around the world and is best identified by the scalloped front edge of its head. This shark reaches a length of 3.5m (11.5ft) and has a brownish-grey dorsal surface. Scalloped Hammerhead Sharks form huge schools and are thought to migrate with changes in water temperature.

WHERE TO SEE

Schools are seen at many locations around the planet, including dive sites off Australia, Papua New Guinea, the Philippines, Malaysia, Indonesia, Japan, the Maldives, Egypt and Mexico. Encounters at these locations are never guaranteed as the sharks are often seasonal and unpredictable. However, the three destinations where divers regularly see incredible schools of these sharks are the Galápagos Islands, Malpelo Island off Colombia, and Cocos Island off Costa Rica. At these islands there are numerous dive sites where Scalloped Hammerheads are still seen in large numbers, giving divers an unforgettable experience.

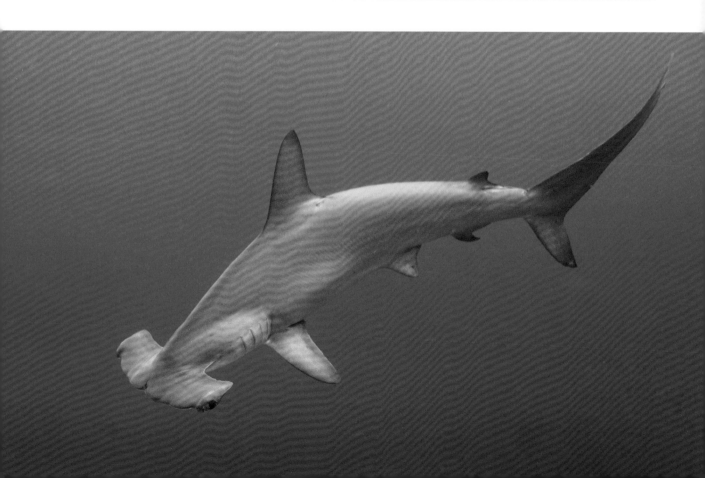

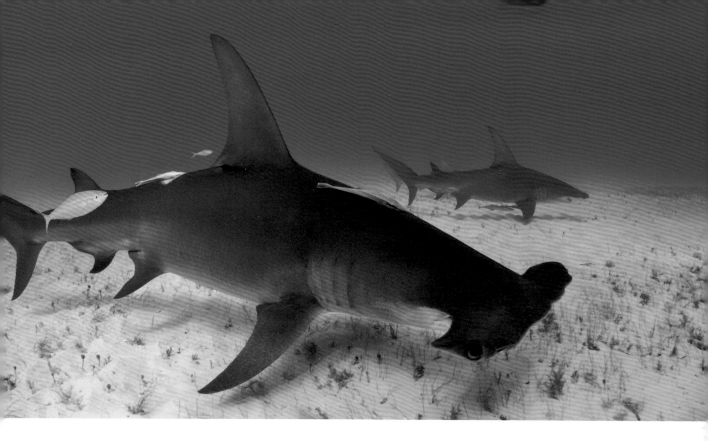

GREAT HAMMERHEAD SHARK *Sphyrna mokarran*

Growing to a length of 6m (19.7ft), the Great Hammerhead Shark is quite an impressive sight. It is found around the globe in tropical to warm temperate waters. Easily recognised by its large size and very tall dorsal fin. Generally a solitary creature and will boldly approach a diver, especially if there are baits in the water.

The Great Hammerhead is a ferocious predator that feeds almost exclusively on rays. One was once observed in Bermuda to chase and hit a stingray to the bottom with its head before biting it. These sharks have been found with dozens of stingray spines jutting out of their head and mouth, a defence that doesn't seem to deter or slow them down at all.

WHERE TO SEE

This species is rarely seen by divers and most encounters are quite brief, with only a fleeting glimpse of the shark. They are occasionally attracted to shark feeds, and other sharks appear to be wary of them. The only location where divers can guarantee an encounter with one of these impressive sharks is off Bimini in the Bahamas. In the past decade shark feeds off Bimini Sands have attracted groups of Great Hammerhead Sharks during the winter months from December to March.

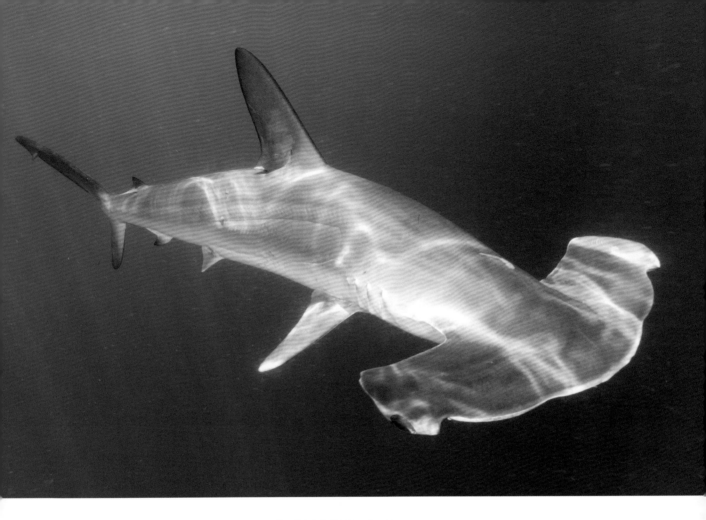

SMOOTH HAMMERHEAD SHARK *Sphyrna zygaena*

Looks very similar to the Scalloped Hammerhead, but has a smoother edge to its head. Growing to a length of 4m (13ft), this species occurs around the world in temperate and subtropical waters. It is found in both shallow water and in oceanic habitats. Known to migrate to warmer waters during the winter months, and often found in large schools.

WHERE TO SEE

Encounters with Smooth Hammerhead Sharks are very hit and miss. They do turn up at shark feeds from time to time, but there are no destinations where divers can guarantee an encounter. Places where they are sometimes seen include Los Cabos off Mexico and Maui, Hawaii, USA.

OPPOSITE – A diver encounters an Eastern Fiddler Ray, *Trygonorrhina fasciata*.

DIVING WITH RAYS

Rays are very closely related to sharks and can simply be considered as flattened sharks. With 13 families and more than 630 species, the rays are as diverse and varied as their shark cousins, and just as fun to dive with.

Rays typically have a disc-shaped head with fused pectoral fins, and while most have an elongated rod-like or whip-like tail, others are misidentified as sharks as they have shark-like tails. The easiest way to identify a ray is by the location of the gills, as all rays have gills on their ventral surface, while sharks always have their gills on their side or back.

Rays typically have small blunt teeth and most species feed on small fish or invertebrates, generally dug out of the sand, where most ray species live. The largest rays, the mobula rays and manta rays, are filter-feeders and consume plankton. Most rays give birth to live young, except for the skates which lay eggs.

At many dive sites around the world divers are more likely to encounter a ray than a shark, especially with the decline in shark numbers due to overfishing. Some ray species are wary of humans and flee on the approach of a bubble-blowing alien, but many species completely ignore divers and are easy to approach and observe. There are also a few rays that seem to enjoy the company of people and take delight in swimming around awestruck divers.

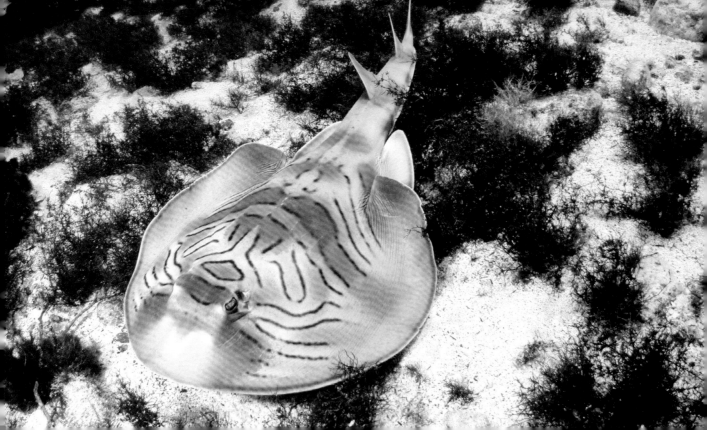

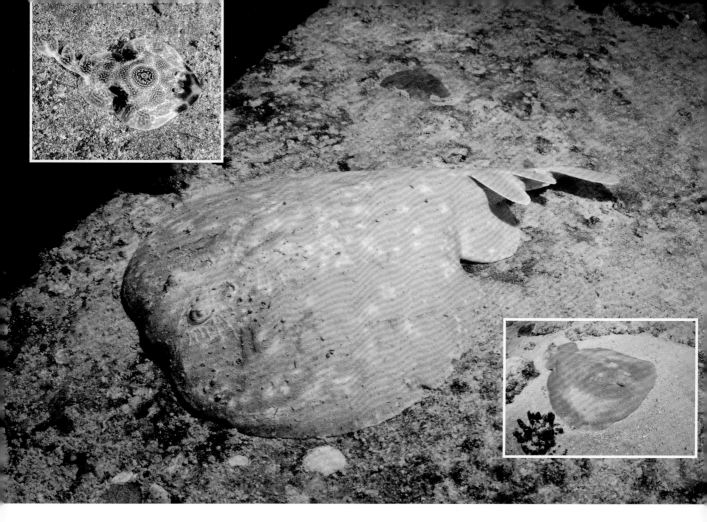

ABOVE - Electric rays vary greatly in shape as can be seen in these species: Panther Electric Ray, *Torpedo panthera* (MAIN IMAGE); Bullseye Electric Ray, *Diplobatis ommata* (TOP LEFT); and Coffin Ray, *Hypnos monopterygius* (BOTTOM RIGHT).

ELECTRIC RAYS

The strangest family of rays that divers will encounter are the electric rays. Around 70 species are known, and all have a small chubby disc and a short tail. Able to generate electric shocks of up to 220 volts via modified muscles, any diver that has touched one of these creatures never forgets the experience. Like all ray species, electric rays are docile and they only use electric shocks to stun prey and for defence. Electric rays are not always easy to find, as they like to hide under the sand, and most divers discover them by accident. Once found, they are easy to observe and photograph, as they are slow swimmers and usually don't bother to swim away.

SHOVELNOSE RAYS

With a head like a ray and a body like a shark many people mistakenly think that shovelnose rays are sharks, but like all rays they have their gills on the ventral surface. This family of rays contains 45 species that either have a triangular or circular-shaped head. Also known as guitarfish, shovelnose rays can get quite large, with some growing to a length of 3m (9.8ft), but most species are around 1m (3.3ft) long. Like most rays, shovelnose rays are generally found on sandy bottoms, and generally like to hide under a layer of sand, but other species also hide amongst seagrass and under kelp. Divers can often get quite close to shovelnose rays to observe and photograph them.

BELOW - These pictures show just a few of the shovelnose ray species that divers can encounter: Banded Guitarfish, *Zapteryx exasperata* (TOP LEFT); Southern Fiddler Ray, *Trygonorrhina dumerilii* (TOP RIGHT); White-spotted Shovelnose Ray, *Rhynchobatus australiae* (BOTTOM LEFT); and Yellow Guitarfish, *Rhinobatos schlegelii* (BOTTOM RIGHT).

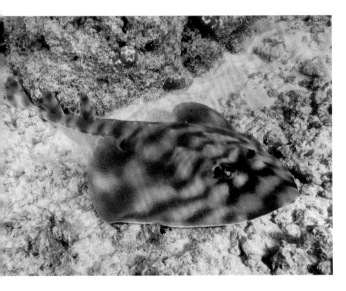
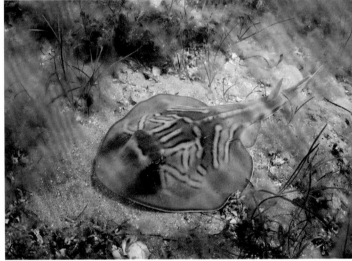
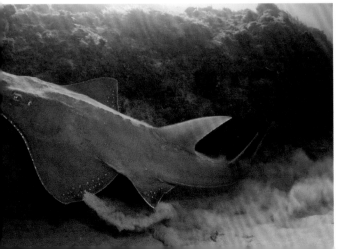
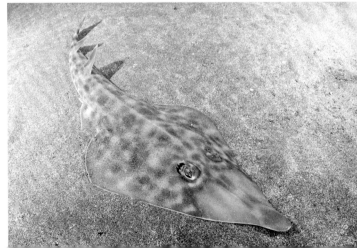

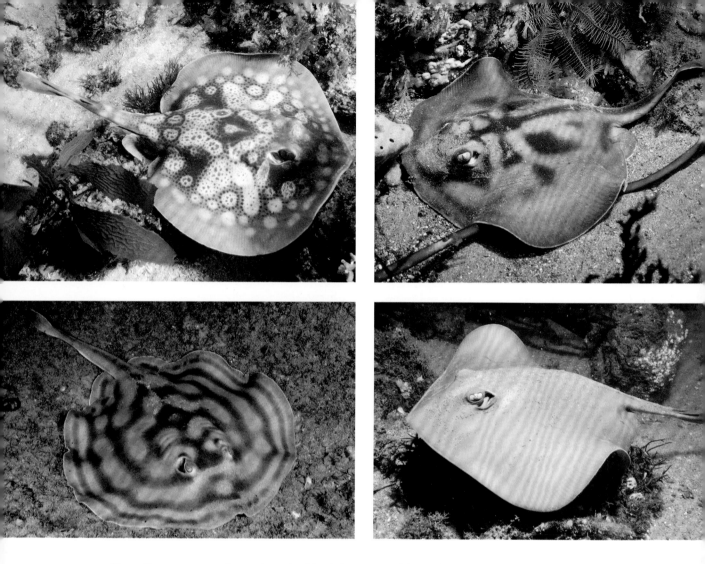

ABOVE - Tiny stingarees are often coloured with elaborate markings. In these pictures are: Circular Stingaree, *Urolophus circularis* **(TOP LEFT)**; Banded Stingaree, *Urolophus cruciatus* **(TOP RIGHT)**; Bullseye Stingaree, *Urobatis concentricus* **(BOTTOM LEFT)**; and Common Stingaree, *Trygonoptera testacea* **(BOTTOM RIGHT)**.

STINGAREES

The stingarees look like a smaller versions of stingrays and typically have a small round disc and a short tail. This family contains around 40 species, which are mostly found in Australian waters. Stingarees are very skittish, and spend most of the day hidden under a layer of sand, taking off in an explosion of particles when a diver gets close. They appear to be less skittish when found in groups, when they are often observed laying on top of each other. Stingarees have a small tail barb and will use it to defend themselves if stepped on or cornered.

168

STINGRAYS

The large stingray family contains more than 70 species, most of which are found in shallow water. Stingrays vary greatly in size and shape. Some are only 30cm (12in) wide, while others grow to almost 3m (9.8ft) wide, some have short tails, while others have long whip-like tails and their disc can be round, oval or kite-shaped. Stingrays also vary greatly in their behaviour and temperament. Many small species are wary of humans and flee before a diver can get anywhere near them, while larger species are bold and will allow a diver to approach very closely. While most stingrays are quite docile, almost all have dagger-like tail barbs that are used for self-defence, and they will use them on divers that grab or corner them. The best stingray encounters generally occur at locations where they are fed. These rays are accustomed to divers and scramble all over them. The barbs on these rays are generally not an issue, but their powerful jaws are, as when searching for food they can munch on fingers, which is like getting your fingers crushed in a vice.

BELOW - A sample of stingrays divers often encounter: Southern Stingray, *Dasyatis americana* (TOP LEFT); Smooth Stingray, *Dasyatis brevicaudata* (TOP RIGHT); Blotched Fantail Ray, *Taeniura meyeni* (BOTTOM LEFT); and Blue-spotted Fantail Ray, *Taeniura lymma* (BOTTOM RIGHT).

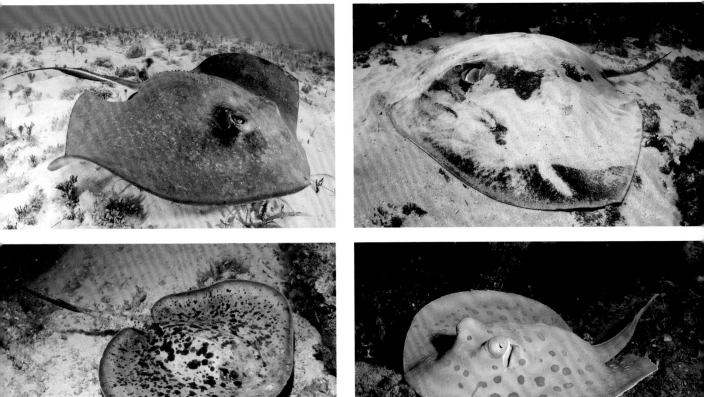

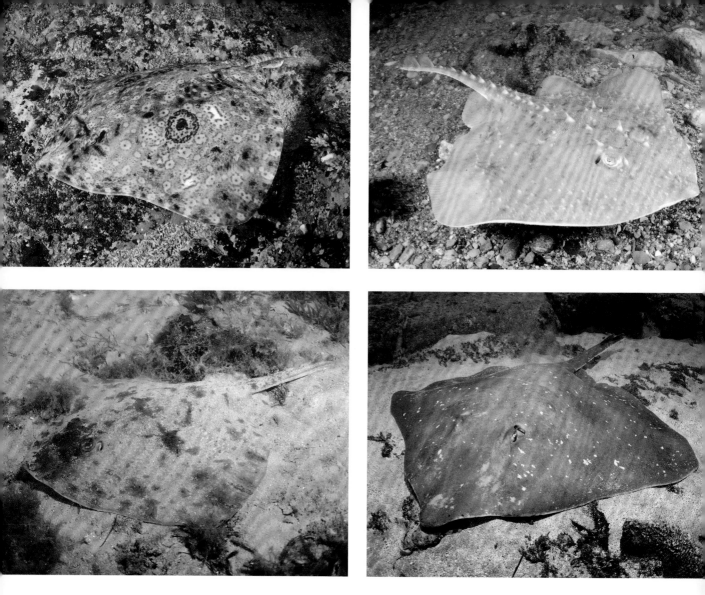

ABOVE – Skates are fascinating rays and come in a range of shapes, sizes and colours, including: Starry Skate, *Raja stellulata* **(TOP LEFT)**; Thorny Skate, *Amblyraja radiata* **(TOP RIGHT)**; Thornback Skate, *Dentiraja lemprieri* **(BOTTOM LEFT)**; and Melbourne Skate, *Spiniraja whitleyi* **(BOTTOM RIGHT)**.

SKATES

The skates are the most primitive of all the rays and lay eggs called mermaid's purses. Skates look very similar to stingrays, but lack a tail barb. For defence they have sharp thorns on their disc and tail. More than 200 species of skates are known, and most species live in deep water. However, divers do encounter shallow-water skates in temperate waters, and most of these species allow divers to approach quite closely.

SAWFISH

With a body like a shark and an elongated snout studded with teeth, the sawfish are one of the most unique families of rays. Found in tropical waters around the world, they regularly move from saltwater to freshwater, and most species live in murky estuaries and rivers, so are rarely seen by divers. Another reason that divers rarely encounter sawfish is they are highly endangered, with all five species facing extinction due to fishing pressures. Sawfish use their formidable snout for feeding and defence, and with some species growing to 7m (23ft) in length, they are a spectacular creature to see underwater. Considering their large size and fearsome saw, sawfish are wary of divers and often difficult to get close too.

BELOW - The Smalltooth Sawfish, Pristis pectinata, is rarely seen by divers; this one was encountered in the USA off Jupiter, Florida.

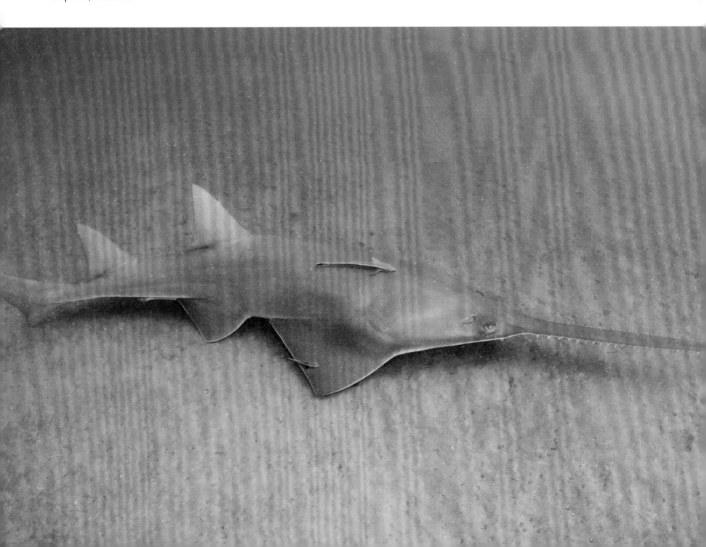

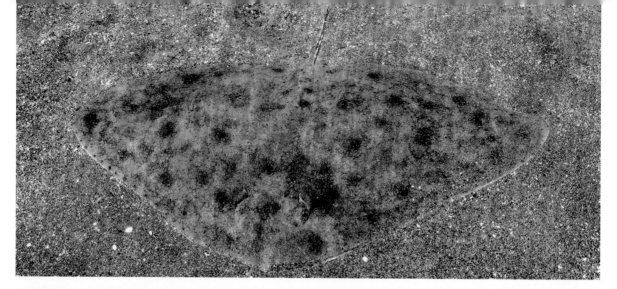

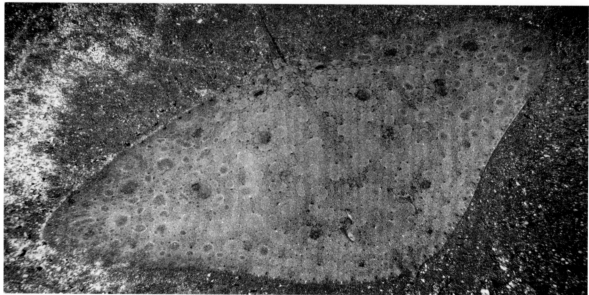

ABOVE - The Japanese Butterfly Ray, *Gymnura japonica* **(TOP)**, is found in many parts of the Northwest Pacific, but is most commonly seen off Japan. The Spiny Butterfly Ray, *Gymnura altavela* **(BOTTOM)**, is found in the Atlantic, and best seen around the Canary Islands.

BUTTERFLY RAYS

One of the strangest rays a diver will encounter are the butterfly rays. This family contains 14 species, all of which have a very flat body, elongated pectoral flaps and a very short tail. These rays vary in width from 1–3m (3.3–9.8ft), and many live in murky estuaries. Butterfly rays are difficult to find, as with a covering of sand they are almost invisible. They are also wary of divers, and when uncovered they tend to swim off into the blue.

COWNOSE RAYS

Cownose rays are closely related to eagle rays and at first glance look very similar, but these rays have a very differently shaped indented head. This family contains eight species. Generally found in vast schools in tropical and subtropical waters, cownose rays are very wary of divers and almost impossible to approach. However, watching a large school of these rays swimming overhead in a flock-like formation is a magical experience.

BELOW – A massive school of Australian Cownose Rays, *Rhinoptera neglecta* (MAIN IMAGE), swarm off Brisbane, Australia. An Atlantic Cownose Ray, *Rhinoptera bonasus* (INSET), encountered off Isla Mujeres, Mexico.

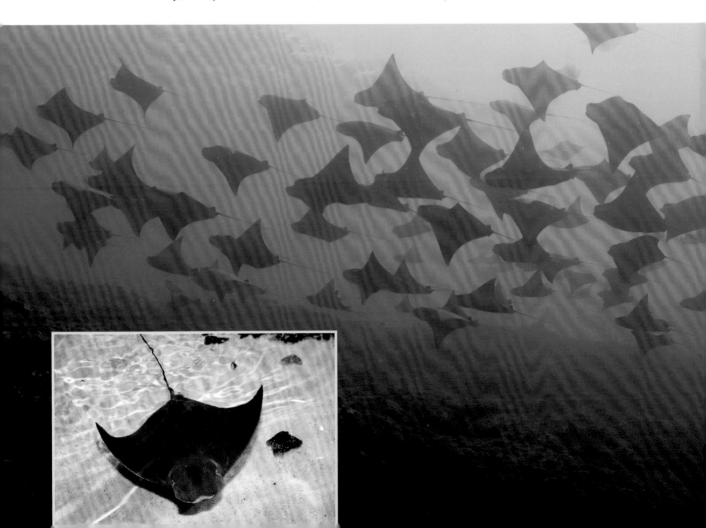

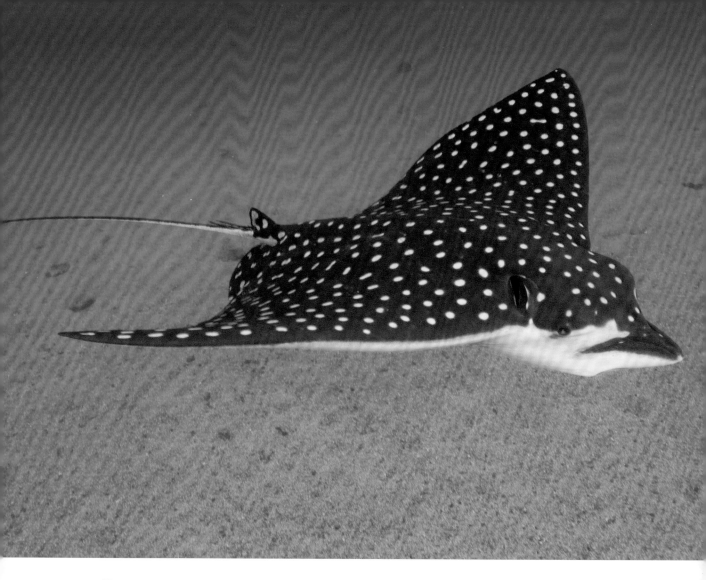

ABOVE - The most common member of the eagle ray family divers encounter on reefs around the world is the Spotted Eagle Ray, *Aetobatus narinari.*

EAGLE RAYS

Graceful eagle rays are a joy to watch as they glide and soar around a reef. This family contains 22 species, all of which have tail barbs. They feed on the bottom, but spend most of their time cruising in mid-water, favouring areas with currents, and will often hover motionless, without any effort, even in strong currents. Eagle rays are often difficult to approach, as they are wary of divers, but occasionally a bold one will allow a diver to get very close or take great delight in circling around and investigating.

DEVILRAYS

The manta and mobula rays both belong in the devilray family. These large rays have a wide mouth flanked by cephalic fins, which are used to funnel plankton into their mouth. The mobula family contains ten species, which vary in width from 1–5m (3.3–16.4ft). They differ from manta rays in having a narrow head and the mouth on the ventral surface, while many species also have tail barbs. Often found in large schools, mobula rays are always difficult to approach and flee when a diver gets too close. The manta ray family contains only two members that are much larger than the mobula rays and also much more diver friendly. These majestic rays are very tolerant of humans photographing and observing them, and many even enjoy playing with divers, soaring around them and also hovering overhead so that exhaled bubbles can tickle their belly. These wonderful rays have a very curious nature and are thought to be the most intelligent of all the elasmobranchs.

BELOW - The Reef Manta Ray, *Manta alfredi* (MAIN IMAGE), is a majestic and very friendly ray, while the Atlantic Mobula Ray, *Mobula hypostoma* (INSET), is a much more shy creature.

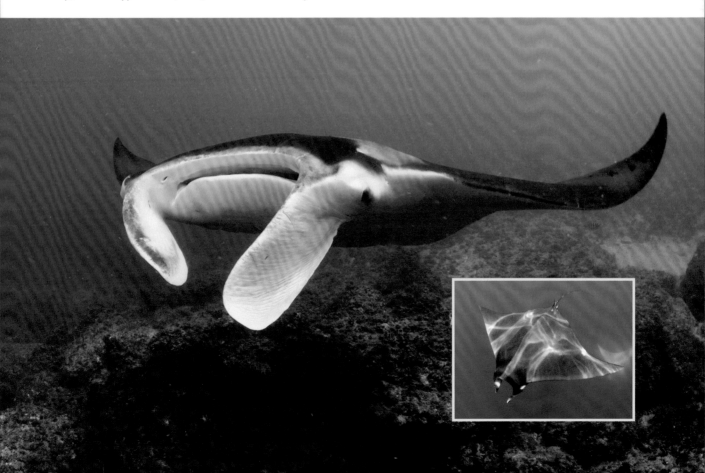

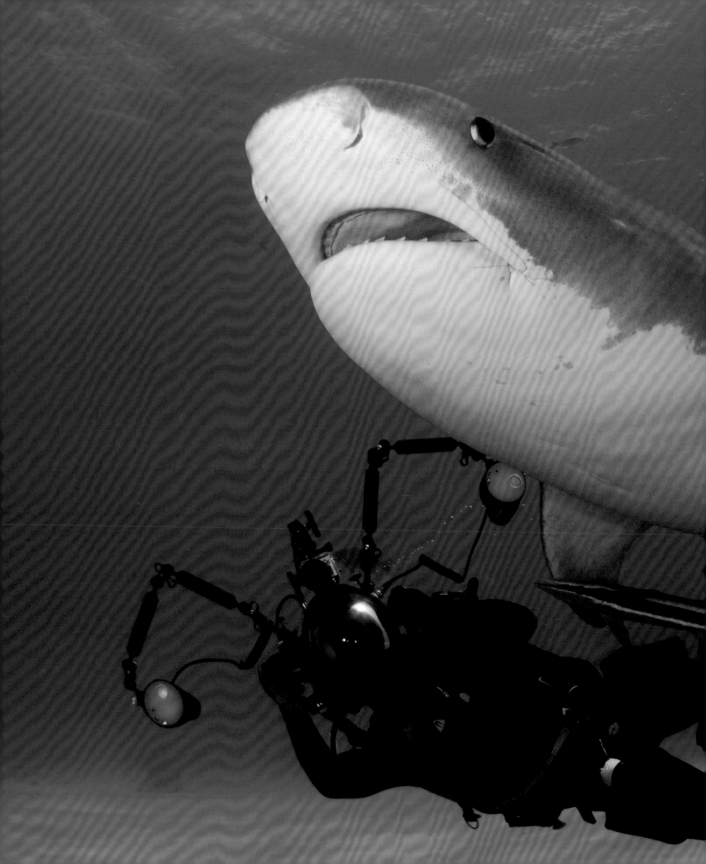

PHOTOGRAPHING SHARKS

Diving with sharks is a lot of fun and will get the heart pumping, but photographing sharks is a completely different matter, as the authors will attest. Between the two of us we have seen a lot more shark species than we have managed to photograph, as the shy and wary nature of many sharks makes them very challenging to capture with a camera.

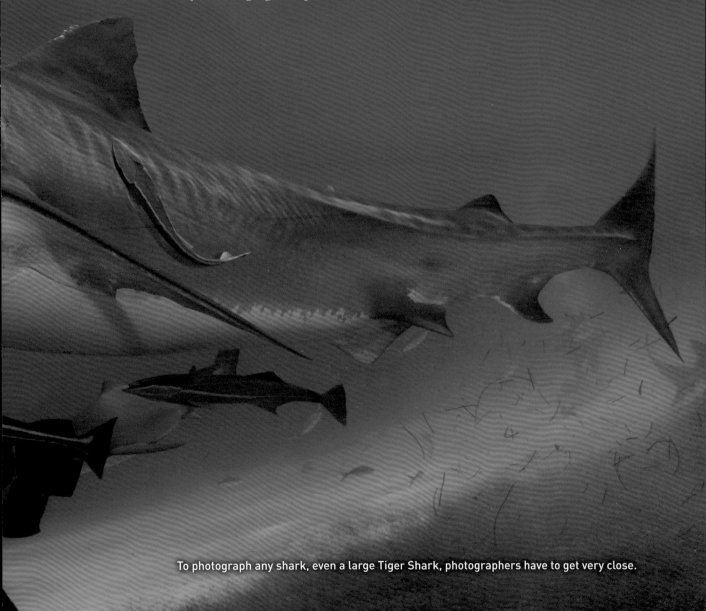

To photograph any shark, even a large Tiger Shark, photographers have to get very close.

Unlike wildlife photography on land, which is mainly done with a telephoto lens from a distance, to get good photographs underwater divers need to get close to the subject. The great majority of shark images are taken with a wide-angle lens, and in most cases the photographer was a maximum of 2m (6.6ft) from the subject. Water absorbs light and is also full of floating particles, so it doesn't matter if a diver is using a compact camera, a DSLR camera or a video camera – to get good images or video of sharks they need to be close.

This is when problems arise, as many shark species don't like divers getting close, so knowing a little about shark behaviour and how to approach sharks is important. Unless baits are in the water, many shark species are wary of divers and will not let them approach within 10m (33ft). Bottom-dwelling species such as wobbegongs, catsharks and horn sharks are usually much easier to approach, but the best way to get close to any shark is by slowing your breathing and approaching slowly from the side. This technique works for most bottom-dwelling species and also a few free-swimming sharks. However, for many shy species divers need to employ a bit more stealth. Try hiding behind rocks, avoiding eye contact and ignoring the shark completely, so they feel confident enough to sneak up and investigate. Of course there are other free-swimming sharks that are curious and bold, such as the Blue Shark, Oceanic Whitetip and Grey Nurse Shark. With these species divers can generally wait for them to come in close before snapping off images.

BELOW – The trick to photographing most large sharks, like this Great Hammerhead, is to get low and get close.

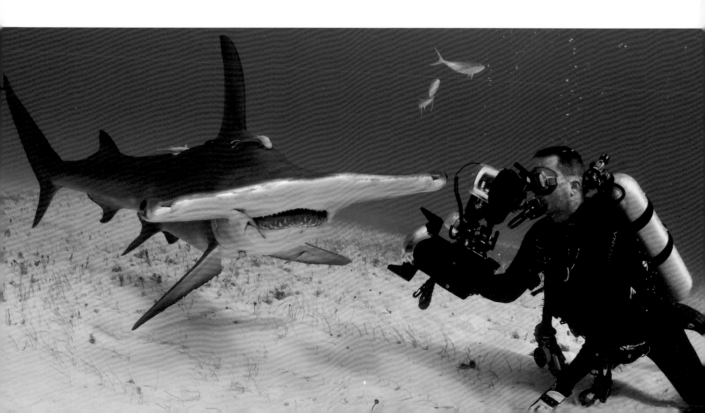

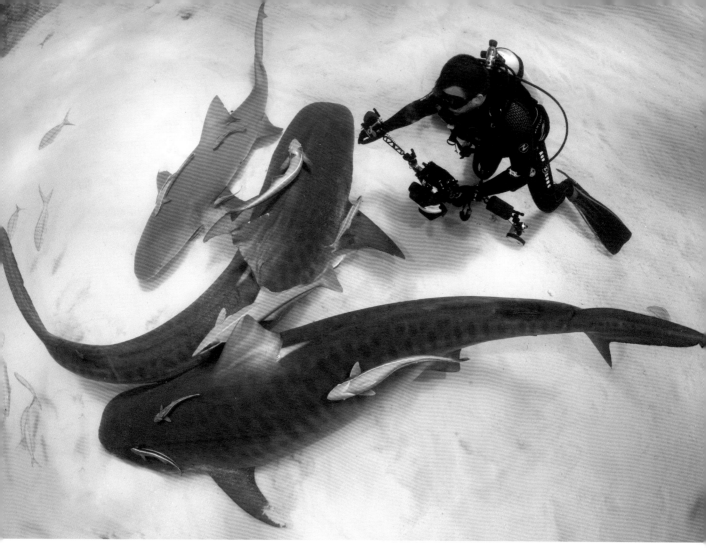

ABOVE - Don't get stuck behind the viewfinder, with a wide-angle lens you can often shoot from the hip and keep an eye on the sharks at all times, which is helpful when you have two Tiger Sharks cruising around you.

While a wide-angle lens is preferable for most shark species, a macro lens is also good for getting nice portrait images of smaller species such as the catsharks and epaulette sharks. Many of these species are best seen at night and a macro lens will allow divers to get great close-up images of a shark's head or eye as it rests on the bottom or searches the reef for food.

Lighting the shark is another challenge with shark photography. Natural light can be used for larger species such as Whale Sharks and Basking Sharks (strobes are generally banned when photographing these species), and also for species encountered near the surface, like Blue Sharks and Great White Sharks. A bit of fill flash is also recommended when close to the surface to instil more colour into the image.

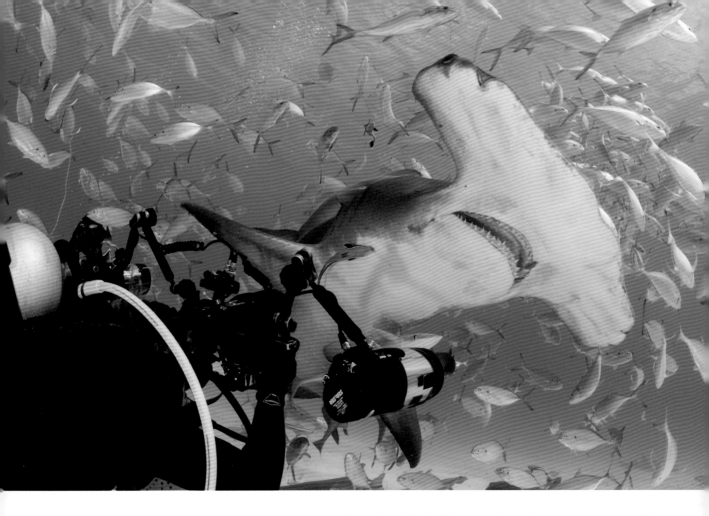

ABOVE - Sharks are not the only animals attracted by baits at shark feeds. Photographers often have to contend with masses of fish that can sometimes obscure the sharks.

Once below 6m (19.7ft), most colours are absorbed by water, so a strobe or light is always recommended. An external strobe or video light is the best investment an underwater photographer can make, as these light sources not only bring colour to the subject, but also reduce the chances of backscatter. However, backscatter can be a problem when using external light sources at shark feeds, as food particles inevitably end up in the water column. The best solution to avoid backscatter at shark feeds is to have the light source well away from the camera and also regularly review the images in the LCD screen. Photographers can also minimise backscatter by moving up-current from the food source so these food particles don't end up in front of the lens. Another problem often faced at shark feeds is other fish. Numerous fish turn up for free food and can often obscure the sharks. Sometimes the feeders will try to lure the fish away with extra pieces of bait, but often photographers simply have to time their images for when the fish part.

As for camera settings for photographing sharks, using manual settings is highly recommended to control the f-stops and shutter speeds. Free-swimming sharks require fast shutter speeds of 1/125 of a second or higher to freeze the action. But when photographing bottom-dwelling sharks resting in dark water, divers can get away with slower shutter speeds of 1/30 or 1/60. Your choice of f-stop will naturally be dictated by the shutter speed, but f8 is always a good starting point, assuming the photographer is using an ASA of 100 or 200. With advances in digital camera technology faster ASA settings can now be used and still give great results, and are a must when photographing some shark species. Photographing Pelagic Thresher Sharks at dawn at Malapascua in the Philippines is a good example, as no strobes are allowed. The only way to photograph these impressive sharks is to crank up the ASA to 3000 or above, set the camera to shutter priority of 1/125 and let the camera select the f-stop.

Photographing sharks with auto settings on the camera will generally produce good results, but does have limitations at times. Divers may find they get blurry images of a fast-moving shark if the

BELOW - Chasing sharks with your camera is never ideal as most sharks are wary of divers and will simply swim away.

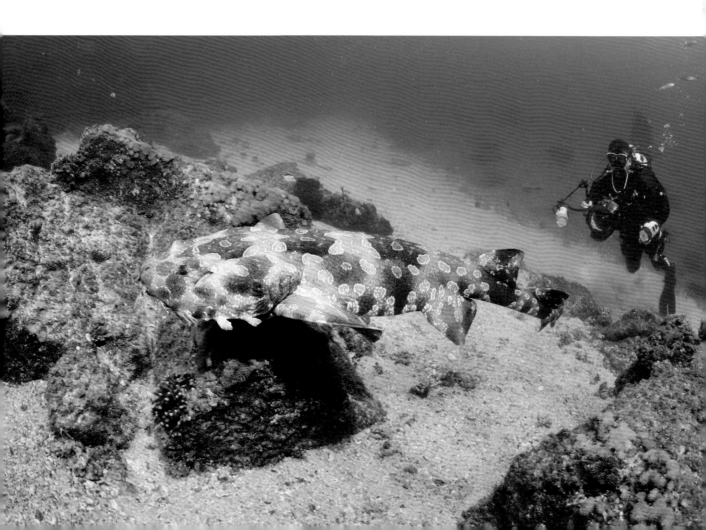

camera hasn't selected a fast enough shutter speed. Divers may also find that the camera underexposes or overexposes the image on free-swimming sharks, depending on the background and the position of the shark. Almost all sharks have a white belly and darker back and sides, and this strong contrast can confuse the camera sensor. Divers can generally avoid this issue by shooting either more of the belly or more of the back.

Composition can either make or break a great shark image. In general it is best to fill the frame with as much of the shark as possible. Also having the shark swimming into the frame is much better than an image with the shark leaving the frame, as it instantly engages the viewer. Another consideration is the background, and sometimes the foreground, as these can often make or break a great shark image. Positioning a diver in the image is a great way to add scale and also a human element, but if the diver is looking away or just randomly swimming through the background it can be distracting. Working with a dive model is the way to go, but they need to be on the same page and understand what the photographer requires. Other background distractions can be anchor lines, bubbles, rubbish in the water and baits. If photographing free-swimming sharks on reefs, try to capture a colourful coral or

BELOW - Bottom-dwelling sharks like Port Jackson Sharks are fun and easy to photograph as they allow divers to get very close.

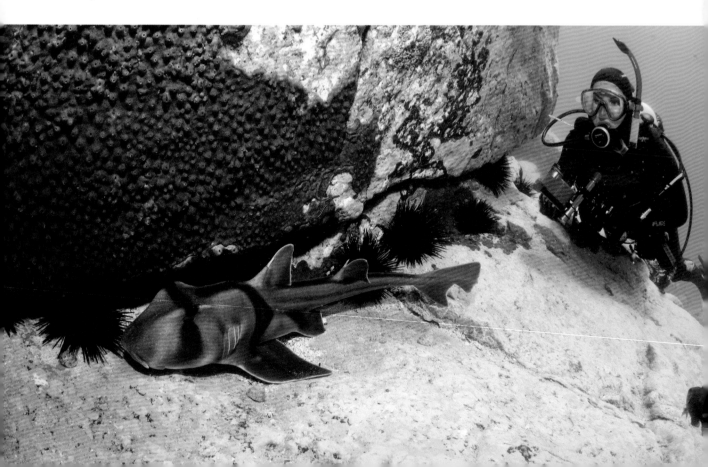

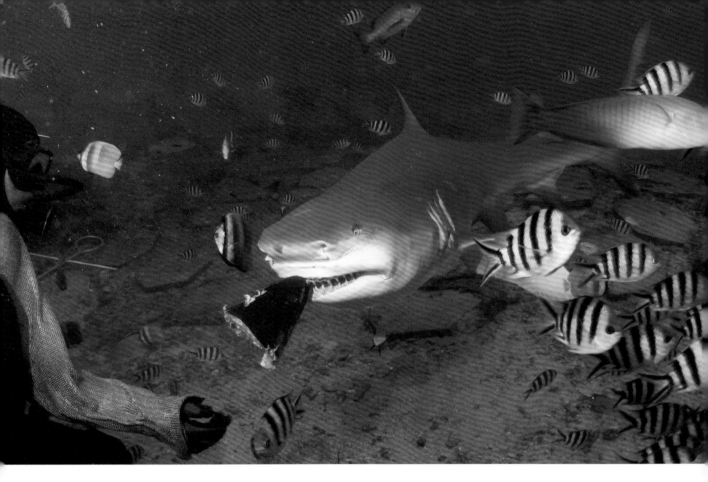

ABOVE - Photography at shark feeds is never easy, as the action is thick and fast and easy to miss. Always try to get as close to the feeder or bait box as possible, so you can capture the moment when the shark takes the food, like this Sicklefin Lemon Shark in Fiji.

sponge in the foreground. When photographing bottom-dwelling sharks, try to get down to eye-level with the shark for a more pleasing composition.

When photographing shark feeds always be aware of the sharks around you. Don't keep your eye glued to the viewfinder, but take it off every few seconds so that you know where the sharks are and what is happening around you. This also ensures that you don't miss a spectacular image, as often the action might be happening behind or beside the diver. Photographers have been bitten at shark feeds by not paying attention, and some have also had a spare camera snapped up by a curious shark because they were not watching what was happening around them.

Finally have fun photographing sharks and don't get stuck behind the viewfinder. Lower the camera every now and then and soak up the experience as well.

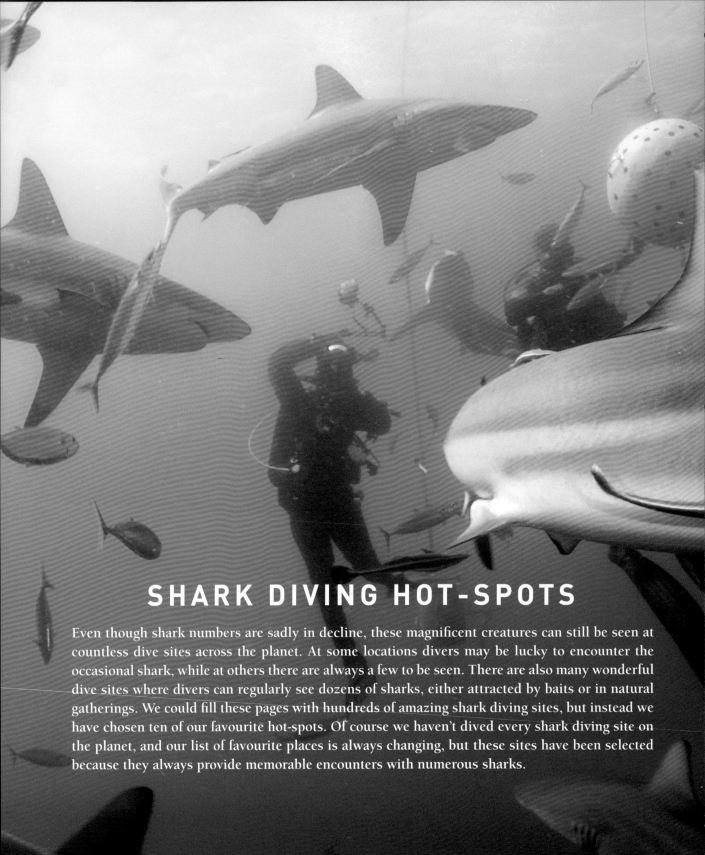

SHARK DIVING HOT-SPOTS

Even though shark numbers are sadly in decline, these magnificent creatures can still be seen at countless dive sites across the planet. At some locations divers may be lucky to encounter the occasional shark, while at others there are always a few to be seen. There are also many wonderful dive sites where divers can regularly see dozens of sharks, either attracted by baits or in natural gatherings. We could fill these pages with hundreds of amazing shark diving sites, but instead we have chosen ten of our favourite hot-spots. Of course we haven't dived every shark diving site on the planet, and our list of favourite places is always changing, but these sites have been selected because they always provide memorable encounters with numerous sharks.

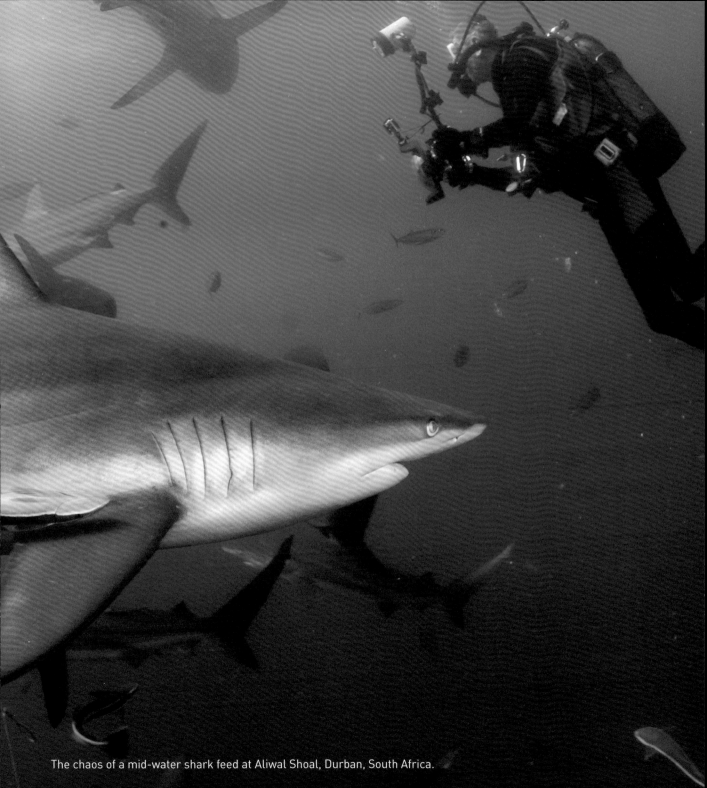

The chaos of a mid-water shark feed at Aliwal Shoal, Durban, South Africa.

FISH ROCK, SOUTH WEST ROCKS, AUSTRALIA

Australia is a great location to see sharks, as it is home to many unique shark species. While divers commonly encounter them on the Great Barrier Reef and Ningaloo Reef, the best area to see a good variety of free-swimming and bottom-dwelling shark species is the New South Wales coastline. Many popular dive destinations are found in New South Wales, with one of the best being South West Rocks.

Located on the mid-north coast, around 465km (289 miles) north of Sydney, South West Rocks is a lovely holiday town with wonderful beaches. For the diver the main attraction is Fish Rock Cave, a magical sea cave which is 125m (410ft) long and runs right through Fish Rock. This cave varies in depth from 12–24m (39–79ft) and is always a fabulous dive. However, great dives can be had anywhere at Fish Rock, as this is one sharky dive site.

Grey Nurse Sharks are the big attraction, with dozens seen on most dives. The sharks are mostly concentrated in the gutters at the south end of Fish Rock, but can be encountered anywhere around the rocky outcrop, even in the shallow cave entrance. At peak times (May to August) more than 100 sharks can be seen packed into the gutters. There can be so many sharks that they bump into each other and sometimes into divers. Grey Nurse Sharks are typically seen year-round, but the numbers fluctuate with the seasons as the sharks migrate north and south.

Wobbegongs are also common, with Spotted, Ornate and Banded Wobbegongs in residence year-round. Spotted and Ornate are the most common, with dozens generally seen on most dives. The Banded Wobbegongs seen here can be huge, more than 2.5m (8ft) long, but they are less common and divers will generally see two or three at most. Another common shark species is the Blind Shark, although these small sharks are harder to find, as they hide in ledges and under rocks.

Fish Rock is also one of the only places in Australia where schools of Scalloped Hammerhead Sharks can be seen. Unfortunately, encounters are never guaranteed with these spectacular sharks. Bull Sharks are another species seen at Fish Rock, but being wary of divers, don't expect a close encounter. The only other shark species regularly seen at Fish Rock is the Bronze Whaler. These impressive sharks are more common during the summer months and have been known to buzz divers while they do their safety stop.

FISH ROCK DIVE DATA
Sharks – Grey Nurse Shark, Spotted Wobbegong, Banded Wobbegong, Ornate Wobbegong, Blind Shark and occasionally Scalloped Hammerhead Shark, Bull Shark and Bronze Whaler.
Visibility – Generally 12–18m (39–59ft) on average.
Best Shark Time – Year-round.

OPPOSITE - Grey Nurse Sharks (TOP) patrol the gutters at Fish Rock, while small Blind Sharks (BOTTOM) hide in the ledges.

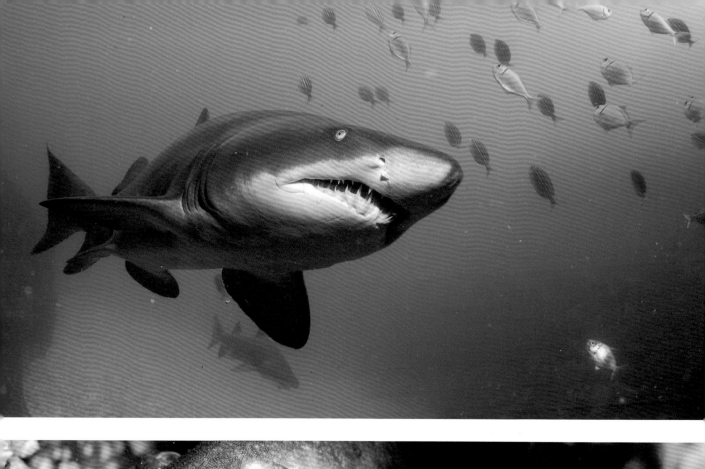
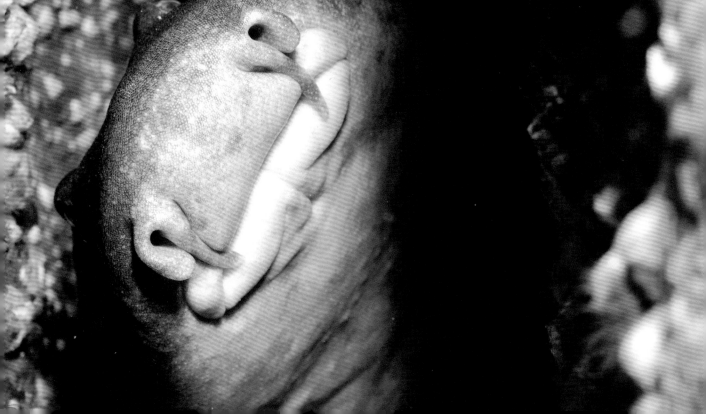

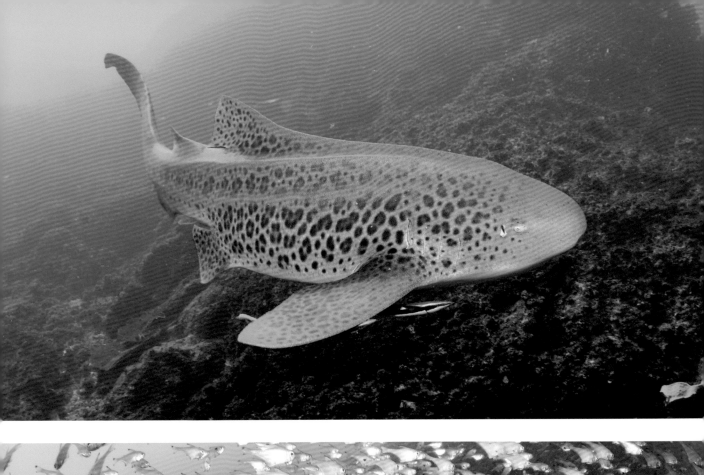

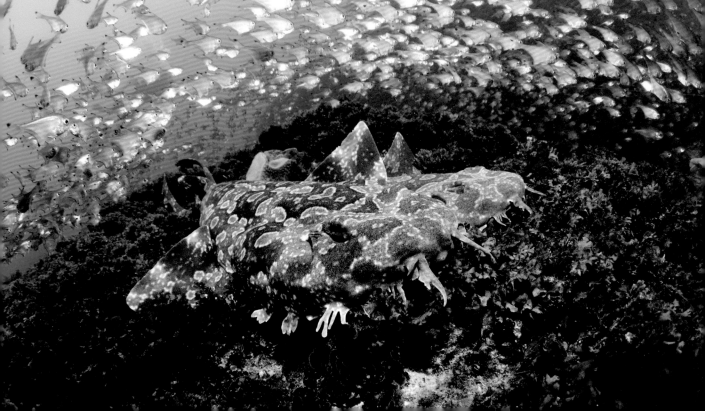

JULIAN ROCKS, BYRON BAY, AUSTRALIA

Byron Bay is located on the northern coast of New South Wales. A popular destination with backpackers, surfers, hippies and holidaymakers, the area has lovely beaches and is surrounded by rainforest-covered hills. For the visiting diver there are rocky reefs and shipwrecks to explore, with the most popular dive site being around a rocky island called Julian Rocks.

All around Julian Rocks are gutters, ledges and caves to explore in depths from 6–25m (20–82ft). This marine reserve is located in subtropical waters and as such is a mixing pot of tropical and temperate species. Reef fish, pelagic fish, gropers, stingrays, manta rays, eagle rays and turtles are common, as are a good variety of sharks.

If divers want to see wobbegong sharks, and lots of them, Julian Rocks is the place to go. Three species of these bottom-dwelling sharks are common here – Spotted, Ornate and Banded. Jump into the water anywhere and divers will see wobbegongs littering the bottom, resting in caves or jammed into ledges. On most dives several dozen can be seen, but sometimes it can be more than 100, making this one of the most unique shark dives on the planet. Other bottom-dwelling species seen here include Blind Sharks, Brown-banded Bamboo Sharks and the occasional Colclough's Shark. These sharks are quite shy and tend to hide under rocks and ledges, so are a little harder to find.

During the summer months (from December to April) Leopard Sharks invade Julian Rocks. At peak times divers might see more than a dozen, but generally divers encounter between 2–6. Grey Nurse Shark is another seasonal visitor, and while they can be seen at almost any time of the year, their numbers are greatest during the winter months, between May and October. These docile but fierce-looking sharks like to hover in the gutters at the eastern end of Julian Rocks, and at peak times a dozen or more can be seen.

Julian Rocks is a wonderful location to dive at any time of the year, and is the sort of site where unexpected species can turn up, as divers have also seen Bull Sharks and a surprising number of Great White Sharks during the winter months.

JULIAN ROCKS DIVE DATA
Sharks – Spotted Wobbegong, Banded Wobbegong, Ornate Wobbegong, Blind Shark, Brown-banded Bamboo Shark, Leopard Shark, Grey Nurse Shark and occasionally Colclough's Shark, Bull Shark and Great White Shark.
Visibility – Generally 10–15m (33–49ft) on average.
Best Shark Time – Year-round.

OPPOSITE - Leopard Sharks (TOP) are summer visitors to Julian Rocks, while abundant Spotted Wobbegongs (BOTTOM) are seen year-round.

THE BISTRO, BEQA LAGOON, FIJI

At one time Beqa Lagoon was renowned for its wonderful soft corals, but in recent years it has become more famous for its sharks. It all started back in 1997, when local dive operator Aqua Trek began dumping fish scraps on a local reef to see if they could attract a few sharks. They got permission from the local village to use Lake Reef for this experiment, as it had a lot of dead coral from coral bleaching. After several months of regularly dropping fish scraps on the same spot, they decided to have a look and see what they had attracted. They were amazed by the numbers of sharks patrolling the reef, especially large Bull Sharks.

Over the next few months they started to hand-feed the sharks, and then took out customers to experience the thrill of seeing so many large sharks. They called the dive site The Bistro, and today it is one of the best shark dives in the world.

The Bistro site is 18m (59ft) deep, on a sloping reef, and also features two scuttled shipwrecks. A rock wall defines the feeding area, and divers sit behind this and watch the 50–100 sharks attracted to this sensation site.

The main stars of this shark feed are the Bull Sharks. Always an impressive sight, these powerful sharks have been well trained by the feeders and if they don't follow the rules they don't get the food. There are always about a dozen Bull Sharks in attendance, but numbers do drop during the breeding season (from November to January) when romance is in the water.

Even more impressive at times are the Silvertip Sharks. These fast-moving sharks zip around the divers and come much closer than the Bull Sharks, often only inches above divers' heads. More sedate are the slower-moving Sicklefin Lemon Sharks and Tawny Nurse Sharks. Dozens of these large sharks patrol both sides of the wall, but will turn on a surprising burst of speed if they claim one of the baits.

Also commonly seen at every feed at The Bistro are Whitetip Reef Sharks and Grey Reef Sharks. Smaller than the other sharks they tend to stay behind the wall and patrol the upper reef slope, but every now and then a sneaky Grey Reef Shark will zoom in and grab one of the baits. Blacktip Reef Sharks are also commonly seen, but these shy sharks like to remain in the shallows.

The most impressive visitors to The Bistro are the Tiger Sharks. Generally only one Tiger Shark turns up to the show, but sometimes two make an appearance to spice up the action. These large, slow-moving sharks quickly take over the feed, as the other sharks are very wary of them and give them right of way. Unfortunately, Tiger Shark appearances are unpredictable, and several weeks can go by without a visit.

The Bistro is not the only shark-feeding site in Beqa Lagoon, as the success of this venture prompted other dive operators in the area to do their own shark feeds. The same shark species are also seen at Shark Reef and The Cathedral, and tagging studies have found that the sharks moving between all three sites.

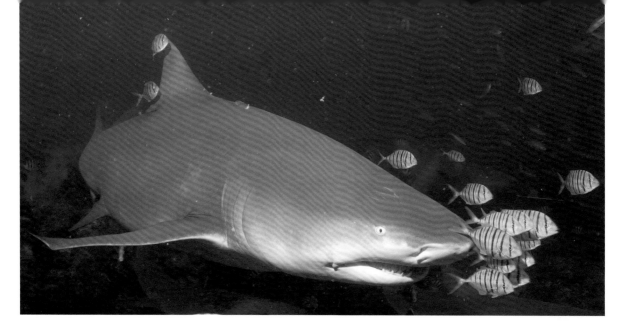

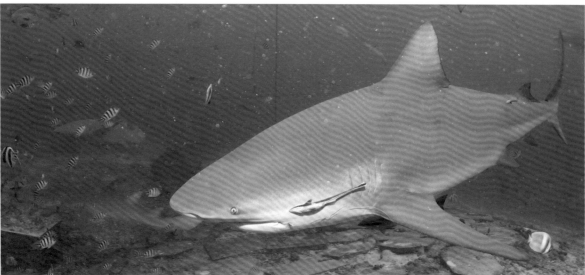

ABOVE – Sicklefin Lemon Sharks **(TOP)** are the most unique species seen at The Bistro, but the Bull Sharks **(BOTTOM)** are the main stars at this shark feed.

THE BISTRO DIVE DATA

Sharks – Bull Shark, Grey Reef Shark, Whitetip Reef Shark, Blacktip Reef Shark, Tawny Nurse Shark, Silvertip Shark, Sicklefin Lemon Shark and Tiger Shark.

Visibility – Generally 12–20m (39–66ft).

Best Shark Time – Year-round, but fewer Bull Sharks from November to January.

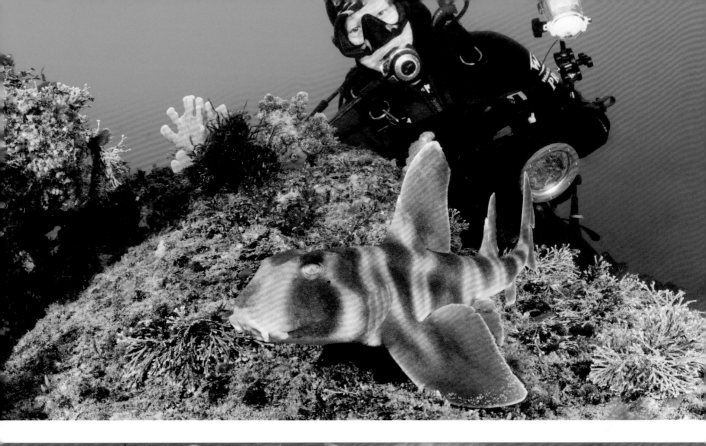

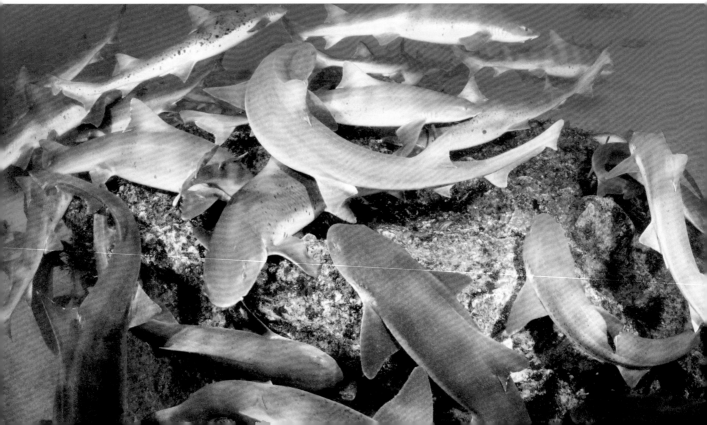

SHARK SCRAMBLE, ITO, JAPAN

This dynamic shark and ray feed is conducted on a 20m (66ft) deep sand flat next to a lush volcanic reef covered in soft corals. The feed takes place near Ito; a tiny fishing village two hours south of Tokyo.

It took local diver Kan Shiota five years to habituate the houndsharks to the presence of divers. Initially, they would not even tolerate his presence so he had to leave the bait on the rocks and return later to see if they had eaten it. Half a decade later, the sharks have grown much bolder and will happily swim within touching distance of the excited divers.

After anchoring the boat, the divers join the feeder on the black volcanic sand. Generally, there are already scores of Banded Houndsharks and Red Stingrays waiting at the feeding site by the time the group descends. For the first half of the dive Kan guards the bait while the divers enjoy the sharks in relatively good visibility. Then, once photographers in the group have taken their images, he opens the crates and starts hand feeding some of the sharks and rays.

Eventually, Kan tips over the bait and spills the remaining fish onto the rocks. At this point, mayhem ensues. The sharks lose all of their inhibitions and tumble over one another to reach the bait before it is all gone. This is where the name 'Shark Scramble' comes from. The sharks and rays often become so frenzied that they kick up inordinate amounts of sand, lowering visibility but creating a spectacle that is not to be missed!

Once the food is depleted, the sharks and rays instantly calm down and resume slowly cruising around the reef while scanning for overlooked morsels. Some rays settle onto the sand to rest and digest their breakfast. This is a great time to sneak up on them for portraits.

It is worth keeping an eye open for Japanese Thornback Rays that sometimes mix in with the Red Stingrays. Lucky divers may also run into a Japanese Angel Shark but they are quite rare in the area. Once the feed is over, a systematic search of any nearby overhangs will often turn up one or two Japanese Horn Sharks resting in the shadows until nightfall.

SHARK SCRAMBLE DIVE DATA
Sharks and Rays – Banded Houndshark, Japanese Horn Shark and rarely Japanese Angel Shark.
Visibility – 10–20m (33–66ft).
Best Shark Time – Year-round but diving conditions are better from April to October.

OPPOSITE - The main attraction at the Shark Scramble are dozens of Banded Houndsharks (BOTTOM), but lucky divers may also encounter a lovely Japanese Horn Shark (TOP).

TOMAKOHUA PASS, FAKARAVA ATOLL, FRENCH POLYNESIA

There are dive sites around the world with bigger sharks and areas with greater species diversity, but it would be difficult to find a dive site that has more sharks than the south pass of Fakarava Atoll. In fact, the entire atoll is so shark-infested that it has been designated as a UNESCO Marine Biosphere Reserve.

During the incoming and outgoing tides, when the currents in the channel pick up speed, it is not unusual to see 200 or more sharks at any given time. A conservative estimate of 400–500 sharks during the course of a dive is not unreasonable.

Divers drop onto a slope at the side of the pass and cling to the reef while the sharks fin slowly past them, up current. The school is mostly composed of Grey Reef Sharks but it is common to see 20 to 30 Silvertip Sharks mixed in. A handful of large, but timid, Blacktip Sharks usually show up too, but stay on the far side of the pass away from the divers. On the floor of the pass there are also small groups of Whitetip Reef Sharks, facing into the current while they rest on the bottom.

The parade of sharks continues for as long as the current rushes by. Any shark reaching the end of the pass peels off and drifts back downstream, only to fall back into formation and repeat their upstream progress. Why they do this, time after time, is somewhat of a mystery. It may be some type of social behaviour or perhaps an opportunity to hunt for fish that are swept downstream by the ripping currents.

When it is time to ascend, divers have a final sharky surprise in store. In the shallows next to the pass, there is a protected area dubbed the swimming pool. For decades, local fishermen have cleaned their catches here, discarding scraps that are gratefully devoured by enormous Napoleon Wrasse and tiny Blacktip Reef Sharks.

During a safety stop, it's not unusual to see a dozen Blacktip Reef Sharks swimming along the slope, but upon surfacing the action actually intensifies. Conditioned to the sound of fish scraps landing on the surface, the sharks rush towards any similar noise. Consequently, slapping the surface with the palm of a hand will illicit a very close inspection from any shark within range.

TOMAKOHUA PASS DIVE DATA
Sharks – Grey Reef Shark, Silvertip Shark, Blacktip Shark, Whitetip Reef Shark and Blacktip Reef Shark.
Visibility – 20–30m (66–98ft).
Best Shark Time – Year-round.

OPPOSITE - Divers exploring Tomakohua Pass will literally see hundreds of Grey Reef Sharks, as can be seen from these pictures.

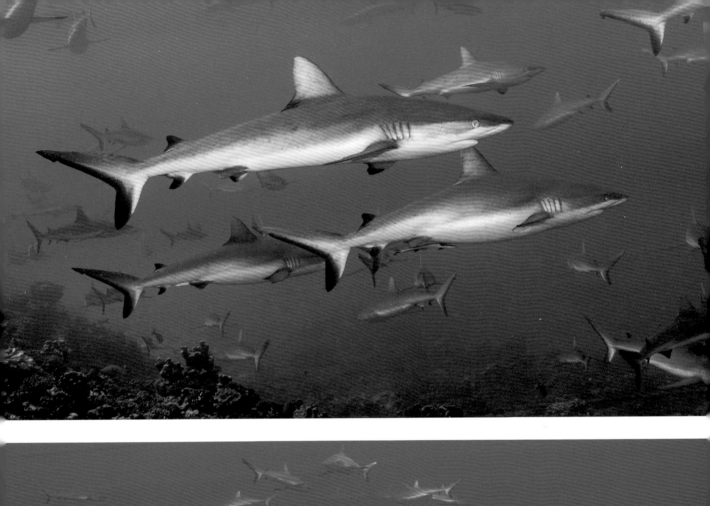
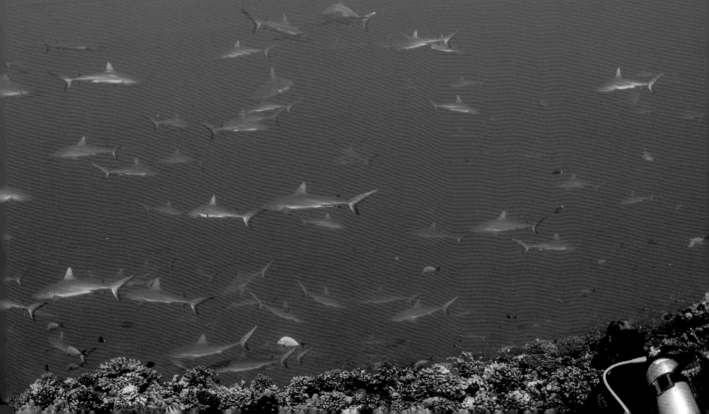

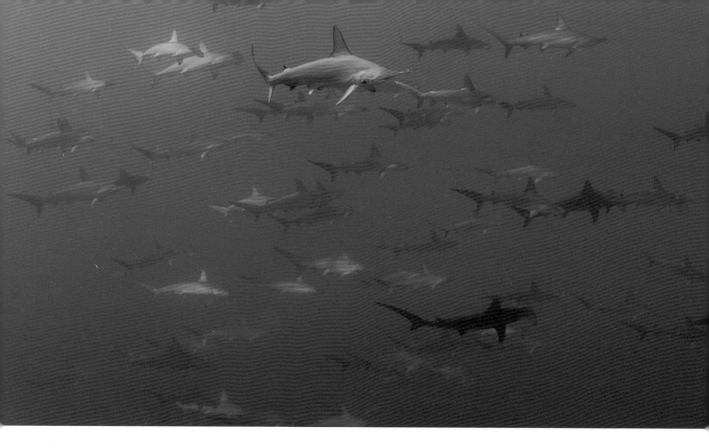

Schools of Scalloped Hammerhead Sharks (ABOVE) are a big attraction at Malpelo Island, but divers looking for a rarer species head to the depths to see Smalltooth Sandtiger Sharks (BELOW).

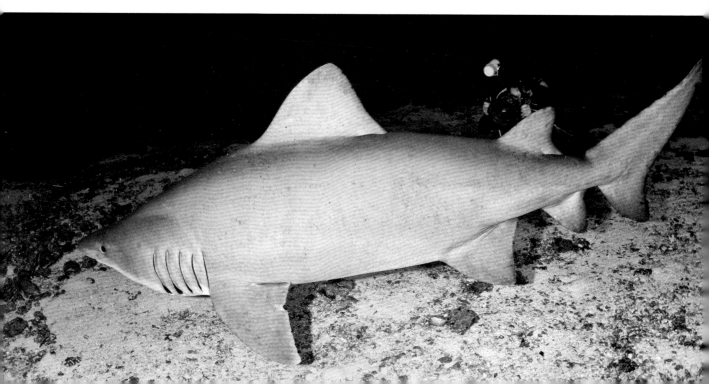

MALPELO ISLAND, COLOMBIA

Malpelo Island is a mile-long outcrop of rock, a 40-hour boat journey west of the Pacific coast of Panama. Its inhospitable volcanic ledges are completely uninhabited except for three species of endemic lizards and a platoon of Colombian soldiers charged with protecting it from the rest of Central America.

Although barren above the waves, Malpelo's submerged reef ledges are teeming with life that is fed by nutrient rich deep-water upwellings. Pelagic species abound including huge aggregations of Scalloped Hammerhead Sharks that constantly circle the island. The hammers form polarised schools hundreds strong. Occasionally, a few sharks break formation, swimming up to cleaning stations where the attendant wrasses and angelfish remove their parasites that have accumulated during their long ocean voyages.

Galápagos Sharks also abound, and Silky and Silvertip Sharks can be sighted on many dives but not in such great numbers as the Scalloped Hammerheads. Whitetip Reef Sharks are also very common on shallow slopes where they huddle together in crevices avoiding the attention of their larger cousins.

Taking advantage of rising sea temperatures, over the last few years Tiger Sharks have also started to colonise Malpelo's well-stocked reefs. During the summer months, Whale Sharks can often be seen circling the main island. These ocean giants tend to be much larger than the ones seen in the Caribbean or further west in the South Pacific and Indian Oceans.

In the cooler winter months the Whale Sharks take their leave, however this is the time lucky divers have the chance to encounter rarely seen Smalltooth Sandtiger Sharks on the island's deeper ledges. These broad-bodied cousins of the Grey Nurse Shark are usually found at abyssal depths, but for a short period each year they enter relatively shallow water. Even then, they generally remain below 60m (197ft), but this does not stop many intrepid divers from swimming down to see them. Although descending to the Smalltooth Sandtigers is something only experienced divers should attempt, once down at their level, the sharks are quite docile, allowing very close approaches.

There are other great spots in the Eastern Pacific such as Cocos Island and the Galápagos Islands where similar shark aggregations occur, but the encounters at Malpelo are hard to beat.

MALPELO ISLAND DIVE DATA

Sharks – Schooling Scalloped Hammerheads, Galápagos Shark, Silky Shark, Silvertip Shark, Smalltooth Sandtiger Shark, Whitetip Reef Shark, Whale Shark and the occasional Tiger Shark.

Visibility – 10–40m (33–131ft).

Best Shark Time – Most species year-round, but Smalltooth Sandtigers are more common from January to April. Whale Sharks are more common in the warmer summer months.

FISH TALES, GRAND BAHAMA, BAHAMAS

The Bahamas is one of the best shark-diving destinations on the planet. At locations across this island nation divers can encounter sharks naturally and at well-organised shark feeds. One of the most famous shark dives in the Bahamas is a site called Tiger Beach, but nearby is an even better site called Fish Tales.

Located off the west end of Grand Bahama, Fish Tales is an isolated rocky reef in depths from 10–14m (33–46ft), with an adjacent sandy plain. This reef is covered in corals and reef fish, and is also a good place to find invertebrate species. However, everyone dives this site to see sharks. As soon as the dive boat pulls up at Fish Tales the sharks appear, even before the baits are lowered. It is common to have dozens of Lemon Sharks cruising around on the surface at the back of the boat, which makes getting into the water a challenge.

Once in the water the sharks are generally fed on the sand, and joining the Lemon Sharks are numerous Caribbean Reef Sharks, Nurse Sharks and usually a few Tiger Sharks. The action is incredible, especially with several Tiger Sharks cruising slowly around and occasionally bumping the divers. This is one site where divers have to be aware of what is happening at all times. All the Tiger Sharks that visit Fish Tales also visit nearby Tiger Beach, and are well known to the boat crews, with names like Hook, Emma and Princess.

While the Tiger Sharks are impressive, the Lemon Sharks are the most curious and laid back, and settle on the bottom right beside divers for a rest or a bit of cleaning. The Nurse Sharks are also a lot of fun, and usually crowd the feeder box until they are given several tasty morsels. The most hyperactive attendees are the dozens of Caribbean Reef Sharks. These graceful sharks zoom around the divers and feeders, but wary of the Tiger Sharks, they only sneak food occasionally.

Once the food runs out, the sharks casually mingle around the divers, and one of the best things about Fish Tales is that divers can get images of the sharks cruising over sand, rock or reef. The dive doesn't end when divers ascend to do their safety stop, as the Lemon Sharks and Caribbean Reef Sharks continue to circle, and many safety stops are stretched to more than 30 minutes. People can also have a great time just hanging off the duckboard with the Lemon Sharks. The shark action at Fish Tales is unbelievable.

FISH TALES DIVE DATA
Sharks – Tiger Shark, Lemon Shark, Caribbean Reef Shark, Nurse Shark and the occasional Great Hammerhead Shark.
Visibility – Generally 20–30m (66–98ft).
Best Shark Time – Year-round.

OPPOSITE - The Tiger Shark (TOP) action at Fish Tales is hard to beat, with divers sometimes surrounded by three or more of these lumbering sharks. Even getting in the water at Fish Tales is fun, with Lemon Sharks (BOTTOM) hanging around the duckboard.

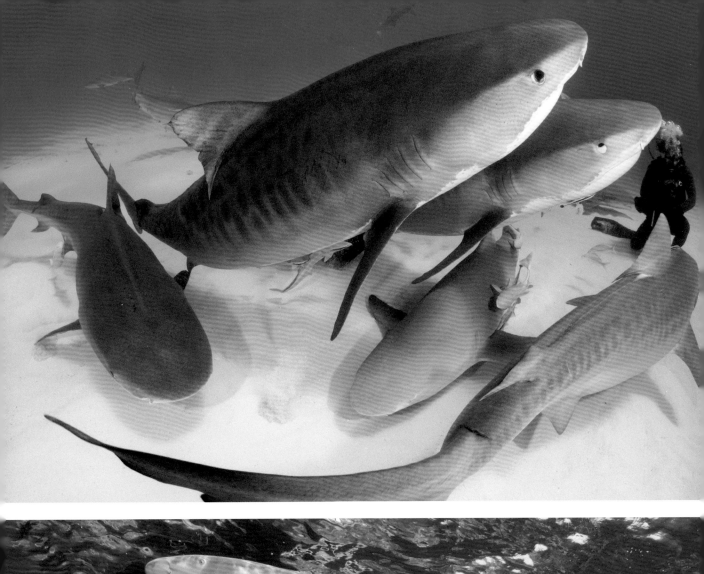
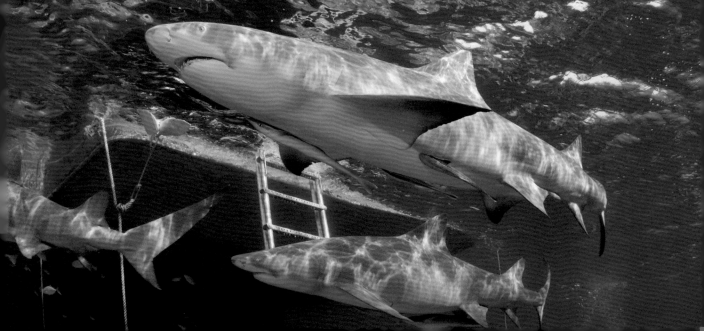

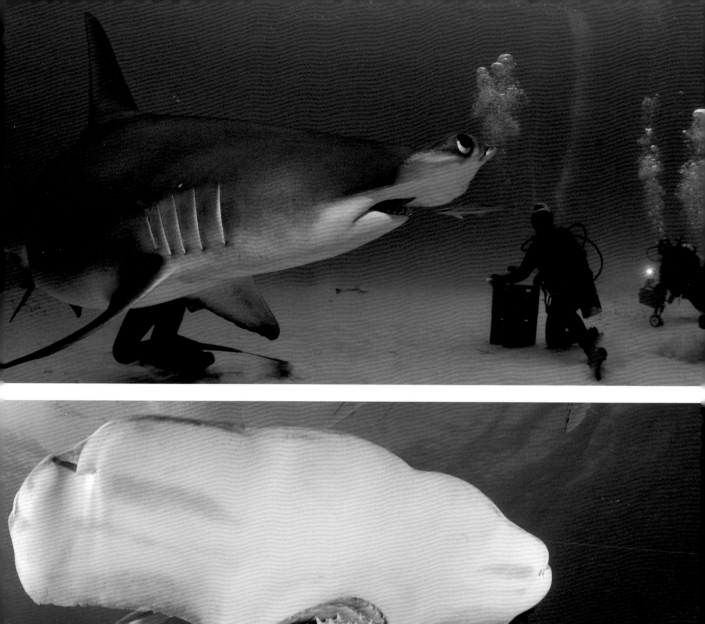
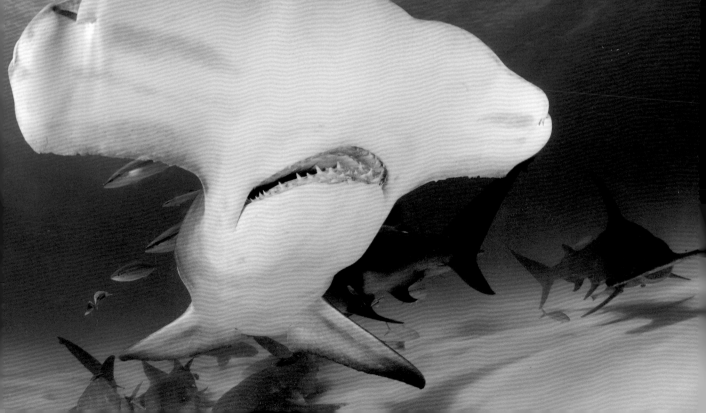

BIMINI SANDS, SOUTH BIMINI, BAHAMAS

At almost any shark feed in tropical waters there is a remote chance that a Great Hammerhead Shark will turn up and join in the action. The largest member of the hammerhead family is an unpredictable creature that is rarely seen by divers. Until recently there was no dive site where an encounter with one of these magnificent sharks could be guaranteed. So when news that a dive site in the Bahamas had been discovered with a good population of Great Hammerheads, divers started to flock there.

Located off the west coast of South Bimini is a sandy seabed only 5m (16ft) deep where Great Hammerhead Sharks gather during winter to feed on the local rays. The dive site doesn't really have a name, as apart from the sharks there is only sand and a little seaweed, but it is often called Bimini Sands after the nearby marina. While local fishers have always known about the Bimini Great Hammerhead Sharks, they were not widely heard of until they were studied by the Bimini Shark Lab. This led to local dive operator Stuart Cove chumming for the sharks with great success in 2012, and since then Bimini Sands has become a shark-diving hot-spot.

Diving with a pack of 4–6 Great Hammerhead Sharks, which vary in size from 3–4.5m (10–15ft), is an incredible experience, and a little unnerving at first. With baits in the water, these large sharks show no fear and come very close to inspect divers and the food. Once the heart rate settles and divers realise that these majestic sharks are curious and cautious, they can enjoy one of the best shark dives on the planet.

Joining the Great Hammerhead Sharks are generally a dozen or more friendly Nurse Sharks that try to stick their nose into the bait box each time it is opened. Less welcome are the Bull Sharks which patrol the edge of the feed but are too wary to take the baits. However, they like to sneak up behind people, so divers have to constantly watch their backs. If too many Bull Sharks arrive they can displace the Great Hammerheads, and when this happens the baits are removed from the water and the boat relocates to another site nearby. On rare occasions a Tiger Shark may also appear at this feed, but having several Great Hammerhead Sharks cruising around divers is what makes Bimini Sands such a special shark dive.

BIMINI SANDS DIVE DATA
Sharks – Great Hammerhead Shark, Bull Shark, Nurse Shark, and rarely Tiger Shark.
Visibility – Generally 20–30m (66–98ft).
Best Shark Time – December to March.

OPPOSITE - Close encounters with Great Hammerhead Sharks make Bimini Sands a very special shark diving hot-spot.

MILLER'S POINT, FALSE BAY, SOUTH AFRICA

Most divers head to False Bay to enjoy encounters with Great White Sharks. Watching these behemoths breaching in the pursuit of Cape Fur Seals at Seal Island is definitely a spectacle not to be missed, but False Bay has much more to offer. A short boat ride from Simon's Town, Miller's Point is a kelp-covered wonderland inhabited by lumbering Broadnose Sevengill Sharks, up to six species of catsharks, and shy Spotted Gully Sharks.

Unlike many impenetrable kelp forests around the world, the foliage in False Bay is mostly Bamboo Kelp – a species with a single long stalk and fronds that lay on the surface so the reef below is exposed and easy to swim over. When the visibility is good, it's a thrilling sight watching the prehistoric-looking Broadnose Sevengill Sharks weaving between the kelp stalks on their slow, methodical search for food.

As well as the captivating cowsharks, it's not unusual to see scores of catsharks swimming around the coral heads or tucked into crevices awaiting the cover of darkness. Two species are abundant – the Dark Shyshark and the beautifully patterned Puffadder Shyshark. Pyjama Catsharks and Leopard Catsharks can also be seen on most dives by spending some time searching under ledges. Very lucky divers may also see a Yellowspotted Catshark or a Tiger Catshark, but these two species usually live out on the sand or in deeper water.

There is one more shark that calls Miller's Point home. The elusive Spotted Gully Shark. Although this species is relatively common in the area, it remains hidden in caves during daylight hours. There are many caves undercutting the reef and a systematic search should reveal a few Spotted Gully Sharks lurking in the shadows. Once discovered, they will quickly flee, so photographers should be on high alert as there are rarely second chances with this species.

The catsharks and gully sharks are year-round residents in False Bay but the Sevengills disappear in the spring. However, Miller's Point is a beautiful site that is worth diving whenever you have the opportunity.

A word of caution: Sevengill Sharks are a favourite prey species of Great White Sharks. White Sharks rarely venture into the kelp forest, but one or two could be patrolling nearby, so when following any sharks out onto the sand, it is important to remain vigilant.

MILLER'S POINT DIVE DATA
Sharks – Broadnose Sevengill Shark, Dark Shyshark, Puffadder Shyshark, Pyjama Catshark, Leopard Catshark, and occasionally Yellowspotted Catshark and Tiger Catshark.
Visibility – 2–20m (6.6–66ft). Heavily affected by surge during the winter months.
Best Shark Time – Year-round.

OPPOSITE - Most divers explore Miller's Point to see large Broadnose Sevengill Sharks (TOP), but this area is also a great spot to see small catsharks such as this Dark Shyshark (BOTTOM).

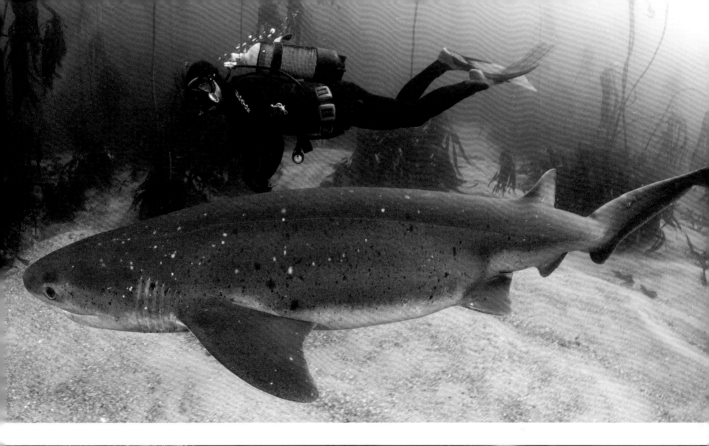
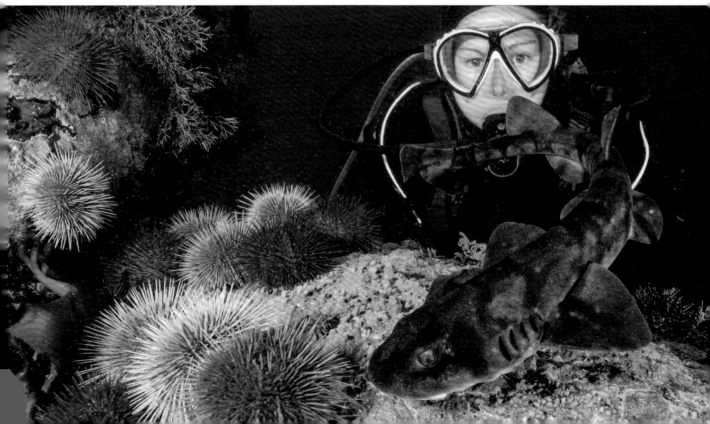

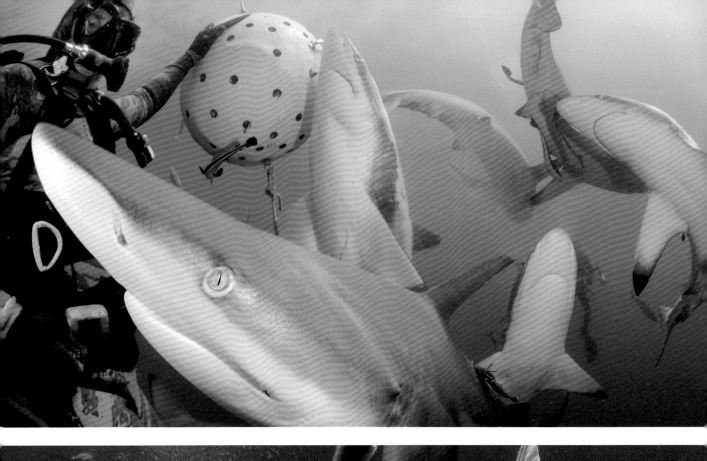
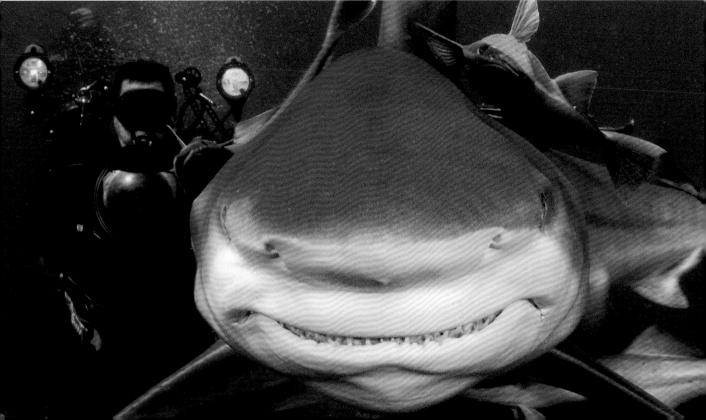

ALIWAL SHOAL, DURBAN, SOUTH AFRICA

South Africa's Aliwal Shoal is a rocky reef system adorned with colourful sponges, soft corals and a healthy assortment of fishes and invertebrate life. The most commonly encountered sharks on the reef are Grey Nurse Sharks, known locally as Raggies or Spotted Ragged-tooth Sharks. During the cooler winter months, these snaggle-toothed predators form large mating aggregations. They can be seen virtually anywhere on the reef but they prefer cave entrances or large overhangs. On a good day, it is possible to see 50 or more hovering in one spot.

Although the Raggies are a nice distraction, the main event at Aliwal Shoal is an extreme shark feed that attracts Tiger Sharks and lots of Blacktip Sharks of the oceanic variety. During the warmer summer months, divers can expect to see 5–6 Tiger Sharks of varying sizes but the real draw are the Blacktips. Up to 2.5m (8.2ft) in length, Blacktip Sharks are powerful predators that make intimidating dive buddies. This is a wide-ranging species, but in most places where divers encounter them they are extremely shy and hard to approach. Not so at Aliwal Shoal. It is quite common to have 40–50 beefy Blacktip Sharks attending the feed and they will happily make close passes or even bump divers if they are close to the chum slick.

Other sharks that occasionally show up at the feed include Dusky Sharks, Bronze Whalers and Bull Sharks. On rare occasions, lucky divers have also seen Great White Sharks.

Unlike most shark feeds, where the encounters take place on the bottom, at Aliwal Shoal the bait crate is suspended about 6m (20ft) below the surface over deep water, so the sharks may arrive from any direction including above or below. This means that the feeder has to be extra vigilant while handing out scraps to the dinner guests.

If the sharks are well behaved, the feeder may invite experienced divers to position themselves right next to the crate where they can get dynamic shots of the sharks devouring fish.

At the end of the dive, the Blacktips often follow the divers right up to the boat, looking for more food. Some feeders keep a little bait in reserve so that photographers can hand-cam over the side of the boat to try to get split images of the sharks breaking the surface; a great way to finish off a world-class shark dive.

ALIWAL SHOAL DIVE DATA

Sharks – Tiger Shark, Blacktip Shark, Grey Nurse Shark, and occasionally Dusky Shark, Bronze Whaler Shark and Bull Shark. Rarely Great White Shark.

Visibility – 5–20m (16–66ft).

Best Shark Time – Grey Nurse Sharks in winter, Tiger Sharks in summer. Blacktip Sharks are present year-round.

OPPOSITE - Dozens of Blacktip Sharks (TOP) are attracted to the mid-water shark feed at Aliwal Shoal. A normally shy Blacktip Shark (BOTTOM) smiles for the camera at the same location.

REFERENCES AND FURTHER READING

Aitken, K. (1998). *Green Guide: Sharks and Rays of Australia*. New Holland, Sydney.

Bannister, K. (1989). *The Book of the Shark*. New Burlington.

Compagno, L., Dando, M., and Fowler, S. (2005). *A Field Guide to the Sharks of the World*. HarperCollins, London.

Ellis, R. and McCosker, J. (1991). *Great White Shark*. Stanford University Press.

Ferrari, A. and Ferrari, A. (2002). *Sharks*. Firefly, Toronto.

Hennemann, R. (2001). *Sharks and Rays: Elasmobranch Guide of the World*. Ikan.

Last, P. and Stevens, J. (1994). *Sharks and Rays of Australia*. CSIRO, Collingwood.

Michael, S. (1993). *Reef Sharks and Rays of the World*. Sea Challengers, Monterey.

Mojetta, A. (1997). *Sharks: History and Biology of the Lords of the Sea*. Five Mile Press.

Parker, S. (2008). *The Encyclopedia of Sharks*. New Burlington.

ACKNOWLEDGEMENTS

The authors have dived around the world looking for and photographing sharks of all shapes and sizes. This book would not have been possible without the support of many amazing divers and many wonderful dive operators. We would like to thank the following...

Argentina: Juan Carlos Mattioli (Intersub Buceo).

Australia: Mike Ball (Mike Ball Dive Expeditions), Chris Eade, Phillip Hobbs and Trina Baker (*Spirit of Freedom* and Tusa Dive), James McVeigh (Big Cat Reality), Ruth Appleyard (Heron Island Resort), Vicki Mullins (Lady Elliot Eco Resort), Lisa and Jim Edwards (Nautilus Supercat Brisbane), James Griffith (Manta Lodge and Scuba Centre, Brisbane), Mark Robertson (Go Dive Brisbane), Deb and Ted Aston, Stuart Ireland, Rod and Christina Gray (Blue Bay Divers, Byron Bay), Giacomo Cavazzini (Sundive, Byron Bay), Jon Cragg (Fish Rock Dive Centre, South West Rocks), Ron Hunter (Dive Forster), Dave Harasti, Darryl Stuart (Narooma Charters), Martin and Cathie Thackray (Montague Island Charters), Mary Malloy, Alan Beckhurst, Margaret Flierman, Geoffrey Whitehorn, Mick Baron and Karen Gowlett-Holmes (Eaglehawk Dive Centre), Greg Lowry, Kristin Anderson and Exmouth Diving Centre.

Bahamas: Neal Watson Jr., Sean Williams and Grant Johnson (Neal Watson's Bimini Scuba Center), Scott Smith and the crew of the *Dolphin Dream* and Vincent and Deborah Canabal (Epic Diving).

Canada: Earl Lowe (Abyssal Dive Charters) and Sylvain Sirois.

Chile: Stefano Bagoni (Las Tacas Dive Resort) and Eduardo Sorensen.

Egypt: Bryony Barton-Carroll (Emperor Divers).

Fiji: Brandon Paige (Aqua Trek) and Andrew Cummings (Beqa Adventure Divers).

Japan: Kan Shiota (Bommie Dive Center) and Kenji Ichimura.

Malaysia: Ah Gan and Ronnie Ng (Bubbles Dive Resort, Palau Perhentian).

Maldives: Bryony Barton-Carroll (Emperor Divers).

Mexico: Rodrigo Friscione Wyssmann (Solo Buceo), Fernando Aguilar Choy (Club Cantamar) and Jorge Chino Loria, Ramon Magana and Carlos Estrabeau (Phantom Divers).

Papua New Guinea: Dik Knight (Loloata Island Resort) and Linda Honey (Tufi Resort).

Philippines: Andrea Agarwal (Thresher Shark Divers, Malapascua) and Phil McGuire (Sogod Bay Scuba Resort).

South Africa: Morne Hardenberg and Brocq Maxey (Shark Explorers) and Walter Bernardis (African Watersports).

United Kingdom: James Fairbairns (Sealife Surveys).

USA: Bobby Purifoy (Olympus Dive Center), John and Bobbi Dickinson (Florida Freedivers), Joe Romeiro and Brian Raymond (Pelagic Expeditions) and Eli Martinez (SDM Adventures).

And finally we would like to thank our loved ones for supporting and sharing in our shark diving adventures, Helen Rose and Laura McColl.

INDEX